Making Progress:
From
Paragraphs
to Essays

Making Progress: From Paragraphs to Essays

Ellen Andrews Knodt

Pennsylvania State University, Ogontz Campus

HarperCollins*Publishers*

Sponsoring Editor: Jane Kinney
Project Editor: B. Pelner
Design Supervisor: Mary Archondes
Text Design: R. David Newcomer Associates
Cover Design: Carrington Design
Cover Illustration/Photo: Paul Silverman, Stock Photos Inc.
Production Assistant: Linda Murray
Compositor: Graphic Typesetting Service, Inc.
Printer and Binder: R. R. Donnelley & Sons Company
Cover Printer: Lehigh Press Lithographers

Making Progress: From Paragraphs to Essays

Library of Congress Cataloging-in-Publication Data

Knodt, Ellen Andrews.
    Making progress: from paragraphs to essays / Ellen Andrews Knodt.
      p.   cm.
    Includes index.
    ISBN 0-673-38332-6 (Student edition) — ISBN 0-673-47865-3 (Instructor's edition)
    1. English language—Rhetoric.   2. English language—Paragraphs.
3. Essay.   I. Title.
PE1408.K6884   1991
808'.042—dc20   90-21420
                                                                 CIP

91 92 93 94   9 8 7 6 5 4 3 2 1

Contents

PART V   Understanding Grammar and Usage   211

Preface

Making Progress: From Paragraphs to Essays is based on the assumption that learning, like writing, is a recursive process. Students need to see the writing process modeled in many different writing situations, and they need to practice each stage of the process many times to develop confidence and proficiency in writing. Furthermore, they need to be able to write paragraphs and essays on a variety of subjects, some rooted in their direct observations and personal experiences, some based on interpretation of information gathered from other sources. To help students meet these needs, Parts I and II of the text emphasize writing that is close to the students' lives, that is based on their observations and personal experience. These initial sections introduce the writing of paragraphs. Part III extends students' knowledge of the writing process to the multiparagraph essay while continuing to focus on familiar subject matter. Part IV allows students to grow cognitively by giving them opportunities to incorporate into their writing information gathered from outside sources, such as they will most likely have to do in other college courses.

Each chapter in Parts I–IV emphasizes the recursiveness of the writing process by taking students through the essential stages of the process: "Understanding Purpose and Audience," "Generating Ideas," and "Writing and Revising." Each chapter, building on what the students have already learned, adds new information to expand the students' writing skills. Following the sequence repeatedly enables students to internalize the process in a way they couldn't were it to be presented only once, at the beginning of the text.

The "Understanding Purpose and Audience" sections emphasize the importance of these concepts to the content and structure of a given piece of writing. Through exercises, students are led to understand how changing the audience may change the form, content, vocabulary, and nearly everything else in the piece. Discussion of a writer's purpose is linked, in part, to the rhetorical strategy or strategies chosen to accomplish what the writer intends the reader to get from the writing. Each chapter focuses on a particular rhetorical strategy, to acquaint students with these useful organizational patterns, while recognizing a writer's need to combine patterns to communicate his or her ideas. Following the assumption that students are more comfortable writing initially about what they know firsthand, these strategies are presented arranged from the concrete and the familiar to the more abstract. Similarly, assignments and exercises in each chapter are arranged from simpler ones to more complex ones, and there are enough exercises to allow instructors to focus on those that meet their students' needs.

The "Generating Ideas" sections introduce students to a variety of invention techniques keyed to the assignment in each chapter. These techniques, which include, among others, observing, freewriting, asking questions, listing, and keeping a journal, enable students to conquer the "tyranny of the blank page" and help prevent writer's block and other barriers to fluency.

The "Writing and Revising" sections emphasize ways to impose order on ideas so that readers will understand what the writer intends them to understand. "Global" revising for content and organization precedes advice on editing individual sentences. A "Revision Checklist" ends each chapter.

Throughout the stages of the process, from invention to revision, *Making Progress* encourages collaborative learning through "Working with Peers" sections, which provide activities for students in pairs or small groups to help each other become better writers.

Many student examples provide users of the text with realistic models of the ongoing writing process. In addition, at the end of each of Parts I–IV are three professional readings keyed to the material just discussed. Questions on the professional readings allow for reader response, analysis of writing techniques, and a writing journal suggestion to encourage integration of the reading with the student's own experience.

Following the four parts on rhetoric is a part emphasizing practical use of Standard English. Each chapter in this Part V has a quick review of grammar principles, which is all some students may need, followed by a more complete discussion of each principle, with exercises that often require students to generate sentences, not just hunt for errors. Terms are defined in ways accessible to students while providing a common vocabulary for instructors and students to analyze language. This part also has "Working with Peers" sections, like the earlier parts of the text, focusing on the abilities of groups of students to compose collaboratively as a way to improve their grammar and usage as well as their other writing skills. Each chapter in Part V ends with a chapter review chart to provide an aid to memory.

Above all, *Making Progress* encourages students to become better writers by presenting them with sequences of exercises and assignments that build their confidence as they move successfully through the text.

Acknowledgments

A textbook author truly appreciates the term *collaborative,* recognizing the encouragement and wise advice of so many people. I would like to thank, first of all, my students at Penn State University, Ogontz Campus, who continue to teach me about what works and what doesn't work in the writing classroom. My colleagues Leonard Mustazza and Robert McCaig gave me much-needed moral support, recognizing that a writing teacher may have trouble finding time to do her own writing. A special thank you goes to Ellen Furman, who suffered through early drafts of the manuscript with me and whose many suggestions have been incorporated into the text. At HarperCollins, I would like to thank Anne E. Smith and Constance Rajala for their good humor, authorial support, and excellent editorial acumen, and Jane Kinney and Kimberley Neat for guiding the text through the publishing process. I appreciate also the many reviewers who helped shape the final version of the text through their suggestions: Christopher Gould, University of North Carolina at Wilmington; Peggy Harbors, Nashville Tech; Paul Hunter, North Lake College; Linda Hanson Meeker, Ball State University; Gratia Murphy, Youngstown State University; Mark Reynolds, Jefferson Davis State Junior College; Gretchen Starks, Community College of the Finger Lakes; Rinda West, Oakton Community College; and Mindy Wright, Ohio State University.

Among many influences on my thinking, I wish especially to recognize Linda Flower, Richard Young, and others at Carnegie-Mellon University, who stimulated me to investigate the writing process.

Finally, I wish to thank my husband, Ken, and my son, Andrew, for their patience, love, humor, and good advice over the long haul.

Ellen Andrews Knodt

PART I

Beginning with the
Basics: Observation

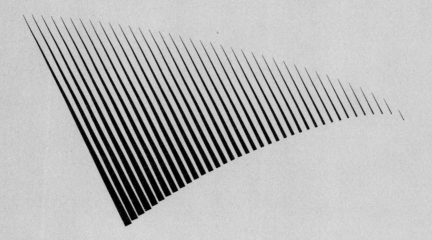

One of the ways people learn is by observing what other people do. Children, for example, watch and listen to adults and other children and learn everything from how to express themselves in language to how to color or play tag. Much of their observing is automatic—they are not aware of watching or listening to someone. As people get older, they often *consciously* observe someone—cooking a favorite dish, fixing a leaky faucet, changing the oil in a car, planting tomatoes—because they want to learn how to do something. If you have held a job, chances are that you went through a training period when you first were hired that showed you the procedures you were to follow on the job. You had to observe your fellow workers and listen to instructions.

Learning to be an effective writer also begins with observation—observing what other writers do when they write, and expressing your own observations in writing. Some of what you will learn in the next two chapters will make you more conscious of your powers of observation, which will make it much easier for you to write about what you gather through your senses of sight, sound, smell, taste, and touch.

CHAPTER 1

Writing Basics

Thinking About the Writing Process

In this chapter you will have the chance to practice writing as you review part of the writing process. To say "*the* writing process" is somewhat misleading, because there are actually many writing processes. Writers approach the task of writing in quite individual ways. Some people plan extensively before they write, using lists, notes, or formal outlines. Others dictate their ideas or compose at a typewriter or a word processor without having written their ideas down beforehand. Some people use a writing process we could call "midnight madness," composing the entire piece of writing from start to finish the night before it is due.

While there are many ways to approach the writing process, everyone can benefit from learning more about it. The writing process is also not as orderly as sometimes presented in textbooks, because writers, being human, change their minds, have false starts, or think of other ideas midway in a writing situation. If you have ever seen the manuscripts of famous writers, you know how many cross-outs, notes written in the margins, and other corrections there are. Most writers make many changes between the beginning stages and the end product. While a textbook can never show all the creative ways people use the writing process to communicate their ideas, it can acquaint you with some strategies that studies of effective writers have shown to be useful and that may make writing easier for you. With these thoughts in mind, let's begin looking at writing basics.

Understanding Purpose and Audience

Two basic writing principles may affect almost every other choice you will make when you write.

The preceding statement may be hard to believe. After all, you have to make many choices when you write. You choose a subject. You choose words that will express your ideas about the subject. You arrange the words in sentences and paragraphs. What are these principles that are so important as to determine all other choices?

Two Basic Writing Principles

1. Purpose: Know why you are writing.

2. Audience: Know your reader.

To understand how these principles influence other decisions writers make, you need to see how they apply to some common situations. Because the principles of purpose and audience apply to any situation, whether writing or speaking, let's consider two speaking situations.

If you were going to ask your friend for a loan or the dean of student affairs at your college to fund a certain activity, would you approach each of them in the same way? Would you say the same things? In this case, the purpose—asking for money—may *seem* the same, but let's look at it more closely. If you are asking a friend for money, it will probably be for something you need personally—books, tuition, household expenses. On the other hand, the money the dean authorizes for a student activity would not go to you alone but to the group you represent—for example, the student government—to pay for the activity, perhaps a calendar of events to be distributed to all students. Therefore, though you are asking for money in both cases, the reasons you give for your request will differ. That is, the purpose of your request alters the way you ask for the money.

Also, since a friend is a familiar audience, you can speak more informally than you would to the dean. The dean might also need more information, such as cost estimates from the printing company, before agreeing to your request. Friends might well ask for detailed information, too, before parting with money, but it is even more likely that the dean will ask for additional facts. So both the different purposes and different audiences for these situations determine what you say and how you say it.

Let's take another common speech example: Does a football coach talk to the players at halftime the same way he speaks at the annual sports banquet? Most of us would answer no. Here again the same speaker has two different purposes and two different audiences. The halftime speech is a pep talk to get the players to give their all in the second half of the game. The language is very informal, perhaps even profane. The sports banquet, on the other hand, is a more formal occasion for handing out awards to players, and the coach's speech will reflect that formality.

As was said earlier, writing situations also reflect differences between purposes or readers. Let's take two common, practical writing situations: writing a department store to inquire about your bill and writing the same store to inquire about getting a job. What purpose do you have in each case? What do you hope to accomplish in each letter? What kinds of information would each letter contain? Besides determining *what* you would say, would your purpose change *how* you would say something? For example, would your choice of words or tone be different from one situation to the other?

Although the department store is the same in both cases, is the audience for each letter the same? Who would be the likely reader of the first letter? of the second? What would each reader look for in the letter directed to him or her? If you understand that the customer service representative needs a clear explanation of the problem with your bill and some proof that what you say is correct, and the personnel representative wants to know how your training and experience can meet the needs of the department store, you will be able to communicate effectively with them. If you really don't consider your readers' needs, you may write a letter that gets no favorable action at all.

If most of your writing has been done in school rather than at a job or at home, you may have thought of writing only for your classes and teachers. But there are many purposes for writing and many different types of readers. Learning to adjust your writing to the purpose and the reader will help you become a more effective writer.

Here are some common purposes for writing:

1. *To entertain*—jokes, stories, poems, diaries

2. *To inform*—explanations, directions, reports, definitions, summaries

3. *To prove*—articles providing evidence supporting an idea, essay exam answers, lawyers' briefs

4. *To judge*—articles determining the value of something, or enabling a choice to be made between two things, recommendations

5. *To solve problems*—analyses of causes of problems and of solutions for the problems, reaching conclusions on a proper course of action, such as hiring a new person or introducing a new product

Besides writing for a variety of purposes, your readers also may vary. You may at times be writing for one of the following readers:

1. Yourself—journals, diaries, poems, stories

2. People close to you—letters, notes, directions, recipes

3. People you know more formally at school, in your community, or on the job—papers for instructors in college courses, letters to the city council, letters to the local newspaper, reports to people you work for or who work for you

4. The public, or people you may not have met—letters to employers for jobs, letters to members of Congress or senators, articles or letters for magazines or newspapers

WRITING APPLICATION: Adapting to an Audience

Before going any further, let's consider what has been discussed and apply it to some new situations. The difference in the content of the letters that you write in this Writing Application may help you to see that the message greatly depends on the purpose and the reader of the message.

A. Write a note to an out-of-town friend inviting him or her to visit. Mention some plans you have for places to go or events to attend when your friend comes.

B. Write a letter to a faculty member or your boss inviting him or her to speak at a meeting of your class or other campus group. Include information about when the visit could take place and what you would like the person to speak about.

WORKING WITH PEERS

Compare your letters with your classmates' efforts. What differences in content or style do you see in the letters written for two different audiences?

Generating Ideas

If you know why you are writing and who your reader will be, you will probably have a topic to write about. That is, most writing is done in reaction to a specific situation: for instance, writing a letter to apply for a job, preparing a report that solves a problem, writing an essay exam for a class. Sometimes, though, you will be given a writing task that is more "open-ended," such as when a college instructor assigns a term paper on "any aspect of this course." The audience of such a paper is your instructor, and the purpose is to show the instructor that you have read in depth and understood a subject related to the course. However, finding a topic one is interested in and developing it can be troublesome for many students.

How does one find material to write about? Basically, you can only write about things you know, unless you use your powers of imagination, and there are three main ways you get such knowledge:

1.   Using your powers of observation to notice what is going on around you, including your senses of sight, hearing, touch, taste, and smell

2.   Using your past observations and experiences to interpret and comment on your or others' actions

3.   Using information gathered through reading or other sources, that is, using other peoples' observations and experiences

In this text, you will use these three ways to find subjects on which to write and to develop them, and you will begin with observing.

Observing and Listing

What is meant by observing? Observing is using your senses to gather information from your environment—the people, places, and things around you. Observing means *really* looking, listening, smelling, touching, and even perhaps tasting!

Many people *think* they are observing, but if asked to tell what it was they saw, they cannot. If you have ever been a witness to an accident, you may recall that everyone who saw the accident had a slightly different version of what happened. Or perhaps you have been the subject of a classroom experiment: Someone rushes in your class and yells something like "the sky is falling" and rushes out. Your instructor tells you to write down a description of the person and what the person said. In this experiment, how many accounts do you think will be alike? Usually the accounts differ considerably.

To be an effective writer, you need to train yourself to be really observant. Becoming truly aware of what is going on around you can give you much information about a subject so that when you write you will be able to give your readers details that interest them and provide them with complete information.

Think about reporters assigned to cover a department store fire. When they arrive on the scene, they must observe carefully to gather information for their stories. They will note the size of the fire by seeing how many stories of the building seem to be involved, the number of fire companies at the scene, the possible spread to nearby buildings. They will watch carefully the activities of the firefighters: Are they still evacuating people from the building, what steps are they taking to get the fire under control, are their efforts working? By observing the scene and perhaps interviewing firefighters and other people, the reporters can write their stories so that their readers will feel they were eyewitnesses too.

WRITING APPLICATION: Observing and Listing

Take 5 to 10 minutes and observe your classroom. List what you see, hear, or smell. For example, what do the students look like? What are they wearing? How is their hair cut? What are the walls of the classroom like? What color are they? What kinds of desks are there? What is their condition? What sounds do you hear in the class? outside in the hall? outside the building? What smells do you notice? You need not write complete sentences. Words or phrases are fine. Your list:

Sights:

Sounds:

Smells:

WORKING WITH PEERS

Next, compare your observations with your classmates. What things did they notice that you didn't?

Although a one-time observation of something like a fire scene or a classroom may give you useful information to write about, sometimes you may need to observe a person or a place over a period of time to develop material to write about. Because it's very hard to remember specifically what you see, hear, or smell for any length of time after observing, whether it was once or many times, you will need to write down your observations to serve as material later for something you will write.

Using a Writing Journal

One way to become an even more effective observer and writer is to keep a writing journal, a small notebook that fits easily in a pocket or purse to use when you are observing. Besides helping you to remember what you observe, the act of writing things down helps you pay closer attention to what you are observing. The journal can be used effectively in other ways to record your experiences or thoughts about issues you read about in newspapers or learn about on television or in other classes you are taking.

You should write in your journal regularly—at least three times a week. Your instructor may give you class time to write in your journal or may make specific assignments of things to be observed or issues to be discussed in your journal. When not assigned to write anything specific, you should feel free to write anything at all, but the following suggestions may give you some ideas with which to start.

Suggestions for Journal Entries

1. Write about any experience from your childhood: getting lost, travels, friends and problems with friends, bad and good school experiences, games you played, favorite toys, being reckless.

2. Think about the words *fear, values,* and *prejudices* and make a list of things you fear, value, or are prejudiced against.

3. Write about your name. Why were you so named? How do you feel about your name? Tell about any experiences relating to your name.

4. What kind of person are you? What are your strengths? your weaknesses?

5. Record a vivid dream, an incident that happened during one of your college classes, or an incident at work.

6. Discuss your favorite television programs, movies, sports teams, sports that you play, or music to listen to or play.

The following example of a student's journal entry shows an observation being recorded, and the Writing Application that follows will give you a chance to develop your ability to observe and record your observations in your journal.

Journal-Bridal Falls

hot day-people sweat, all ages
brows wet, shirts clinging, wet places under arms,
*   around necks, some people wear bathing suits,*
path to falls rocky
low water, trickles over rocks
people are wading or standing under falls
boy (4 yrs) on father's shoulders
water is warm, but still feels good
rocky under foot, feet hurt and slip

people climb up slippery rocks to ledge
one man wears a straw hat—brim fills with water
*   and tips over*
dark-skinned man, looks Italian, slips on ledge,
*   almost falls, people go ``ooh''—ledge had slime and*
moss growing on it

WRITING APPLICATION: Using a Journal to Record an Observation

Imagine that you are a private investigator on a stakeout or a foreign journalist assigned to write an article on an American scene.

Observe a place where you live or work or one you simply find interesting and take notes in your journal on what you see, hear, or smell. Try this for at least fifteen minutes each day for at least two days. If possible, observe more than once each day. The place can be your house, apartment, or dorm room and its surroundings—the neighborhood or campus where it's located. Or you may prefer to observe the office, shop, factory, or restaurant where you work, or any other place that an investigator or journalist might find intriguing.

In order for this to be a productive activity, you really have to act as a recorder of events, of sounds, of how your surroundings look, of people you see or hear—in short, you need to be actively aware of everything around you.

WORKING WITH PEERS

Share your observations with your classmates by reading your journal or telling what you saw. Write down any questions they ask you so that you will remember them to answer later. Your classmates' questions:

Recognizing and Using Specific Details

When you shared what you had observed, did you find that what some people said was more interesting than what others said? Ask yourself which of your classmates' observations were the most interesting. Why were some more interesting than others?

The answer may be that some of the observations were more specific than others. Details are usually more interesting than just general ideas. If a society reporter writes that she attended a star-studded party, you want to to know names, places, the works! You want more details than just that famous people were there. You want to know that Cher was seen nibbling cucumber sandwiches while talking with Meryl Streep and Jack Nicholson.

As another example, think about what would happen if a newspaper covering a story about a fire printed only that a fire caused damage to a building on the waterfront. People would stop reading the newspaper. They want to know how big the fire was, what started it, how much damage it caused, exactly where it was, and so on.

Compare the two versions of the following student observations. Which is more interesting and helps you to "see" what the writer saw?

A.	B.
Kids play on my street.	Two twelve-year-olds on skate boards zigzag madly from curb to curb.
The streets are dirty.	Beer cans and a broken bottle of Gallo port lie in the gutter while cigarette wrappers swirl in the breeze.

The observations in the first column *tell* you that kids are playing and that the streets are dirty, but the ones in the second column *show* you by giving you details you can picture or otherwise relate to your senses.

If you were a witness to a crime and the police asked you what you saw, which of the following would be more helpful to say? "I saw a man snatch a lady's purse and run away" or "I saw a tall man with short, black hair and wearing a bluejeans jacket take the woman's black handbag and run south on 12th Street." In the second case, the details make the eyewitness account much more helpful to the police. Writers need to train themselves to use specific, concrete language that *shows* rather than *tells*.

ACTIVITY 1

To give you practice in recognizing sentences that are more specific, the following exercise has groups of three sentences on the same topic. Circle the one that gives the *most* specific picture to the reader. The first one is commented upon to show you the various levels of being specific.

1. a. The comedian was funny. (A general statement—a reader doesn't know what kinds of jokes were told.)
    b. The comedian told exaggerated stories about his childhood. (More specific—a reader knows now that the comedian used his childhood as a subject but doesn't know what the specific jokes were.)

    c.   The comedian described his embarrassment over being suspended from school for starting a fire in a trashcan behind the gym. (Most specific—the reader knows a specific incident the comedian used.)

2.   a.   Almost fourteen inches of rain fell during our vacation.
        b.   We had bad weather during our vacation.
        c.   It rained a lot when we were on vacation.

3.   a.   My cousin is a very nervous person.
        b.   My nervous cousin fiddles with her hands.
        c.   My nervous cousin bites her fingernails and cracks her knuckles.

4.   a.   The rock star was really strange.
        b.   The rock star's behavior was unusual.
        c.   The rock star swallowed a live turtle.

5.   a.   The politician falsified information on his income tax return for the last five years.
        b.   The politician was dishonest.
        c.   The politician didn't tell the truth about how much money he had earned.

You can *show* a reader what you have observed in several ways. One way is to add adjectives (tall, short, long-haired, heavy-set) or adverbs (quickly, slowly, hesitantly). These words help create clearer pictures in a reader's mind. Compare "The lady got on a bus" with "The huge, shapeless lady slowly got on a crosstown bus." Prepositional phrases (in the room, at the window, on the chair) are also used as modifiers to clarify a picture in the reader's mind. Using our previous sentence, we could add "The huge, shapeless lady in the faded calico dress slowly got on the crosstown bus." If you would like more information about these modifiers, see Chapter 11, in Part V.

Another way to make a sentence *show* rather than *tell* the reader something is to make the subject or verb more exact. Changing the subjects and verbs can do wonders for dull sentences:

"The cheese was old" becomes "The limburger smelled rotten."

Try your skill at making a basic sentence more specific in the following activity.

ACTIVITY 2

Make each of the following sentences clearer by adding modifiers that will create a picture of a specific person or place. Be imaginative and try to create a "mini-drama" in each sentence. The first one is done to give you an idea of the possibilities.

1. A man walked.

   A tall, leather-faced man in a worn leather jacket walked bowlegged up to the block-long bar.

2. A child cried.

3. A car crashed.

4. A woman laughed.

5. The family bought a house.

6. The athlete won a game.

7. Snow fell.

8. A storm hit the city.

9. The book was checked out.

10. The horse trotted.

WORKING WITH PEERS

In groups, choose the best examples of "mini-dramas" from Activity 2 and share them with the rest of the class.

ACTIVITY 3

Make each of the following sentences more detailed by adding modifiers as you did in Activity 2 or by changing some words to be more specific. Replace verbs like "is" and "are" with more specific actions if you can. Change nouns like "man," "woman," and "people" to words that characterize them, like "lawyer" and "doctor," or name them, like "George," "Martha," "the Smiths." Watch out, too, for words like "nice," "interesting," "awesome," and "terrific." They have become so overused as to lose their meaning. Replace such words with more exact words. The first one is done to give you the idea.

1. The crowd at the concert dressed alike.

   The loyal fans at the Grateful Dead concert wore black leather jackets, tie-dyed shirts, and shoulder-length hair or shaved heads.

2. Certain movies appeal to different people.

3. Riding a bus is interesting.

4. The doctor's waiting room was old.

5. Streets were under construction.

6. Clothes are too expensive.

7.   My best friend is nice.

8.   The young people stood at the corner.

9.   The necklace was beautiful.

10.   The traffic was heavy.

WORKING WITH PEERS

Choose five of the best sentences from Activity 3 from your group and share them with the rest of the class. Be prepared to explain why you think they are good.

   Now that you have practiced observing and making observations specific, you are ready to put your observations into complete sentences. You may wish to consult Chapter 10, on writing complete sentences, to help you with the following Writing Application.

WRITING APPLICATON: Writing the Observation As Sentences

Write in complete sentences your observation from page 9 of a place you live in, work at, or find interesting, using the lists or notes you wrote in your writing journal. Be as specific in writing down the details as you can. You may wish to write your observation just as you observed it, telling what you saw and when. You want your reader to experience the place as vividly as you observed it.

WORKING WITH PEERS

Exchange your written observations with one or more of your classmates. Ask readers to suggest sentences that could be made more specific. Also ask them to check the completeness of your sentences.

Focusing on a Main Point

After observing and writing up the observation in sentences, you should decide what the main point is that you want to communicate to the reader about your subject.

Readers need to have a clear idea of what a writer is saying. If a writer meanders from one idea to another or presents a list of unrelated details, readers will not understand what they are reading. Unfocused writing can easily leave a reader asking "Why am I reading this? What is the point?" In order to avoid such confusion, writers focus their writing on a central point.

Finding Dominant Impressions

Before you know what your clear point is, you have to have an idea of the overall impression you are trying to share with the reader. Is this place dull, lively, run-down, or well kept? You need once again to think about your purpose for writing and about the reader, and to ask, "What picture or idea about this place do I want to create in my reader's mind?" Since your observations may have included many different sights, sounds, and smells, you may now be forced to focus your attention on the details that create the dominant impression the reader is supposed to understand.

ACTIVITY 4

Read the following lists of sentences from two students' observations. What dominant impression do you get from the list of things observed? The first list has a suggested answer.

List 1:

Three ducks in formation search the pond for unsuspecting fish.

Three male students talk on a bench by the duck pond.

A female student is reading a paperback book at the base of a large tree.

Four squirrels, searching for winter food, carefully scour the ground for nuts.

A lonely tree stands defiantly in the center of the duck pond.

A large barren rock pokes through the green grass.

Dominant Impression:

I get the impression of a quiet campus scene.

Now write your impression of the following list:

List 2:

A crowd of boys argues over a game of basketball.

Several large men try to settle the football schedule with a bored park manager.

Automobiles screech to a halt at a quick-changing red light.

Women stick their heads out of windows to see what the commotion is. They
  yell at their children to stay out of the street.

Old men on porches discuss the chances of the Phillies winning a pennant. A
  Mets fan razzes them and then is quiet.

A fistfight between a tall, husky boy and a smaller but also heavy boy ends in
  a draw. Both their noses are bleeding.

Dominant Impression:

Sometimes writers start with a main idea or a dominant impression that is already in their minds; that is, from the start they have an idea they wish to communicate to their readers. Then they observe a scene or in other ways gather evidence to support their idea. Let's say, for example, that you begin with the idea that "My house is a crazy place at dinner time." What observations might support that idea? You could note that your baby sister bangs her spoon in the high chair, that telephone surveyors call to ask questions about cemetary lots, and that your ten-year-old brother is likely to spill his milk. All these are details that provide evidence that what you say about your house at dinner time is true. In the next exercise try your hand at adding details to a dominant impression.

ACTIVITY 5

For each dominant impression, add three sentences that will provide details to support the idea. The first one has a suggested list of details.

1. My apartment building is well kept.

    a. *The landlord repairs broken shutters, crumbling steps, and cracked driveways promptly.*

    b. *Inside, the halls are clean, and the walls are freshly painted.*

   c. *The tenants' apartments are redecorated before each tenant moves in.*

2.   Our family's home is desperately in need of repair.

   a.

   b.

   c.

3.   The food in the cafeteria is not fit for human consumption.

   a.

   b.

   c.

4.   My grandmother's house is old-fashioned.

   a.

   b.

   c.

5.   My room is a mess.

   a.

b.

c.

You may have noticed that a sentence that gives a dominant impression of an observation gives a focus or direction to what follows. As was said earlier, such a focus or direction is important to your readers, for it helps them to understand what you are writing about. Since everything you write has a purpose and is directed to an audience, it follows that a focus or direction statement that helps the audience to understand your purpose is important.

If you have ever heard somebody ramble on about a subject, you may have heard a frustrated listener say, "Get to the point." Listeners and readers need to have a clear idea of what the speaker or writer is saying or else they will "tune them out." To avoid being "tuned out," you can provide your readers with some reason for reading, usually an idea you want them to understand. One way to help the reader understand the main point is to use a topic sentence at the beginning of the paragraph to provide this important focus.

Writing a Topic Sentence

A topic sentence is a statement about a subject that shows the main idea and the writer's attitude towards it. A topic sentence gives the reader a clear sense of what the paragraph will be about. In fact, it forms a contract between the writer and the reader. Through the topic sentence, the writer says, "I agree that this paragraph will be about this subject and nothing else." The reader says, "I understand that this paragraph will be about this subject. "If writers change the subject from what the topic sentence says, they are "breaking the contract. "Their readers then may become confused and may not be able to follow their ideas.

Usually a topic sentence contains one or more words that show the writer's attitude toward the subject as well as what subject is being discussed. So a paragraph that begins "My Uncle Martin has several annoying habits when he eats" will be different from one that begins "My Uncle Martin tells fascinating stories at the dinner table." Both of them concern the same general subject—Uncle Martin—but the writer's attitude and the specific subject being discussed are different in each case.

Try the next activity to sharpen your sense of focusing an observation.

ACTIVITY 6

Circle the word or words in the following topic sentences that show the writer's attitude toward the subject.

1. My brother's eating habits are disgusting.

2. I must confess that I am a very fussy eater.

3. My once-quiet neighborhood has become very noisy.

4. My friend Jean is a true humanitarian.

5. I had a difficult adjustment to make when I entered college.

6. The weather on my last vacation was not ideal.

7. My political science professsor has some annoying habits that distract the class.

8. The landscape architect created an exotic garden for the building's courtyard.

9. Knowledge of first aid is essential for a kindergarten teacher.

10. Many horror movies have highly predictable plots.

WORKING WITH PEERS

In pairs or small groups, choose three of the preceding topic sentences and write three sentences for each that provide details to support the main idea, as expressed in the attitude word of each one. Here is one example.

EXAMPLE

Many horror movies have highly predictable plots.

a. *They always involve a pretty girl who has lost her way or is alone somewhere.*

b. *Like Freddy Kruger, the murderer or the monster on the loose has always been wronged somehow and is out to get revenge.*

c. *The murderer usually disappears or is defeated but in a way that leaves his reappearance possible.*

1.

   a.

   b.

   c.

2.

   a.

   b.

   c.

3.

   a.

   b.

   c.

Sometimes writers think they have written a topic sentence that will give direction to a paragraph, but they have been too general or have forgotten the attitude word altogether. Read the following sentences and revise them to improve the focus. Be prepared to discuss your revisions in class.

ACTIVITY 7

Improve the focus or direction of the following sentences by making sure each includes a clear attitude towards the subject. You may also wish to make the subject more specifiic. The first one has been revised as an example.

1. My family goes to the seashore every summer.

    My family enjoys both the beach and the board-walk in Ocean City, New Jersey, each summer.

2. I have been dating the same person for five years.

3. I eat when I watch television.

4. Susan joined an exercise club.

5. Going to college is quite an experience.

Now let's look at topic sentences in the context of paragraphs. As mentioned before, a topic sentence serves as a contract with a reader, letting him or her know what the paragraph will be about. It has another advantage as well. It helps the writer stay on the subject and not stray from the main point. Look at the following brief paragraph as an example.

Too Many Kids

My neighborhood has changed from not many children to too many. No one can keep a lawn free from bike tracks as kids ride across corners on their way to each others' houses. And every week or so I pick up a new ding or scratch on my car from a bike ridden too close to my car parked in the street. However, the bikers don't cause the only problems. Kids on skateboards make walking on sidewalks hazardous as they zigzag none too expertly past. Skateboards are also noisy, clattering across the seams in the sidewalks early on a Saturday morning. I got so I would long for a rainy day when the bikers and skateboarders would stay inside. Much to my dismay, on rainy days the kids make dams around the storm drains so they can splash in a kid-made lake and scream excitedly. As I think about it, my attitude toward the neighborhood kids might change if I were twelve instead of nineteen. I'd probably be right out there with my bike, skateboard, or swimsuit enjoying my playmates instead of complaining that there are too many kids!

The topic sentence here expresses the writer's opinion that there are too many children in the neighborhood, and each of the supporting details *shows* the reader why the writer feels that way. Lawn tracks, car scratches, sidewalk-hazards, and noise give readers concrete reasons for understanding the writer's feelings. Also, nothing strays from the idea of the topic sentence to confuse the reader.

Topic sentences may be constructed after you have gathered information on a topic, or may just occur to you as a judgment or statement of attitude when you first think of a subject. In the first case, you need to look over your information and try to find a main idea, a point that will sum up your observations for your reader, and then try to state that point clearly in a complete sentence. In the second case, you will already have your main point but will want to express it in a complete sentence.

Pitfalls in the Process

Although asking a question at the beginning of a paragraph can hint at the subject to be discussed, a question is not a topic sentence. A question may be answered in several different ways, and it is the answer, *not* the question, that can be the topic sentence. For example, in the paragraph "Too Many Kids," if the writer had begun with the question "Are there too many kids in my neighborhood?" the reader would not know whether the answer was yes or no until the writer revealed his or her attitude in an answer to the question.

Similarly, although a title may give a hint as to your subject, a title is not a substitute for a topic sentence. You need a complete sentence that expresses the subject and your attitude about the subject.

While it is true that not every writer uses a topic sentence for every paragraph, learning to write topic sentences can help writers organize and present their thoughts more clearly. As you will see later in the text, you may find situations that don't call for topic sentences, and that's fine. For now, you can make sure the idea in your paragraph is clear to the reader by including a topic sentence.

WRITING APPLICATION: Writing a Topic Sentence

From your writing journal observation that you turned into sentences in the Writing Application on page 14, write a topic sentence that includes an attitude word that captures the character of the place.

WORKING WITH PEERS

Exchange topic sentences with your classmates, and ask them what they expect the accompanying paragraph will be about, based on their understanding of your topic sentence. Is their understanding of the attitude you have toward the place you wrote about the same as your understanding? Explain.

Keeping the Focus Clear

You may notice that your topic sentence could include only a few details from your earlier observations. This is a common occurrence. Observation includes many different factors: the weather, what people are doing, how a street looks, background noises, and the like. But in a topic sentence expressing a writer's main idea, the focus is narrowed to one particular quality so that the reader will understand the main point. Compare this experience to that of a camera operator who at first takes a sweeping panorama of a scene and then zooms in for a close-up.

The topic sentence also forces writers to include in a paragraph *only* those details that support the main idea. Thinking of the way movies are made may help clarify the process: Directors frequently film many versions of one scene or even many different scenes before choosing just which ones will create the effects they wish the audience to see. The alternative versions or whole scenes are lopped off and left on the cutting room floor. Many actors have been surprised at the final screening of a film because several of their scenes may have been cut or eliminated during the editing process. For example, if you have seen the film "The Big Chill," you may recall the opening scene of the dead man being prepared for burial. What you didn't see was a whole series of scenes of the character when alive, played in flashback by Kevin Costner. His entire part ended up on the cutting room floor! The aim of the film maker in carefully choosing scenes is a well-paced, coherent movie, and the writer must make similar kinds of choices to produce coherent paragraphs.

Selecting and Omitting Details

The following activities will help you sharpen your sense of what belongs with a topic sentence and what must be left out. The key here is to read each sentence and ask if it is related to the main idea as expressed in the topic sentence. Other ideas might be developed in other paragraphs, but in order not to confuse the reader, only those details that support the idea of the topic sentence should be included in this paragraph.

ACTIVITY 8

In each of the following sentence groups, specific observations have been listed to support a topic sentence. Check each statement to determine if it supports the topic sentence. Cross out any that do not.

1. My grandmother's hands tell the story of her hard-working life.

   a. The skin is hard and calloused from working in a shoe factory.

    b. The fingernail on the thumb of her left hand is deformed because of an accident with the machine that stamps out pieces of leather.

    c. She is the kindest, most unselfish person in the world.

    d. Brown spots on the back of her hands are evidence of many hours working in the sun in her garden to raise vegetables for the family table.

    e. My grandfather's hands are quite expressive too.

2. My brother's bedroom should be condemned as a health hazard.

    a. A broken screen on the window allows insects to gather whenever the lights are on.

    b. People enjoy coming to his room because he has an appealing personality.

    c. A two month's collection of dirty gym socks sits in one corner of the room.

    d. Candy-bar wrappers and pizza boxes with some remaining moldy crusts cover his desk.

    e. He is the only one in the family who has not changed his sheets since New Year's.

3. Our summer cottage is desperately in need of repair.

    a. The entire family enjoys going there to escape from the pressures of city life.

    b. The columns on the front porch are leaning.

    c. The back door swings on one rusty hinge.

    d. The house is large enough for my family and a couple of our friends.

    e. The boards on the living-room floor are cracked and splintered in places.

4. My brother-in-law's car attracts attention wherever it goes.

    a. All four doors are painted different colors.

    b. It backfires every time he accelerates or brakes.

    c. He bought it from a used car dealer for $500.

    d. I think he paid more than it was worth.

    e. Huge clouds of smoke pour out of the tail pipe.

    f. The muffler scrapes the ground when the car bounces, causing sparks.

    g. It gets very low gas mileage.

Now read the student paragraph in the following activity and try to pick out sentences that do not support the topic sentence.

ACTIVITY 9

Underline the topic sentence in the following selection. Next, cross out sentences that seem unrelated to the topic sentence. Finally, list the specific details that support the dominant impression.

Urban Despair

A reporter roving the city sees despair on many faces. The shivering woman standing in the street holding her crying baby despairs as she watches a fire consuming her apartment building. Her other children cling to her skirts, too shocked to cry. Their eyes show their anguish at losing all they had. I wonder what caused the fire. Was it faulty wiring, children playing with matches, careless smoking? Fire department officials warn us that smoke detectors can save lives. On another corner, despair is an old, shaggy, homeless man, wandering the streets, begging for money. His downcast, vacant eyes show his shame and his helplessness. Clusters of young men hanging out on street corners in mid-morning aimlessly wait for something to happen. Their tense faces contrast with their casual posture and emphasize the despair of no job, no future. Rush hour commuters entering or leaving the city may not see the faces I have seen, but they are everywhere, and it is sad.

List of Supporting Details:

Writing a topic sentence that expresses your main idea and selecting details to support the idea will go a long way to help your reader understand what you are trying to communicate. To give you practice in these skills, see the following Writing Application.

WRITING APPLICATION: Writing Warm-Up

From the ideas you have written in your writing journal, select one important experience, value, or opinion that you think will help your instructor get to know you as a person. Write a topic sentence that expresses the main idea and your attitude and then support the topic sentence with several specific details. Your instructor may share a similar passage with you so that you can get to know him or her better also.

CHAPTER 2

Developing a Paragraph by Observation: Description

Thinking About Description

Describing things fully and accurately has many advantages in college and in careers after college. For example, a biology or chemistry student may have to observe the results of experiments in the lab and write up his or her observations. A film or drama student may need to describe an actor's gestures, costumes, or voice for a review. On the job, someone might need to record observations of a production process, an employee's performance, or a customer's reaction to a product. Teachers must observe students; doctors and nurses must observe patients; lawyers must observe jury behavior; and police depend on observing criminals and potentially dangerous situations for their very lives. Many of these observations will need to be recorded in writing through various kinds of reports.

In Chapter 1 you learned the importance of purpose and audience in writing, and you practiced writing topic sentences supported by specific details. This chapter builds on what you have learned, adding additional strategies for writing and revising a paragraph. The chapter follows a student paper from the starting stages to the final paragraph so that you can see how one student composed his ideas. You have several choices of topics for the assignment and should consider your purpose in writing and your proposed reader as you make your choice. Additional topics are found at the end of the chapter.

Understanding Purpose and Audience: Topics for an Observation Paragraph

1.   Write a paragraph in which you encourage a reader to come to live where you do or discourage him or her from moving to your area. You may assume that the reader is your age, shares your interests, and has asked you for your opinion. You could assume that someone you know is moving from another state or transferring from another college to your area. Would he or she find where you live pleasant, attractive, and affordable? Your purpose is to give your reader enough information about where you live so that he or she will be able to accept your recommendation about moving or not moving there.

2.   Observe a place where people eat, and describe its atmosphere. Choose a cafeteria, a pizza place, a luxury restaurant, a "theme" restaurant, a fast-food place, or any other dining establishment. Assume your description will appear in the campus newspaper, so your readers for the most part will be fellow students. Your purpose is to acquaint readers with places to eat in the area.

You may find the following strategies for gathering information helpful in addition to the lists and the writing journal you used for Chapter 1. Continue to employ your writing journal to discuss any topics that interest you. Use it too to get started with this assignment.

Generating Ideas

As you saw in Chapter 1, observation focuses on the senses—what can be seen, heard, touched, smelled, or tasted—and on the present—what is going on at the time you are observing. Making lists or notes or using a writing journal are useful for gathering information for this assignment. There are, however, other techniques to plan what you will say in this paragraph. You will learn several of these techniques in the following pages.

Asking Questions

The first such technique is asking questions. Almost everyone knows the journalist's questions: Who? What? When? Where? Why? How? These questions can be very helpful in developing ideas for any writer. You may wish to try out these questions on your topic. The following example assumes I am doing the assignment based on where I live.

Who?   My reader is someone who has asked me if she should come to live in Philadelphia.

What?   What do I think about Philadelphia? What are its advantages?
             I could mention the museums, the sports teams, the convenient
             location to other cities, such as New York and Washington, the
             historical atmosphere, the affordable housing. What are the dis-
             advantages? Problems with government services, such as dirty
             streets, a decaying public transportation system, lack of sup-
             port for public schools. What does my reader care about? If
             she is of my age and interests, she is a college teacher of
             English, so she would be interested in the colleges in the area.
             (This question can develop many leads.)

When?   When is she planning to move?

Where?   Where would I recommend that someone live in Philadelphia?
             There are so many areas and neighborhoods, each with its own
             charm and character. Old City and Society Hill are expensive
             but convenient to Center City. West Philadelphia would be close
             to the University of Pennsylvania. Chestnut Hill has a suburban
             feeling.

Why?   Why does she want to come here? This question would be
             important to answer because it might affect the rest of my
             recommendations.

How?   I am not sure about this question. It could be how long have I
             lived here or how long will she stay? Or it could be how will she
             find a job or a place to live?

As you can see, some of these questions are better than others for generating thoughts on a topic or pointing to areas that need to be investigated.

Another technique that may be helpful for this assignment is to ask questions your reader would want to know about your subject. Putting yourself in
your reader's place is often a good way to decide what information to include
in a paper. The following activity should be based on the topic you have chosen
for the assignment given at the beginning of the chapter.

WRITING APPLICATION: Asking Questions a Reader Might Ask

List questions here that a reader might ask about your topic. By asking these
questions, you begin to put yourself in your reader's frame of mind, which
should help you provide him or her with the necessary information.

1.

2.

3.

4.

5.

6.

7.

8.

Here is the completed list of questions one student asked about the place he lives in, Atlantic City:

1.   What are the people like who live there?

2.   What can I do there?

3.   Where would I go to school? What are the schools like?

4.   What transportation is available? Do I need to own a car?

5.   How available are the jobs? How well do they pay?

6.   How much do the homes cost there?

7.   What is the climate there?

8.   How is the social life there?

After you have asked the questions that you think your reader would ask, write answers to the questions. This activity may provide you with a focus for your paper. That is, the way you answer the questions will help you to determine your attitude toward the subject for your paper.

WRITING APPLICATION: Answering Your Reader's Questions

Answer the questions you asked, drawing on your knowledge of of the subject and your observations. Work toward deciding on the main idea you wish to communicate to your reader. Answers should be as specific as possible.

Answers to questions:

1.

2.

3.

4.

5.

6.

7.

8.

The student from Atlantic City gave the following answers to his questions. Note that he was more detailed in some of his answers, which indicates that he probably has to find out more about some subjects or perhaps that he is not interested in some of the subjects.

1.   The people are nice, *rich,* some are stuck up, there are old and young people.

2.   Many things to do: work, arcades, Jacuzzis, pool, weight room, beach (in summer), casino

3.   No! The schools are terrible (add more on that).

4.   Public transportation is good. The roads are in poor condition.

5.   There are plenty of jobs, and the casinos pay especially well.

6.   Homes are expensive. Condos cost half a million and more.

7.   The climate is hot in summer and cold in winter.

8.   Social life is terrific for a single male. There are thousands of beautiful women to take out.

Now that you have an idea of what readers may want to know, and of some answers to their questions, you can use another technique helpful in starting a paragraph: freewriting.

Freewriting

This technique involves writing for a certain amount of time (usually 10 or 15 minutes) on a suggested topic. Sometimes people use it when they don't even have a topic in mind, to see what "pops up." The important thing is that the writing be uncensored; that is, write without regard to sentence structure, spelling, or even good logic. Let your mind flow into your pen!

Some people find that this technique really helps them unblock themselves when they are having trouble starting to write. It gets them over the "first-sentence hurdle" that so many writers have, that is, the feeling that the first sentence they write has to be perfect. People who feel this way may spend hours on just the first sentence.

Other people don't like freewriting, and that's fine. It is important to try different generating techniques to see what works best for you. You may also find that one method works well on a particular assignment but not on another, and that's fine too.

WRITING APPLICATION: Freewriting

Write on your chosen topic for 10 minutes, without stopping. Try to write down all the ideas on the topic that come into your head without deciding at this point whether they are worthwhile or not. Don't worry either about the way your sentences look or whether spelling or punctuation is correct.

The Atlantic City student wrote two paragraphs of freewriting, one on the advantages of the city as a place to live and one on the disadvantages. That was fine. He could have mixed both advantages and disadvantages together in one paragraph, because in freewriting anything goes. But he was already organizing his points in his mind, which many people (though certainly not all) do even before they write.

Atlantic City—Freewriting

There are a few reasons why you might want to or not to come to live in Atlantic City. Some of the reasons you might want to is because, first there a lot of people, and most of them are pretty friendly. The beach is a great place to hang out and met girls. There are also some really good job openings like to casinos who pay very well. There are also other jobs around that are kind of fun like parking attendant, a change person in an arcade and other fun things. There is almost always something to do there all year roundand it is p rctically never boring. One really nice thing is you d n't really need a car. Most things are in walking distance and there is also the jitney which is a small bus and that will take you from one end of the city to the other for 75 cents.

Then there are some of the bad reasons. Being that there is a lot of people there are usually lines everywhere. The tourists come from everywhere. There is also a very high crime rate in A.C. luckily not in my immediate neighborhood, but you have to be careful. The public schools in A.C. are VERY poor quality so if you want to go to college you have to enroll in private school. Last there is the price. Apartments and houses are extremly expensive as most land in A.C. now is.

There are also many run down houses throughout the city which takes away from it appearance.

You can see from his freewriting that the student is thinking about the answers to the questions he said a reader might ask. Now that he has quite a bit of material from his question-asking and freewriting, he is ready to begin writing his paragraph into a form his reader will understand. As he does this, he may drop certain of his freewriting ideas and expand others, because rarely does all the preliminary material fit in the final version. His decisions to include some material and reject other ideas will depend on the focus—the main idea he now will decide on.

Writing and Revising a Descriptive Paragraph

Focusing Ideas by Writing a Topic Sentence

Before seeing how the Atlantic City student focuses his thoughts, try your hand at creating a topic sentence from your own question-asking and freewriting. Look at your freewriting. Is there a sentence that sums up your attitude toward the topic? If so, you may already have a working topic sentence. If not, consider what you have thought and written, and then create a topic sentence.

WRITING APPLICATION: Writing a Topic Sentence

Write the main idea of your paragraph in a topic sentence. Remember, it should be a complete sentence that expresses an attitude toward the subject. It will be your "contract" with the reader to discuss this idea.

WORKING WITH PEERS

Exchange your topic sentence with classmates who are working on the same topic. Ask them to tell you what they expect the rest of your paragraph will be about from reading your topic sentence. Since the topic sentence forms a kind of contract with the reader, you need to know just what your reader expects from you. If what they expect is different from what you are trying to communicate to them, you may need to revise your topic sentence.

The Atlantic City student decided to focus his paragraph on the advantages of living in Atlantic City, because he likes living there himself. That meant he had to drop all the disadvantages he thought of in his question-asking and freewriting. As mentioned before, the writing process is not always neat and straightforward. There are frequent stops and detours.

The student's topic sentence is "Atlantic City is one of the greatest places for a teenager to live." With a topic sentence like this, the reader expects to learn the reasons for the writer's attitude. The writer could focus on just one factor, but as you have seen, the Atlantic City student has several reasons for liking his home town. In order to express more than one idea related to the topic sentence, writers can organize a paragraph by using subtopic sentences.

Using Subtopic Sentences to Organize

Now that you have decided on answers to your reader's questions and have written your main idea as a topic sentence, you need to select your information and organize it so your reader will understand your ideas.

Begin to consider two or three factors that you think will best explain your idea. For example, if your preliminary topic sentence is "Students at Capitol State University should not move into Smith Residence Hall," isolate two or three reasons from your observations. Let's say you feel this way because the hall is noisy and because students do not respect each other's privacy. Using as much specific detail as you can, you discuss the noise and the lack of privacy. You introduce each factor in order, using something called the *subtopic sentence*.

In brief form your paragraph will look like this:

(Topic sentence) Students at Capital State University should not move into Smith Residence Hall.
(Subtopic 1) For one thing, the noise there prevents studying, sleeping, or even listening to music.
(details about noise)

(Subtopic 2) If the noise were not annoying enough, the students in the hall have no respect for each other's privacy.

(details about privacy)

If you choose two or three subtopics to discuss, your paragraph is likely to be longer than if you only have one point to discuss, but it will be more complete and more interesting to a reader. Subtopic sentences allow writers to explore an idea thoroughly, while the organized structure enables the reader to follow a more complex discussion easily.

Before working on your own paragraph, practice the following activities.

ACTIVITY 1

Read the following paragraph about a place, and underline the topic sentence twice and the subtopic sentences once. Then answer the questions following the paragraph.

Lake Wobegon Lives

Brainerd, Minnesota, is a great town for the growing child. For one thing, it is nature's paradise. Its location on the upper Mississippi River in an area dotted with lakes offers children the opportunity to swim, water ski, fish, and hike in the summer and to snowmobile, ski, and ice skate in the winter. The air is clean and scented with pine. Besides the outdoors, children experience the friendly atmosphere of a small town that might be described as a place that time forgot. The broad streets with little traffic are safe for children going to and from school. Cheerful "car hops" at the A&W Root Beer stand still deliver frosty-sided mugs of root beer on trays to fit on your partly rolled-up car window. Paul Bunyan and Babe the Blue Ox stand tall at the entrance to the small amusement park that offers rides on "The Whip," a ferris wheel, a small roller coaster, and bumper boats. Brave children venture through the Fun House with its dark mysteries and halls of mirrors. Brainerd is so peaceful and friendly, it is hard to believe that such a town still exists in the modern world.

QUESTIONS:
1. What details support the first subtopic sentence?

2. What details support the second subtopic sentence?

ACTIVITY 2

The following activity first gives you a topic sentence for a paragraph and then provides details to organize into a paragraph with subtopic sentences. Read the topic sentence and the sentences of details. Try to determine two subdivisions of the idea that can be expressed in subtopic sentences that will be supported by two groups of details. Then write the paragraph in the space provided. You may wish to combine some sentences or leave out certain details as you write the paragraph.

Topic Sentence: Meadville, Pennsylvania, is a town that has seen very little change in some ways but a lot of change in others.
Details: Meadville is a small town in northwestern Pennsylvania, located fifty-five miles south of Erie, Pennsylvania.

Meadville has new snopping malls on the outskirts of the city.

Meadville was once a thriving steel-producing town, but most of the plants are now closed.

Many of the town's original buildings from the late 1800s still stand in good condition. The Market House (1870) on Market Street continues to be used as an open-air market place.

High unemployment has caused many long-time residents to move elsewhere, seeking jobs.

Roads in the center of town still have their original brick surfaces.

Allegheny College in Meadville dates back to 1815 and still has buildings from the period. One of the best examples of Federal architecture is Bentley Hall (1820).

Paragraph on Meadville, Pennsylvania:

(Title)

Meadville, Pennsylvania, is a town that has seen very little change in some ways but a lot of change in others.
(1st subtopic sentence)

(Supporting details)

(2nd subtopic sentence)

(Supporting details)

In addition to using subtopic sentences to organize ideas, effective writers frequently use words or phrases called *transitions* to link ideas together. These words that signal additional ideas or changes in subtopics can help readers understand the writer's ideas.

Linking Ideas with Transitions

Besides a clear organization and supporting details, readers need signposts along the way to help them read from idea to idea. Signposts, often called transitions, help the reader to read along smoothly, without a lot of jerky stops and starts. Like a good transmission helps a car to change gears smoothly, transitions help readers.

Common transitions can be grouped according to the ways they connect ideas:

Time Order of Ideas	Additional Idea	Different Idea
first	also	however
second	and	yet
next	moreover	but
then	in addition	on the other hand
As I entered	besides	
meanwhile		

Similar Idea	Ending Idea
or	finally
similarly	therefore
	in conclusion

Example of an Idea	Cause or Effect of Ideas
such as	because
for example	therefore
that is	subsequently
	as a result
	for

Place Order of Ideas
on the left or right
near
next to
above
below

In the earlier paragraph on Brainerd, Minnesota, transitions were used to move from one subtopic to another. "For one thing" introduced the first group of details, and "besides the outdoors" introduced the second group of details.

In the activity that follows, note how students use transitions to help readers understand a description of a place.

ACTIVITY 3

Read the following student observation of a classroom. Circle the transition words or phrases.

Escape from Dalton Hall

Sitting inside a classroom in Dalton Hall is very unpleasant. Around me are four walls painted in a dull green color with paint peeling and plaster falling in many places. Beside me is a blackboard with a large wooden rim that looks as if it came from a little red schoolhouse. The tiles below my feet are three different shades of green. Across the room the window frames appear to be splitting, explaining the cold draft of air from that direction. Finally, the room is small and plain, like a box with only one door, making me feel shut in. I can't wait for class to end and to walk outdoors in the sunshine!

QUESTION
What kinds of transition are used most often in this paragraph? (Refer to the previous lists.)

In the next paragraph, the student used two types of transitions: space and time order. Circle the transitions, and list them under the appropriate category.

A Room of Despair

As soon as I walked into the boxlike apartment, I could tell that an alcoholic lived there. As I opened the door, I was hit in the face by a pungent, damp smell of whiskey and beer. In the room to my right, the television was left on, and only static could be heard. About four feet directly in front of the TV was a small, shabby sofa littered with newspapers, empty potato chip bags, and Budweiser cans. On the floor the rug was hard and worn, with crumbs stuck to the wet fibers soaked with beer. A bowl was tipped over, with popcorn scattered around it in a circle. In the kitchen, the refrigerator door was half open, with the strong smell of sour milk and about five dollars worth of spoiling food. On the open bar that overlooked the TV room were bottles that were either empty or a quarter of the way full of Smirnov vodka, Old Grand Dad whiskey, and Gordon's gin. As I turned to leave, I kicked a shot glass that glided over the hard-worn carpet.

List of place transitions:

List of time-order transitions:

Another way to keep your reader focused on your main ideas is to repeat a key word throughout a paragraph, such as the repetition of the word *room* in the preceding paragraphs.

WRITING APPLICATION: Topic Outline

At this point you may wish to change your topic sentence to reflect two or three subtopic ideas. For example, the earlier sample sentence on Capital University could be changed to "Students at Capital State University who want a quiet place and some privacy should not move into Smith Residence Hall."

Fill in the following outline form with your revised topic sentence, any subtopic sentences with transitions, and a list of specific details to support your main points.

Topic sentence:

Subtopic sentence 1 (with transition)

Supporting details:

Subtopic sentence 2 (with transition)

Supporting details:

Note: You may have more or fewer subtopic sentences than are suggested here. While not everyone finds outlines useful, many writers find that outlines help them organize their ideas.

Below is an outline for the Atlantic City student's paper:

Topic Sentence: Teenagers have many good reasons for wanting to move to Atlantic City.
Subtopic sentence 1: For one thing, there are many year-round activities.
Supporting details: lounges with entertainment, casinos, boardwalk, malls, beaches in summer.

Subtopic sentence 2: Because there is so much going on, there are a lot of people worth getting to know.
Supporting details: friend—Tropicana, friend on fishing trawler, women.
Subtopic sentence 3: Perhaps most important for some teens, Atlantic City has many job openings all year.
Supporting details: casino car parkers, bellhops, room service, other restaurant jobs, lifeguards in summer.

With your outline in hand, you are almost ready to write a first draft for this assignment. But first, you need to consider how you will end your paper.

Writing an Ending

A final feature of a paragraph that helps a reader to understand the writer's ideas is a good ending. Paragraphs don't just stop; they are finished. You wouldn't want your reader to turn the page expecting to read more, only to see that there is no more. You want the reader to know you have finished what you wanted to say.

An ending is the last thing the reader reads, and you want it to help "sew up" the paragraph. There are several possibilities for endings:

1.   Signal the end by using words such as finally, last, or in conclusion.

2.   Restate the main point of the paragraph without actually repeating the topic sentence.

3.   Indicate in a sentence or two the importance of the subject to the reader or to you, the writer. This last suggestion prevents a reader from thinking "so what?" after reading the paragraph.

ACTIVITY 4

Read the following student paragraph on a place as an example of one way to end a piece of writing. Answer the questions following the selection.

Bodybuilder's Choice

Champion's Gym has a great atmosphere for aspiring bodybuilders. As soon as I stepped through the door, I found out that this was the place for the serious athlete. All I could hear were sounds of barbells and dumbbells being clanged together. As I walked toward the desk to pay for my workout, I noticed a display case filled with vitamins for sale. The labels on the cans and jars of vitamins emphasized their importance to the bodybuilder: "dynamic musclebuilder" or "ultra stamina." After the owner gave me my change, I started to walk around to get a better look at the place. Everywhere I looked, there was some kind of hard, sweaty training going on. Just beyond the desk, I saw guys torturing their chests, bench-pressing more than 400 pounds. A little farther in, my buddy was punishing his biceps with heavy curls, and veins were standing out all over his arms. In the back of the gym, I saw a guy with thighs the size of tree trunks doing endless sets of squats with heavy weights. Their examples and the great facilities of the gym lured me in. Now I was looking forward to training and even anticipating the pleasure of pushing my muscles against heavy iron.

QUESTIONS
What kind of ending does the writer use?

Does it help the reader to understand the main point?

What suggestions do you have for a better ending?

What transitions did you notice?

Endings of short paragraphs or papers may be only a sentence or two. Longer papers require more "drawing together" or summarizing of information and can be several paragraphs. Writers of books often make the whole last chapter the ending!

WRITING APPLICATION: Writing an Ending

To write an ending for your observation, ask yourself the following questions:

1.   How did the place make me feel?

2.   What importance does this place have for me or for others?

3.   Why do I want my reader to know about this place?

4.   What should my reader remember about this place?

      The answer to one or more of these questions will help you write an ending to your observation.

WRITING APPLICATION: Writing a Rough Draft of a Descriptive Paragraph

Write a paragraph on one of the topics listed at the beginning of the chapter. Keep the contract with the reader made by the topic sentence—that is, stick to the main point. Use subtopic sentences and transitions to link together related ideas. Support your ideas with good specific details to help your reader to experience the place as you experienced it in your observation. Try to help your reader follow your thoughts by providing transitions between ideas, and "sew up" the paragraph with an appropriate ending.

Revising vs. Proofreading: What's the Difference?

Frequently, the task of getting ideas down on paper is so complex that problems go unnoticed until the writer is finished and has time to reread the paragraph. It is best to think first in terms of revision of the larger issues that may affect the entire piece of writing, such as purpose and audience, before going on to problems that may affect only sentences and words, such as proofreading for punctuation and spelling.

You may wish to think of this process as one of reviewing your intentions for what you have written.

1. Did I remember my purpose for writing?
You want to think again about what you are trying to do in the paragraph. In this case it was to make a reader understand something about a particular place. Did you do that?

2. Did I consider my reader?
As you read your paragraph, you should think about what your readers know about the subject and what they don't know. Are there any parts of your paragraph that would be puzzling to them? Where could you add more information?

3. Did I provide a focus for the reader?
Is there a clear topic sentence that contains an attitude word to provide a direction for the paragraph?

4. Did I keep to the main point?
Read each sentence and check to see that it is related to the topic sentence.

5. Did I provide links between my ideas?
Read your sentences to see whether you have provided the signals or transitions that make it easy for readers to follow your train of thought.

6. Does the ending help make my point?

The ending should let the reader know that the paper is finished and should reinforce the main point or let the reader see the importance of what was discussed.

WORKING WITH PEERS

Exchange your draft with someone else, and have him or her respond to the preceding questions on your draft.

Proofreading for Grammar, Usage, and Spelling

After reading your paragraph through for its support of your topic sentence, its support of one main point, and its transitions, you need to pay attention to the "mechanics" of writing: grammar, usage, and spelling. You may have been surprised to find that this was not the first thing to do in revising a paragraph. But if you think about why mechanics come last, perhaps it will make sense to you. If you add material to make something clearer to the reader, or change the way some sentence is worded to make the linkage between ideas more effective, you will most likely be altering the sentence structure or the punctuation. If you already had revised the paper for mechanics, you might have had to do it again because you made changes. So it makes sense to save this step for last and do it only once.

Some people wonder why attention to the mechanics of writing is important at all. After all, isn't the message the most important thing? Yes and no. Poor sentence structure, spelling, and punctuation distract the reader from your message. Such distractions may be serious enough to make your ideas unreadable, or they may be fairly minor but nevertheless undermine your credibility with the reader ("Why should I believe someone who can't even spell correctly or write a complete sentence?"). In a way, it is like going to apply for a job in torn, dirty clothes. You may have great credentials, but the interviewer will probably form a bad impression before ever finding out how good you are.

Part V suggests strategies for writing effective sentences. You may wish to consult it to help you revise your mechanics. As mentioned earlier, revising of ideas comes before revising of sentences and words. When you are satisfied that your ideas are expressed clearly and completely, then proofread for errors in mechanics.

Here are some hints to help you proofread:

1. Read your paper out loud. That way you may hear an error that your eyes might have missed.

2. Next, read backwards, from the last sentence to the first, instead of in normal order. This way of proofreading a paper will help you avoid the

tendency we all have to read what is in our minds instead of what is actually on the paper.

Using a Revision Checklist

What follows is a revision checklist that calls attention to the features of a paragraph. Note that the questions direct someone to check the major content features of the paper before considering mechanical problems.

Revision Checklist

1.   Is there a topic sentence? What is the attitude word in the topic sentence? Does the attitude word reflect the main idea in this paragraph?

2.   Are all the sentences of the paragraph related to the main idea expressed in the topic sentence?

3.   What transitions are used to help the reader move from sentence to sentence in the paragraph?

4.   Are there enough specific details in the paragraph to enable a reader to "picture" the place?

5.   What is the conclusion? Is it effective?

6.   Are there any mechanical errors?

WORKING WITH PEERS

To practice using the revision checklist before applying it to your paragraph, in pairs or small groups go over the following first draft of the Atlantic City paper, which contains several errors. Before correcting the errors, apply the questions of the checklist to the paper

Atlantic City (Rough Draft)

Atlantic City is one of the greatest places for a teenager to live. First, there is always something to do all year around. A.C., unlike most other shore towns, doesn't close after October. In my building alone there is enough to do to keep a person busy for awhile. For example we have an indoor pool with snack bar, a health spa, pool and ping pong tables, resturaunts, and lounges with entertainment by people like David Brenner, Steve Martin, and Andy Williams to name a few. Then near-by there is the Board Walk, a few malls, the casinos, some movie theaters, resturaunts, and dance clubs. Because there is so much going on and so many people, there are a lot of people worth getting to know. One of my new friends is the son of an owner of the Tropicano casino. Another friend works on a fishing trawler. And there are thousands of women so that one's social life is usually booked up. Most important for teenagers is the many job openings there are. Summer is the only time that it is harder to get a job. Summer is also the time of year when the city is very crowded. Traffic can get really terrible then. Working for the casinos is a lot of fun and it pays very well. Casino jobs include parking cars, where you get to drive other peoples' Porches, BMWs, and if you're lucky mabey a Lamborghini. There is also bell hops, room service, and when you turn 21, the bars and casinos themselves. Teenagers, who usually get bored easily, will find nothing boring about Atlantic City.

WRITING APPLICATION: Writing the Final Copy

Using your classmates' suggestions on your rough draft and your own editing and proofreading, write a final copy of your paragraph.

ADDITIONAL WRITING TOPICS: OBSERVATION

1. Observe places where people wait for something, such as a doctor's office, a ticket line, a traffic jam, a line for a bank teller, outside an elevator. Describe the people and their actions as they wait. Assume you are an impatient person and that you are making this observation to see if you can learn anything about waiting. You are therefore writing for yourself.

2. Observe people at a shopping mall, a rock concert, a county fair, a football game, a large lecture hall on campus, or another place where large numbers of people gather. Assume you are writing a column on people for a local newspaper, pointing out modern fads and behavior. Your readers are interested in "What's Hot" and "What's Not," and your observations should provide plenty of specific details to satisfy their curiosity.

Readings for Part I

Timeless Beauty
CHARLES KURALT

NEWPORT, OREGON. In the second week of June, the coast of Oregon is alive as at no other time of year. I don't mean alive with people, although the weekend salmon fishermen are crowded into the bars and cafés along the bay front here in Newport. To see the kind of life I'm talking about, you have to leave town and drive down this magnificent coast along the cliffs and headlands. Golden splashes of scotch broom bank the road, improbably beautiful in the sun. The bright green coastal meadows are carpeted with daisies, and the fragile white flowers contrast with the sturdy dark trunks of towering Douglas fir, the spruce and hemlock, the myrtle and cedar. Everything that blooms is in bloom in the Oregon June: azaleas and rhododendron and, back at the edge of the forest, wild roses.

You look to the left and up to see all this. But if you do, you will be missing all the life that is to the right and down, below the cliffs at the edge of the sea. There are seals down there, and sea lions emerging from their caves to frolic in the surf, and seagulls and cormorants, and murre birds, which look like miniature flying penguins, skimming beyond the breakers. The sand crabs scuttle along the beach, the sculpins dart through the tidal pools, and otters roll in the coral sea.

cormorants: web-footed sea birds
murre birds: diving sea birds
breakers: waves
sculpins: spiny fish
heath: low shrub

In this season there is too much of life to see it all. To the south, inland from Pistol River, there is a wilderness area where the rarest of flowers grows, a kind of heath called *Kalmiopsis leachiania*. The Kalmiopsis is a living fossil, much studied. The visitor regarding with awe the burst of life and beauty in the second week of June, and wondering how many springs this has been going on, learns that the Kalmiopsis has been blooming now for 65 million years.

"Timeless beauty" is an expression that has meaning in June and the coast of Oregon.

QUESTIONS

Before answering questions that focus on specific features of the writing, think about this passage and discuss in your writing journal what you thought was important and how you reacted to the reading. Then answer the following questions, if assigned.

1. Kuralt celebrates the forms of life he sees during June in Oregon. What forms of life does he admire in these paragraphs?

2. How does he organize his descriptions? That is, what details go into each separate paragraph?

3. What transitions between paragraphs does the author use?

4. Could this description be written all as one paragraph? If yes, what would be the topic sentence? Would there be any subtopic sentences? Explain.

5. Note the vivid verbs Kuralt uses to describe the actions of the animals: "frolic," "scuttle," and "dart." Think of three other animals and the action verbs that would apply to them:

Animal	Action verb

Writing Journal Suggestion: If you could choose your favorite time of year in a favorite place, what would it be? Why?

The Ngong Farm
ISAK DINESEN

I had a farm in Africa, at the foot of the Ngong Hills. The Equator runs across these highlands, a hundred miles to the

North, and the farm lay at an altitude of over six thousand feet. In the day-time you felt that you had got high up, near to the sun, but the early mornings and evenings were limpid and restful, and the nights were cold.

limpid: perfectly clear

The geographical position, and the height of the land combined to create a landscape that had not its like in all the world. There was no fat on it and no luxuriance anywhere; it was Africa distilled up through six thousand feet, like the strong and refined essence of a continent. The colours were dry and burnt, like the colours in pottery. The trees had a light delicate foliage, the structure of which was different from that of the trees in Europe; it did not grow in bows or cupolas, but in horizontal layers, and the formation gave to the tall solitary trees a likeness to the palms, or a heroic and romantic air like fullrigged ships with their sails clewed up, and to the edge of a wood a strange appearance as if the whole wood were faintly vibrating. Upon the grass of the great plains the crooked bare old thorn-trees were scattered, and the grass was spiced like thyme and bog-myrtle; in some places the scent was so strong, that it smarted in the nostrils. All the flowers that you found on the plains, or upon the creepers and liana in the native forest, were diminutive like flowers of the downs,—only just in the beginning of the long rains a number of big, massive heavy-scented lilies sprang out on the plains. The views were immensely wide. Everything that you saw made for greatness and freedom, and unequalled nobility.

no luxuriance: not fertile
essence: true nature
foliage: leaves

cupolas: rounded domes

clewed up: raised up

thyme: plant used to flavor food
bog myrtle: plant
creepers: vines
liana: woody vine that climbs on trees
diminutive: small
downs: a high, treeless area of England

sojourn: visit

The chief feature of the landscape, and of your life in it, was the air. Looking back on a sojourn in the African highlands, you are struck by your feeling of having lived for a time up in the air. The sky was rarely more than pale blue or violet, with a profusion of mighty, weightless, ever-changing clouds towering up and sailing on it, but it has a blue vigour in it, and at a short distance it painted the ranges of hills and the woods a fresh deep blue. In the middle of the day the air was alive over the land, like a flame burning; it scintillated, waved and shone like running water, mirrored and doubled all objects, and created great Fata Morgana. Up in this high air you breathed easily, drawing in a vital assurance and lightness of heart. In the highlands you woke up in the morning and thought: Here I am, where I ought to be.

profusion: large number or amount
vigour: strength

scintillated: sparkling
Fata Morgana: a mirage or illusion

assurance: confidence

QUESTIONS
Before answering questions that focus on specific features of the writing, think about this passage and discuss in your writing journal what you thought was important and how you reacted to the reading. Then answer the following questions, if assigned.

1. What sentence of paragraph 2 expresses Dinesen's attitude toward the landscape? What details support her ideas about the landscape?

2. What does Dinesen call the air in paragraph 3? What details explain what she means?

3. Dinesen says in paragraph 3 that the "air was alive over the land." What does she compare the air to?

Writing Journal Suggestion: Comparisons help you to understand things in a different way than you might ordinarily think about them. Have you ever seen air you could describe as alive? Where? What did it look like? Can you think of another natural object, such as a cliff, a lake, a woods, that you might characterize as being alive or like a person or animal? Write about it.

Muroc

TOM WOLFE

elevations: altitude

terrestrial: land-based
evolution:
  development
vegetation: plants
Japanese bonsai:
  dwarf trees
silhouette: dark
  outline
arthritic: a person
  with arthritis or
  pain in the joints

putrid: rotten
prehistoric: time
  before history

throwbacks: an old
  form of life

Muroc was up in the high elevations of the Mojave Desert. It looked like some fossil landscape that had long since been left behind by the rest of terrestrial evolution. It was full of huge dry lake beds, the biggest being Rogers Lake. Other than sagebrush the only vegetation was Joshua trees, twisted freaks of the plant world that looked like a cross between cactus and Japanese bonsai. They had a dark petrified green color and horribly crippled branches. At dusk the Joshua trees stood out in silhouette on the fossil wasteland like some arthritic nightmare. In the summer the temperature went up to 110 degrees as a matter of course, and the dry lake beds were covered in sand, and there would be windstorms and sandstorms right out of a Foreign Legion movie. At night it would drop to near freezing, and in December it would start raining, and the dry lakes would fill up with a few inches of water, and some sort of putrid prehistoric shrimps would work their way up from out of the ooze, and sea gulls would come flying in a hundred miles or more from the ocean, over the mountains, to gobble up these squirming little throwbacks. A person had to see it to believe it: flocks of sea gulls wheeling around in the air out in the middle of the high desert in the dead

grazing: eating
antediluvian:
    primitive, old
crustaceans: sea
    animals
primordial: primitive
ooze: mud

of winter and grazing on antediluvian crustaceans in the primordial ooze.

When the wind blew the few inches of water back and forth across the lake beds, they became absolutely smooth and level. And when the water evaporated in the spring, and the sun baked the ground hard, the lake beds became the greatest natural landing fields ever discovered, and also the biggest, with miles of room for error. That was highly desirable, given the nature of the enterprise at Muroc.

quonset-style: metal
    shelter

Besides the wind, sand, tumbleweed, and Joshua trees, there was nothing at Muroc except for two quonset-style hangars, side by side, a couple of gasoline pumps, a single concrete runway, a few tarpaper shacks, and some tents. The officers stayed in the shacks marked "barracks," and lesser souls stayed in the tents and froze all night and fried all day. Every road into the property had a guardhouse on it manned by soldiers. The enterprise the Army had undertaken in this godforsaken place was the development of supersonic jet and rocket planes.

QUESTIONS

Before answering questions that focus on specific features of the writing, consider this passage and discuss in your writing journal what you thought was important and how you reacted to the reading. Then answer the following questions, if assigned.

1. What specific details about Muroc made it "highly desirable," as Tom Wolfe says, for "the development of supersonic jet and rocket planes"?

2. In the first paragraph, Wolfe uses the terms "fossil landscape," "fossil wasteland," and "prehistoric shrimps," among others, to describe Muroc. What dominant impression do these words create for you, the reader?

3. Another set of terms may create another impression: "twisted freaks," "horribly crippled," and "arthritic nightmare." What do these words describe? Why does Wolfe use such words?

4. How does Wolfe make you understand that Muroc is isolated?

5.   What sentence might serve as a topic sentence for paragraph 1?

Writing Journal Suggestion: Write about the most isolated place you have ever seen. How did it make you feel?

PART II

Writing from Personal Experience

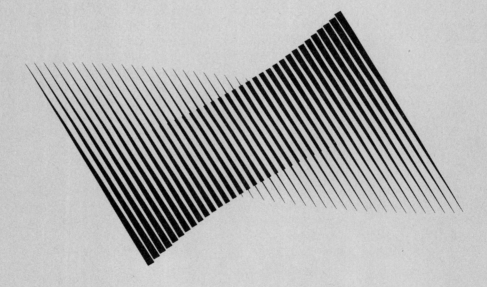

What we observe, being in the present, can be recorded in notes or even on film, videotape, or cassette. What we *have* observed over our lifetimes is embedded in our memories and is, therefore, sometimes more challenging to recall, organize, and express in writing. Nevertheless, our experiences give us insights into human nature and a time perspective that a simple observation does not allow. If we are asked for advice, we often use examples from our experience to illustrate our answer, or we may relate a personal anecdote relevant to the point. In the next two chapters you will learn how to use your valuable experiences to illustrate your ideas with examples or to narrate an incident to explain an idea. Building on what you have learned about the writing process, these chapters will expand your command of techniques to generate ideas, to organize them effectively, and to express them convincingly to your audience.

CHAPTER 3

Developing a Paragraph from Experience: Illustration

Thinking About Illustration

People are constantly observing their surroundings and other people as they go through life. They accumulate a storehouse of such observations. These memories of their personal experiences can serve as a basis for writing. Think of what you have experienced: You have worked at jobs, traveled, lived in different houses or apartments in different neighborhoods or even in different parts of the United States or in other countries, have made friends (or perhaps enemies), have been to school, have been part of a family, and have had hundreds of other experiences too numerous to list. That no two persons have exactly the same experiences makes their individual lives unique, special, and interesting to write about.

Sometimes you may want to discuss incidents that have happened to you or to people you have known to explain an idea to someone or to make a point about something you wish the other person to understand. In other words, you want someone else to benefit from your experience. For example, you might recall a problem with the electrical system of your 1979 Chevrolet to a friend frequently experiencing a dead battery in his Camaro, to help that friend figure out the problem with his car. Or you could write about the three best teachers you had, to illustrate to someone what qualities make for a really good teacher. Or you might remember some of the spectacular plays of a famous sports figure to illustrate just how skilled or deserving of fame he or she may be.

One application of this idea goes beyond your own life experiences. College instructors may ask questions on essay exams that require giving examples of principles students have learned in class. An English professor might ask you to explain what kind of person Daisy Buchanan is in the novel *The Great Gatsby*. You might reply that Daisy is shallow and, as the author F. Scott Fitzgerald puts it, "careless." To give specific examples of Daisy's behavior to support your opinion, you might mention that Daisy seems to have no goals or real purpose in life as she says, "What do people plan anyway?" And you could mention her conduct at the end of the novel as being particularly careless when she lets Gatsby take the blame for the accident for which she was responsible. Giving examples to support a point is very useful in many writing situations.

Before continuing, let's discuss the assignment you will be working on in this chapter. As before, if you wish to write an alternative assignment, there are several topics suggested at the end of the chapter.

Understanding Purpose and Audience: Topics for an Illustration Paragraph

Reader's Digest frequently includes a feature called "The Most Unforgettable Character I Ever Met," which describes the personality and accomplishments of some remarkable person (often not a famous one, just someone ordinary). Assume your college or local newspaper decides that it wants to run a shorter version of such an article each week, length to be 250–300 words, and you decide to submit an article, concentrating on a single quality of a person you know or knew well. The newspaper doesn't demand that the people described all be heroes; in fact, some humorous glimpses into eccentric or unusual behavior would be just fine—and the names can be changed to protect the foolish!

Who is your audience? Whoever reads the newspaper—faculty and students on a campus, or anyone from the community for the local paper. Each audience might differ on what it wants to read. The campus audience might be most interested in campus personalities—faculty members; students with interesting backgrounds or personalities; people who work in the counseling office, the cafeteria; the buildings and grounds crews, and the like. The local newspaper might like portraits of local government officials, teachers, sports figures, or just ordinary people. Whomever you choose, it should be someone you have known and observed for a while.

To get your thinking started, think about anybody you know who has one of the following qualities:

courage	neatness/messiness	creativity
persistence	leadership	mechanical skill
ambition	thriftiness/miserliness	artistic skill
patience	optimism/pessimism	thoughtfulness
imagination	curiosity	dedication

(Additional topic suggestions may be found at the end of the chapter.)

Generating Ideas

Sometimes you may feel that you don't have anything to write about, that you haven't had enough experience to say anything that someone else might find interesting to hear or read. Such feelings are normal; most people feel at some time that their lives are rather ordinary and uninteresting. Sometimes, however, you may feel this way because you haven't really thought about your attitudes or experiences, just as you really hadn't observed the place that you lived. So you need ways to think about your past experience to develop material to write about.

The Writing Journal

In earlier chapters you used a writing journal to record your observations. In this chapter, you can use your journal to explore your memories of the person you will be writing about. You can jot down specific incidents you remember about the person or some of his or her behavior you might later use in your article. If you ever have had a thought while falling asleep or while in the shower that you told yourself you would remember and that you then forgot, you may appreciate the value of keeping a writing journal. Some people even use a small tape recorder to record thoughts they don't want to lose.

WRITING APPLICATION: Using the Writing Journal

For two or three days, let your mind dwell on a person who is a likely subject for your article. Write down your thoughts—no matter how unrelated—as they occur to you. If you can observe the person without calling attention to yourself, include such observations in your journal.

Asking Questions

After entering ideas and observations in your journal, you need to explore your topic further by asking questions about the person, his or her behavior, and what you will say in your article. Try the reporter's questions as they relate to this assignment: who, what, where, when, why, how? One student working on the assignment answered the questions as follows:

Who? Mrs. V, my mother's friend.

What? She is very clean—almost too clean.

Where and When? When she goes out to eat, she cleans the silverware with her napkin and checks glasses for spots. She holds a cup of coffee in her left hand and drinks from that side of the cup. In hotel rooms, she sprays everything with antiseptic. At home she cleans the kitchen after every meal, wiping cabinets, counters, and even the telephone. She asks her family members to comb their hair in only one bathroom. She's trained her Yorkshire terrier to wipe his feet on a mat when he comes in.

Why? She is at war with dirt and germs.

How? I think if I explain the extremes to which Mrs. V goes that people will be amused that someone carries cleanliness so far.

WRITING APPLICATION: Answering Questions

Answer the following questions as completely as you can.

1. Who is my subject?

2. What quality do I find interesting or unusual about this person?

3. Where have I seen this person "in action?" What were the circumstances?

4. When has the person shown this interesting or unusual characteristic? List all the incidents you know about.

5. Why does the person act this way? What motivates him or her?

6. How can I show this person's character to the reader? How can I make the reader understand the person as I understand him or her?

WORKING WITH PEERS

After you have answered the questions, exchange them with another class member and read each other's answers. Do you have any additional questions to ask the other student about the person being discussed? Do you want to know more details than are given? If so, write down questions so that the other student will be able to answer them.

Freewriting

By this time you have given the topic much thought, and it may be helpful to let all that you are thinking "spill" onto a page by freewriting. Remember that freewriting is "uncensored"; that is, you write quickly to get your ideas down on paper without editing for spelling, punctuation, or sentence structure.

WRITING APPLICATION: Freewriting

Freewrite for ten minutes about the person who is the subject of your article. See if you discover any additional memories by letting your mind flow into your pen.

Developing Specific Examples

Now that you have your journal, your questions and answers, and your freewriting to work with, you can begin to select the examples your reader will find most interesting and convincing. Your purpose, you remember, is to illustrate some quality or characteristic of a person for an article in the local newspaper or campus newspaper. In Chapter 1 you learned about the importance of *showing* rather than *telling*, and the key to that was using specific details. In this assignment, the key to success is also being specific, that is, choosing specific examples.

Something else also can happen when you begin to look for specific examples to illustrate a quality or characteristic of a person—you may find yourself altering what you want to say about that person. You might decide that Mrs. V's kindness to your family is more important than her need for a clean house. The writing process does not always proceed neatly from one step to another. People frequently change their minds and revise their plans. If this happens to you, go with your new idea and find specific examples that show that characteristic.

ACTIVITY 1

In this activity are a number of statements about people. Below each statement, write a specific example of behavior that *shows* the reader that the statement is true. The first one serves as an example.

1. My mother is thrifty.
    Specific example:

    My mother hates to throw food away. She saves every scrap of meat, tablespoon of applesauce, or ounce of juice.

2. I have a creative friend.
    Specific example:

3. I once had an unreasonable teacher.
    Specific example:

4. One of my relatives is a mechanical genius.
    Specific example:

5. One of the Olympic athletes seemed especially talented.
    Specific example:

ACTIVITY 2

Read the following student paragraph on Mrs. V (based on the answers to the questions on page 57), and answer the questions that follow.

A Meticulously Clean Person

My mother's best friend, Mrs. V, is a meticulously clean person. She is always on her guard against dirt and germs when she is away from home. Whenever she orders coffee at a restaurant, she always holds the handle of her cup with her left hand because she says fewer people drink from that side of the cup. She also polishes all of the utensils and checks the water glasses for spots before using them. In hotel rooms, she completely sanitizes the closets, drawers, beds, and bathroom with antiseptic before she moves in. At home, Mrs. V is even more meticulous. She will not allow her husband and daughter to comb their hair anywhere in the house except the basement bathroom. Since it is the only room without rugs, hair that falls on the floor can be more easily swept up. The kitchen in her house is always immaculately clean. After doing the dinner dishes, she wipes down everything in the room from the cabinets to the telephone to make sure that there is not a spot of grease or dirt. But the most amazingly clean thing has to be Mrs. V's Yorkshire terrier, Chippy. These dogs have very long hair that usually becomes knotted, but not Chippy's. His hair is always brushed, and the hairs around his face are held back in a barrette. Mrs. V never lets Chippy go anyplace outside, except the yard, where he was trained to go on newspaper. When Chippy is finished, he comes into the house and stands on his doormat and wipes his feet. I know this sounds unbelievable, but I have seen the dog do this myself. While I agree that it is important to be clean, I feel Mrs. V is a bit too meticulous.

QUESTIONS

1.   The writer has a series of examples to illustrate Mrs. V's cleanliness. List those examples of behavior outside the house:

Now list the examples of habits inside the house:

2.   What transitions let you, the reader, know where these incidents occurred? Circle them in the paragraph.

3.   Why does the writer end with the example of Chippy?

After reading this student paragraph, you are now ready to begin writing your own. The next section will help you organize your ideas and write the paragraph.

Writing and Revising an Illustration Paragraph

After you have generated many ideas about your subject person and his or her personality, you are ready to begin to select and focus your ideas for the article you are writing. As was said in Chapter 1, the writer makes a contract with the reader to discuss a specific, limited topic. If the writer keeps the contract, the reader will be able to follow the ideas and understand the article. If, on the other hand, the writer breaks the contract with the reader and strays away from the subject, the reader will become confused. One way to preserve the contract between writer and reader is to have a clear topic sentence at the beginning (or close to the beginning) of the paragraph.

Writing Topic and Subtopic Sentences

Topic sentences, you recall, make a statement about the subject and contain an attitude word that gives the paragraph its focus or direction. For example, a student might write, "My Uncle George is the most generous person I know," and follow that with examples of Uncle George's generosity (perhaps he used to bring mayonnaise jars filled with quarters, dimes, and nickels every time he visited). Or maybe the same Uncle George is a talented wood carver, and the student decides to focus the article on that quality. The topic sentence would then have to be changed to reflect the new focus: "George Berman, my uncle, is one of the best carvers of bird decoys in the East." This focus would then be supported by examples of Uncle George's art and his recognized success in the field. In each of these cases, the paragraph would most likely be rather short, for each topic sentence focuses on one, rather limited subject.

If, however, you have several examples to illustrate a person's character, you may need subtopic sentences to organize your ideas. An example of using subtopic sentences to organize a discussion of a subject is illustrated in the paragraph about Mrs. V that you read earlier. Look back at that paragraph (page 59) and notice how each group of examples is clustered under a transitional subtopic sentence to direct the reader to the three areas in which Mrs. V's cleanliness is evident: outside the house, inside the house, and in the treatment of her dog. In the activity that follows, you will practice writing topic sentences that belong with the examples that follow them.

ACTIVITY 3

For each set of supporting examples, write a topic sentence that makes a statement and has an attitude word to provide focus for the paragraph. The examples that would support the topic sentence are listed. The first one has been done as an example.

1. Topic Sentence: *My fourth grade teacher was a strict disciplinarian.*

   Supporting Examples: Mrs. Skinner used to keep a ruler handy at her desk and would rap a student's knuckles if he or she was not paying close attention to the lesson. She also believed that making a student sit in the corner was a good way to punish the student. She insisted on complete quiet when our class was walking in the hall to the library or lunchroom.

2. Topic Sentence:

   Supporting Examples: One time Bob had a flat tire on the way to my house. Another time his dog had been playing with his car keys, and Bob had to look all over the house before finding them. Several times he said he got a phone call just as he was about to leave the house. It's getting so that I tell him to meet me about thirty minutes before I really need to meet him.

3.   Topic Sentence:

Supporting Examples: Recently, an oil spill near Pittsburgh contaminated the Ohio River and threatened the drinking water of communities downstream. Oyster harvesters on Chesapeake Bay report taking fewer oysters in their days on the water. Even more frightening are reports that a lake near the U.S.–Canada border is polluted by toxic chemicals borne by the wind.

4.   Topic Sentence:

Supporting Examples: Jean donates one Sunday each month to her church's kitchen, where she and other volunteers cook and package meals for the homeless. She also spends time in an inner-city mission, serving food to street people who otherwise would go hungry. Jean and her children participate each year in a walkathon; for each mile they walk, sponsors contribute money to aid the homeless.

5.   Topic Sentence:

Supporting Examples: Leroy never reads directions before he tries to put something together. As a result, he gets even more frustrated when parts don't fit. When he is fixing things around the house, he wants to get done as quickly as possible, so he doesn't wait for the paint to dry before putting on a second coat. He walks on a freshly washed floor because he is too impatient to let it dry first. If you ever are in a traffic jam with Leroy behind you, you will know it. He leans on the horn although no one in front of him can move either.

WORKING WITH PEERS

After writing a topic sentence for each paragraph in Activity 3, discuss your topic sentences with others in your class. You may be surprised at how many variations there were, even though the examples supporting the topic sentences remain the same.

Next, could you expand any paragraphs by using subtopic sentences and additional examples? Choose one to expand and work on it in pairs or groups.

Now you are ready to write your own topic sentence for the article you are writing on a person.

WRITING APPLICATION: Writing a Topic Sentence

Write a topic sentence that makes a statement about a person you know. If the sentence reflects one characteristic of the person's character or personality, you may not need subtopic sentences in your paragraph. If, however, you wish to focus on more than one characteristic, or you will have many examples, you may need subtopic sentences and should include them in this Writing Application.

Beginning the Paragraph

Sometimes, you will want to provide some background on a subject before your reader reads your topic sentence. An introduction to your subject can give your reader a reason for reading your article or help him or her to understand the rest of the article because you could explain any unfamiliar words or situations in the introduction. If what you are writing is short, as is the paragraph you have been working on, then a beginning sentence or two is usually enough. If you are writing an essay of many paragraphs, then an introduction can be a paragraph or longer.

For example, let's take the earlier paragraph on Mrs. V (page 59). That began with the topic sentence "My mother's best friend, Mrs. V, is a meticulously clean person." If the writer had wanted to, she might have discussed how much her mother values a clean, orderly house, how the writer herself likes things to be neat, but how Mrs. V puts everyone she has ever met to shame. In other words, the paragraph might have begun like this:

My family has always prided itself on keeping a clean, orderly house. My mother cleans regularly, and after much nagging in my preteen years, I began to appreciate keeping my room neat and clean too. Similarly, our neighbors' houses are always picked up and freshly dusted and vacuumed. However, no one comes close to Mrs. V, my mother's best friend. Mrs. V is a meticulously clean person. . . .

ACTIVITY 4

Look back at the paragraphs in Activity 3 for which you wrote the topic sentence. Now write a sentence or two to begin each paragraph that will "set the scene" or in some other way lead into your topic sentence. The first one has been done as an example.

1. *Although I went to a good school, I can't remember most of my elementary school teachers, probably because nothing they did really left an impression on my mind. But I clearly remember one who*

frightened everybody. My fourth grade teacher was a strict disciplinarian.

2.

3.

4.

5.

WRITING APPLICATION: Beginning a Paragraph

Write a beginning to your paragraph about a person that will act as a "lead-in" to your topic sentence. Remember to consider your purpose and audience (the local or campus newspaper article you are writing).

WORKING WITH PEERS

Exchange your paragraph beginning with another student or group of students, and find out from them if the beginning you have written effectively sets the scene for the paragraph.

Using Short or Extended Examples

The next decision you have to make is selecting the examples to support your topic sentence. You may have several examples from your writing journal, from the answers to your questions, or from the freewriting you did earlier in this chapter. Now you have to decide which one or ones support your topic sentence. Just as was the case in your observation, you may have examples you can't use because they do not support your topic sentence. Whenever we write, we find ourselves having to narrow down our ideas, and in the process we have to cast some details or examples aside. Sometimes, it seems almost wasteful, but if we don't eliminate ideas that don't support the topic sentence, we will confuse our readers by getting off the track.

You have probably listened to someone who could never stay on a subject but rambled off to a dozen different topics. What did you do? Probably you stopped listening out of boredom or frustration.

As you begin to select examples to illustrate your topic sentence, you have two main choices:

1.   Choose several short examples to support your main idea, *or*

2.   Use one longer, more developed example to illustrate your point.

Using several short examples can keep the reader's interest and provide the reader with enough separate pieces of evidence to be very convincing. The prosecuting attorney probably will bring many witnesses to the stand rather than rely on just one. And if you are writing an answer to an essay exam question, you may want to give several examples to show your instructor that you have read and understood the material thoroughly. On the other hand, if what you are writing does not need to be so persuasive, or if the one example you are presenting is persuasive by itself, then the longer example works well too.

In the earlier paragraph on Mrs. V, the writer used several examples of Mrs. V's behavior to show how concerned with cleanliness she is. As you will recall, the examples were of her behavior first outside the house and then inside the house. It is important to group shorter examples together so the reader doesn't get confused moving from one to another. If the writer had talked about Mrs. V's drinking coffee in restaurants from the wrong side of the cup, and then her making her family members comb their hair in a certain place, and then had gone back to her sanitizing the hotel room, readers would feel as if someone was dragging them from room to room. Instead, the writer was careful to organize the examples logically, first according to location (outside the home, then inside) and then according to the order of importance (ending with the most remarkable example, of the dog wiping its feet). The switch from outside the home to inside the home was signaled by a transitional subtopic sentence: "At home, Mrs. V is even more meticulous." And the episode with the dog is also signaled by a sentence: "But the most amazingly clean thing has to be Mrs. V's Yorkshire terrier, Chippy."

ACTIVITY 5

Read through the following two lists of sentences. For each list, first pick out the topic sentence; make it number 1. Then number the remaining sentences in each list in the order of their importance, using the transition words as clues to what is of greater importance.

A. _____ They are the marketplaces for Spanish gold doubloons, French dueling pistols of ornamental silver, or industrial floor cleaner in economical gallon jugs.

_____ Other oddities include an antique oak commode, displays of martial art weaponry, and vases of tarnished, hammered brass displayed among six-packs of toilet paper.

_____ Flea markets are havens of the unusual.

_____ Even the most suspicious customer is won over by their practiced sincerity.

_____ They can convince a shopper that heat-stamped vinyl is hand-sewn glove leather, or that paper-light tin is hardened alloy steel.

_____ One enthusiastic salesman sounds a trumpet after each sale and bellows, "another satisfied customer," in an attempt to draw more customers to his small table.

_____ Even more unusual than the goods are the merchants who will do almost anything for the shopper's dollar.

_____ Retired laborers, seventeen-year-old entrepreneurs, and ex-carnival games operators compete with each other for the weekend trade.

B. _____ We could count on her to keep track of what we were doing by peeking through her kitchen curtains as she cooked or cleaned up after meals.

_____ But what we didn't count on was her inability to sleep soundly.

_____ She would also quiz her children when they came in from play as to what they had seen in the neighborhood.

_____ Every neighborhood has its snoopy neighbor, and ours was Mrs. S.

_____ She would be instantly awake if a car pulled into a nearby driveway, note the time, look out the window to see who it was and what was going on, and then go back to sleep.

_____ The next day she'd find a reason to talk to our mother about the time we got in the night before.

_____ It did no good to sneak quietly into the house when Mrs. S was the neighborhood watchdog.

If you decide to use one longer example to develop your paragraph, you may find that you are telling a story. That is, your example may be of a particular incident that has a beginning, a middle, and an end. Read the following paragraph as an example.

Brian, my little brother, has an unbelievable imagination. It seems as though, with a little thought, he can turn any area into a mine field, a deserted island, or anything else that he happens to be in the mood to play at that time. For example, one day last year, I was coming home from work when I spotted this rather large orange-and-dark-blue plaid tent in my backyard. When I got closer to the tent, I discovered that it was constructed of three old bedspreads draped over a clothesline with eight cinder blocks holding the ends of the bedspreads to the ground and forming a triangular-shaped tent. My brother and a friend of his were inside the tent, and when I asked what they were doing, they said, "Playing dinosaur land." With a little chuckle, I turned around and started walking away from the tent. I didn't get more than five feet away from it, when this high-pitched scream rang out, and my brother and his friend came running out of the tent hollering "Quick, take cover! Hurry!" Before I knew it, I was hiding behind this bush wondering what was going on. When I asked him what was the matter, he said, "Our tent just got run over by a herd of dinosaurs, and we almost got crushed." My brother thinks up things so quickly that you never know what he is going to do next. He certainly has an active imagination.

The longer example does not always have to be an incident. It can be just a good example of the characteristic you are illustrating. Read the following paragraph as a example.

The most unusual person I have ever met is my high school friend, Martin. Probably the one quality that makes Martin so unique is his sense of humor. Martin had a very rare, almost bizarre sense of humor that he displayed through his drawings and animations. One of my favorites among Martin's characters was Splerg the Merciless. Now, with such a title a person might expect Splerg to be a hulking monster from another planet. But no, he was nothing more than a slug. Martin would have me laughing to tears with his sketches of this ruthless desperado, a lowly slug, striking fear into the hearts of bank managers and public citizens alike by barking out, during one of his notorious bank heists, "Nobody moves and nobody gets hurt!" The idea of a slug terrorizing a city was so ridiculous that a person couldn't help but laugh. All of Martin's humor was similar to this. He had a flair for making such common, everyday things as a slug extremely humorous.

WRITING APPLICATION: Rough Draft

Write a rough draft of your article on a person. Try to begin your paragraph with a sentence or two that "sets the scene" before you present the topic sentence. Use several short examples or one longer example to support your topic sentence. Use appropriate transitions to link your examples together or to signal a change in subtopics.

Ending the Paragraph

As you learned in Chapter 2, your reader appreciates knowing when you have ended your paragraph, because it is confusing to turn the page expecting something to continue only to find that it has, in fact, ended. The ending also helps remind the reader of the "contract" you made when you began the paragraph, that is, the agreement to discuss a certain subject as stated in your topic sentence.

In an illustration you will have been discussing several examples or one longer example to make a point, and you will not want your reader to lose sight of that point. Therefore, your ending sentence may repeat the main point you are making. The Army has a formula for writing that produces nicely organized paragraphs: "Tell them what you are going to tell them, then tell them, and then tell them what you told them." The ending sentences tell readers what you have told them.

ACTIVITY 6

Look back at the paragraphs about Mrs. V, the imaginative brother, and the humorous Martin. How did they end? Did the endings help the reader keep in mind the point the writer wanted to make about each person? Would you change any of the endings of these paragraphs? Discuss these questions in class.

WRITING APPLICATION: Writing an Ending

When you wrote your rough draft, did you end in a way that helps your reader to understand your point? If not, write an ending now that draws together what you have said about the person and reinforces your topic sentence.

Using a Revision Checklist

Now that you have a completed rough draft, you need to revise it before writing the final copy. As before, you should work on the large-scale revisions first—matters involving understanding purpose and audience and main focus—before you tackle the smaller-scale problems like transitions, sentence structure, grammar, and spelling. Use the following revision checklist to help you revise, or get a classmate to read your paper and answer the questions.

Revision Checklist

1. What is the purpose of the article and who is the audience?
   Does the article take into account the audience's needs? Explain.

2. Is there a clear topic sentence making a statement about a person's interesting or important character? Write it here.

3. Does the beginning provide interesting or necessary background for understanding the person and his or her personality? _____
   If the paragraph begins directly with the topic sentence, can you suggest a possible beginning that might be more effective? Explain.

4. What examples does the writer use to support the topic sentence? List them here:

5. Are these enough to be convincing? _____ If not, where should more be added?

6. Are there transitions between examples or major subgroups of examples? _____ Underline the transitions in the draft. If there are not enough transitions, where are additional transitions needed?

7. Do all the examples support the topic sentence? _____ Are there any that should be omitted because they do not belong?

8. What is the writer's ending? Any suggestions for improvement?

9. Are the sentences grammatically correct? Put a check mark in the margin next to any that need attention.

10. Is the spelling correct? Write "sp" in the margin opposite any sentences in which you think there is a spelling error.

WRITING APPLICATION: Writing the Final Copy

After revising your article, write the final copy.

ADDITIONAL WRITING TOPICS: ILLUSTRATION

1. A marketing firm, AD-vice Associates, seeks college students' opinions of television advertisements for several groups of products:

breakfast cereal

shampoo

beer

blue jeans

soft drinks

The firm wants you to choose one of these products and to give your opinion on its advertising: Are the ads effective? silly? offensive to women or other groups? Support your opinion by referring to specific examples of ads for specific brands of these products (e.g., Coke, Pepsi, Dr. Pepper).

2. You are a columnist for a local or campus newspaper asked to write a weekly column entitled "Sports Greats." Each column chooses a current or former athlete who deserves to be called great. Your job is to give examples of the athlete's performance that have earned him or her such praise.

3. Each year, travelers seek vacation places that are adventurous, restful, educational, or scenic or that have some other characteristic. Most newspapers and many magazines have travel editors who give readers the benefit of their experiences—both positive and negative. You have been invited to be guest travel editor for such a publication. First, decide what the reader of the publication wants to know. Then write a brief article about a vacation spot you have visited, illustrating your opinion about it with specific examples.

CHAPTER 4

Developing a Paragraph from Experience: Narration

Thinking About Narration

Everyone likes to hear or tell stories. Children, of course, love bedtime stories, fairy tales, ghost stories at Halloween, and family stories about things that happened when their parents were children (particularly if the stories involve mistakes the parents made). However, this love of storytelling is not confined to children. Sports commentators recount favorite anecdotes about famous coaches like Vince Lombardi or famous players like Hank Aaron as a way of adding interest to a football or baseball broadcast. Newspaper articles or news broadcasts often tell an incident that reporters feel would interest their readers or listeners. For example, some time ago America read and watched the story of the successful rescue of little Jessica, who had fallen into a well in a small Texas town.

Think about the situations in which you tell stories or hear them told. If you have ever been asked, "What did you do today?" or "What did you do last weekend?", you probably replied with a story of some incident. Also, you have undoubtedly listened while friends told you about a traffic ticket, a car accident, or a great party. And who hasn't been held captive by strangers or relatives relating their life stories?

While most of these examples concern stories being told orally, writing about incidents—also called *narration*—is also routine for people in many occupations. Accident reports are filed by insurance agents and police officers. Workers must report accounts of injuries on the job. Lawyers' briefs may include an account of an incident as part of a prosecution or defense of a case. In college, narratives may be required as part of a paper or exam on a novel, play, or short story. You may be asked in a literature class, for example, to write a narrative on the following topic: "In *Huckleberry Finn,* explain Huck's part in the events leading to Buck's death in the Grangerford-Shepherdson feud." Or a history professor may ask for an account of a historical incident such as the assassination of President Abraham Lincoln or General Sherman's march through Georgia during the Civil War.

In this chapter you will use narration as a way of explaining an idea. The story or narrative will, therefore, support a point or an idea that you wish to explain. As before, you first will need to understand the purpose you have in mind and the audience who will read your paper.

Understanding Purpose and Audience: Topics for a Narrative Paragraph

1. You may be the older relative (brother, sister, aunt, uncle, or parent) of a child between the ages of 10 and 18. Because you want to give the child the benefit of your experience, write about an incident that happened to you, or that you witnessed, to make a point about an invaluable lesson you have learned. Consider one of the following areas, or substitute an idea of your own.

car safety	being careless
drinking	importance of family
drugs	a well-deserved reward
honesty	unselfish friendship
an emergency situation	

2. Write an account of an incident to explain your actions to one of the following people. Or think of another situation in which telling a story would serve some purpose or make a point.

a. a police officer about to give you a citation. Tell your version of the event that might excuse you from being held responsible.

b. a coach considering team members for a "greatest effort" award or "player who made the most difference" award. Show the coach through a retelling of a particular incident during practice or during a game why *you* deserve an award.

   c. an employer considering people for a "problem-solver of the month" award. Tell about an incident involving a customer, another employee, or business procedures that shows your valuable contribution to the business.

Additional topic suggestions may be found at the end of the chapter.

As you consider these topics, think carefully about the reader and the writing situation. If your reader is someone younger than you, you need to consider what he or she knows about the subject of your narrative. You want the younger person to be interested enough in your story to read it all the way through and not be confused by unfamiliar terms. If your reader is someone whom you are trying to influence with your story, you need to consider what would be convincing about your narrative, that is, what specific actions of yours you can tell the reader to achieve your purpose.

Generating Ideas

Your Writing Journal

As you think about your reader and your purpose, you may want to write about your thoughts in your writing journal so as to have a record of your thinking to prompt you as you write. The following suggests other effective strategies for generating ideas for a narrative.

At this point you may not know just what to write about. Perhaps no story comes to mind to fit one of the suggested writing situations, and you can't really come up with another. On the other hand, you may have more than one incident in mind about which you can write and may wonder which one would make the best point or best achieve your purpose. In either case, the most effective strategy that you have learned so far is probably freewriting.

Freewriting

As mentioned in earlier chapters, freewriting has the advantage of allowing your mind to flow onto the page without regard to logic, organization, or correctness. This "trial run" can help you dredge up memories you may only half remember at first or help you sort one incident from another. It's important to keep the words flowing from mind to page and not stop to refine or second-guess. This is not the time to say, "Oh, this is dumb" or "Nobody will find this interesting—it's too trivial." Rather, this is the time for discovery.

WRITING APPLICATIONS: Freewriting

Write about any incidents you remember that may be related, however loosely, to the topic suggestions. (If you can't relate an incident to any of the topics, write about any events in your life. Later, you may find an audience and purpose for retelling that event.)

Write for about twenty minutes, and aim for getting down more than one story. As soon as you have written enough of an event that you are sure you will be able to recreate it later, go on to another memory and write that down. In this way you will be able to choose the most powerful event to tell.

If only one story surfaces in the freewriting, go with it and write as much as you can about it—it may already be your most vivid memory. There is no right or wrong way to do a freewriting; you are just that—free.

In the following student freewriting, a bike rider explores two incidents that happened during a recent bike race, either of which might become the basis for a narrative paragraph later. (Spelling has been corrected to make it easier for you to read.)

Sample Freewriting—The Bike Race

Bike race Saturday-beautiful dry fall weather. Saw the worst accident ever. A racer leaned too far over going into a turn. His pedal scraped the ground and he went down and took the next guy down too. They both hit hard. I heard bones snap-it was that loud! Then ten more riders rounding the turn piled up on the first two. What a mess-bike frames everywhere, blood on the pavement. I was lucky to have been just ahead of the accident. But I saw the spot where it happened each time I came around the loop. By the time I came around it was clear but I could still see blood stains and some bicycle parts. After the race I found out that it wasn't as bad as it looked-a broken collar bone, a broken wrist, and some stitches. I sure am careful now about where my pedals are going into a turn.

Another thing-I lost the race because I was stupid. I was in fifth place and within sprinting *distance of the leaders. There were four of them about thirty seconds ahead of me. I decided to go for it. I gained on them. I threw everything I had into it. I thought my legs would die or my lungs explode. I ditched my food and water bottle to lighten my load. I passed them but then I looked back-with that three of them passed me-I ended up fourth when I could have won. My coach talked to me. I knew not to look back but I forgot-I won't forget again. If I had won I would have had enough points for a better rating. That makes me feel even worse.*

Asking Questions to Select Relevant Details

Freewriting may include details that later seem unnecessary, such as the weather or what was eaten for breakfast. As you prepare to write about an incident so that a reader will be able to follow your thoughts, you need to consider how to tell the incident, what to include, and what to leave out.

Deciding what to include or leave out is a matter of judgment. On one hand, you need to give readers a context for the incident. That is, readers need to know what the situation is (is this a bike race, a car rally, a marathon?). Although you can be mysterious in a narrative ("It was a dark and stormy night"), you run the risk of being so mysterious as to cause confusion. On the other hand, you probably have listened to someone tell a real "shaggy dog" story that went on forever, including every small detail—what everyone at a party was wearing, what the hostess served, each conversation rendered word for word, what the weather was like that day, how long it took to get to the party, etc. You need to include enough background and details of the incident to be understood but not so much that you bore your readers.

WORKING WITH PEERS

In class discussion or in small groups, choose which incident you think would be better for the bike rider to develop in a narrative paragraph, and discuss the reasons for your choice. What points would need more details? What points should be left out?

The following activity gives you more practice in asking questions about the details to include in a narrative paragraph.

ACTIVITY 1

Read the following two student narratives. Then answer the questions that follow each.

My Last Game

I was playing basketball for my high school in my junior year. I had played on the junior varsity as a sophomore. We practiced every day. The season was only two weeks away. I was hoping to get a starting job on the varsity team. So one day after practice the coach called me over and asked if I wanted to work on my rebounding skills some more. I said, "Yes." When I went back on the basketball court, there were the junior varsity team tryouts. My coach said for me to just play and grab rebounds. Then the coach split the teams up into groups of five, and we started to play. Since I was the only varsity player on the court, I was doing rather well. The other players tried to play me close because all the coaches were watching, and if they could stop me from playing well, then they could make the team. The game was going on for about twenty minutes when I went up for a rebound in which I jumped the highest I ever jumped before. A player on the other team slipped underneath me and flipped me over on my back. The coaches and players rushed right over, as I was told. The last thing I remembered was soaring high for the basketball and feeling danger when my feet weren't touching the ground. The next thing I knew, I was in the hospital, and the doctors were afraid to move me because they thought my spine was broken. After many hours of tests, x-rays, and questions, the doctor told me I had a severe nerve disorder in my lower back and that I shouldn't play sports again. This was probably the last time I'll ever again play basketball or any kind of sport in serious competition.

QUESTIONS

1. What point does the writer seem to be making with this incident?

2. What would you say the meaning of it is?

   What in it do you find most interesting?

3. Are there places in the narrative where you would like more information? _____ If so, where? Explain.

4. Are there sentences in the narrative that could be left out? _____ If so, which ones? Explain.

Hero or Failure?

Slow-pitch softball is a sport not taken too seriously by many. Imagine yourself playing shortstop in a playoff game in the bottom of the seventh with one out and men on second and third. Your team is depending on you to make the big play to save the game. In your mind you are going through possible plays. Then you suddenly realize the situation. You're standing less than sixty-five feet away from a cannon aiming right for you with a bullet rifling out at eighty miles per hour. Your mind blanks. You don't have time to think. You just react. You dive for the bullet heading right for the hole up the middle. Then the pressure hits you. The thought runs through your head that if you miss it, it's your fault, but if you make it, you're the hero. You lunge, you stretch your glove out, the runners break, and in slow motion you watch the ball enter your glove. When you hit the ground, you jump up with the ball and calmly tag second for the double play. You are the hero.

QUESTIONS
1.   What is the writer's point in telling this incident?

2.   What would you say is the meaning of the incident?
      What in it do you find most interesting?

3.   Are there places in the narrative where you need more information?
      _____ If so, where? Explain.

4.   Are there sentences that could be left out? _____ If so,
      which ones? Explain.

WORKING WITH PEERS

Exchange your freewriting and have your readers answer the following questions. Add new material or leave out portions of your freewriting as their answers to the questions indicate.

1.   Is this an interesting incident? _____

      Should the writer continue to work with this story? _____
      Explain what you found most interesting or what was uninteresting.

2.   If there is more than one incident in the freewriting, does one incident seem most vivid or best serve the purpose and most interest readers?

If so, which? (If two incidents are related to each other and would serve the same purpose, you may want to try to use both of them in your paragraph. For example, the student bike racer might be able to use both the accident he witnessed and his own mistake of looking back to illustrate the lesson of concentrating on fundamentals during a bike race.)

3. Are there places in the narrative where more information is needed in order for the reader to understand it? _____ If so, where?

4. Are there sentences or details that can be left out because they are unnecessary to the reader's understanding of the incident? _____ If so, which?

Understanding Time Order

If you look back at your freewriting or at the earlier sample student freewriting, you can see that a narrative paragraph is frequently written in the order in which events occurred. That is, events have a beginning, a middle, and an end. (Though flashbacks and other breaks in time order are found in narratives, particularly fictional ones, normal chronological order is probably the easiest for writers and readers to understand.) While freewriting, however, writers may jumble the time order, writing down memories without regard to a reader's need for order to make sense of ideas. As you work with your freewriting, make sure your ideas get put into logical order.

Equally important, writers must give readers appropriate signals or transitions to help them follow the events of a narrative. In addition to time-order transitions like *first, second, next, then,* and *finally,* writers use phrases that act as bridges from one part of the narrative to the next. For example, even in his freewriting, the bike racer used "by the time I came around" and "after the race" to show time order.

The following activities ask you to use transitions to indicate time order.

ACTIVITY 2

Read the following pairs of sentences. Fill in the blank at the beginning of the second sentence with an appropriate transition or transitional phrase. There may be several possibilities for each blank.

1. Janet Evans took her position on the starting block. _____, she dove into the water to start her race for a gold medal.

2. Inez takes a shot that rebounds off the top bar of the soccer goal. _____ there is a blinding spray of water and mud as Tania takes another shot.

3. He walked up to my friend, Tony, asking him if he wanted to buy a VCR.
    _____ he asked me if I wanted to buy one.

4. The quarterback moved back into the pocket. _____ he
    dumped the ball off to me.

5. I was really overwhelmed on the first day of school. _____
    I began to adjust to my new schedule and the demands of my teachers.

ACTIVITY 3

The sentences in the following student paragraph have been scrambled. By
following the clues given by the transitions and the sequence of events, put
the paragraph in logical order by numbering each sentence. The first sentence
has been numbered to start you off.

Spitballs

_____ a. To my shock, I had nailed the teacher in her hair with
                    my spitball!

_____ b. If we weren't hitting other kids, we were having contests
                    to see who had the best aim.

_____ c. We made big and small spitballs and projected them
                    through the air by hand or with a straw.

_____ d. One day we got really daring.

____1____ e. In the middle of my fifth grade year, my friends and I
              went through a stage of throwing spitballs in class.

_____ f. I took aim, closed my eyes, and fired.

_____ g. Most of the time we tried to hit other kids across the
                    room.

_____ h. We invented a contest to see who could get the most
                    spitballs to stick on the chalkboard while the teacher was
                    standing in front of it, teaching.

_____ i. After about five minutes, each of us had at least one
                    spitball sticking to the board.

_____ j. To make matters worse, she called my parents.

_____ k. When I heard laughing start, I opened my eyes.

_____ l. The look she gave me made me feel I was two inches tall.

_____ m. After yelling at me, she made me pick up all the spitballs and paper on the floor.

_____ n. I never threw spitballs again, but I still look back and think of the fun I had until I got caught.

_____ o. To make the contest more challenging, I decided to close my eyes and try to hit the board.

WRITING APPLICATIONS: Putting Events in Time Order

Read over your freewriting and arrange the events in time order, that is, which would come first, second, etc., adding transitions or transitional phrases to signal each stage of the incident to your reader.

WORKING WITH PEERS

Exchange your narrative again with a classmate or read it to a small group. Get feedback on your success with presenting the sequence of events and your use of transitions.

Writing and Revising a Narrative Paragraph

You already have an excellent start in writing a narrative paragraph. You have explored topics by freewriting, expanded or narrowed them by asking questions, and have worked to arrange your freewriting in time order. Now you need to reconsider your purpose for writing and make sure the point you wish to make by telling the story to your reader is clear. You don't want your reader to miss the point of your story. One way to make your point clear is to use a topic sentence at the beginning of the narrative, but that way has its disadvantages too.

Beginning a Narrative with a Topic Sentence: Pros and Cons

The advantage of beginning with the point you wish to make is that it leaves no doubt in readers' minds about why they are reading the narrative. You have told them "right off the bat":

> (Student example) "The time I was conned out of fifty dollars was when I finally learned that you get what you pay for."

After the topic sentence, the rest of the paragraph tells the incident that supports and explains the point you have made.

The disadvantage of beginning with the topic sentence may depend on your reader and your purpose. If you would rather *show* your reader through your narrative the dangers of carelessness, the importance of being clear-headed in an emergency, or the value of an unselfish friendship, for example, you may want to begin with the story itself. This way the reader is involved quickly in the story. It doesn't preach or start with a lesson. If you think the reader would be reluctant to read your ideas if you were to begin with the main point, then begin with the story. You can always write an ending sentence to emphasize the story's importance or its message.

However, there is a risk in beginning with the story: The reader may not be interested in your story without knowing why it is being told. You don't want someone thinking "Why am I reading this?" If the story you have in mind is more of an illustration of an idea than a dramatic story in its own right, you may need to start with the main idea expressed in a topic sentence.

WRITING APPLICATIONS: Experimenting with a Topic Sentence

Write a topic sentence for your narrative paragraph that expresses the purpose of your story. Then read the paragraph with it and without it to see which seems more effective to you.

Using Dialogue to Develop a Narrative

Frequently, narratives concern the actions and conversations of two or more people. One way to report what someone says is indirectly: Antonio says that George will come tomorrow. Another way is to reproduce a person's exact words: Antonio says, "George will come tomorrow." Often the direct quotation is more interesting because it puts the reader in the story as it is happening. Read the following student paper as an example of how dialogue can be worked into a narrative.

You Get What You Pay For

The time I was conned out of fifty dollars was when I finally learned that you get what you pay for. It began as just an ordinary day at work. My friend Brian and I were working together and having fun. As soon as the store became busy, the man who was going to swindle us walked in. He seemed to know the perfect time to put the hit on us. First he walked up to Brian and asked, "How would you like a VCR for fifty bucks?" Then he turned to me and asked, "You want in too?" My eyes lit up when I heard him because I had always wanted a VCR of my own. I was overwhelmed by the deal he offered us, a VCR for fifty dollars! We knew that the VCR's were probably stolen, but we just couldn't pass up a once-in-a-lifetime deal. Also, something in his manner told me that the guy was bad news, but I overlooked my suspicions. He said convincingly, "I work for Sony, where I get these as parts. I service what I sell, so if anything ever goes wrong, I'll fix it for you." After all his smooth talking, we agreed to buy them for fifty dollars each. We gave him our money. Then the man said, "The VCRs are in my van. I'll bring them right back." He walked out the door and down the street. I should have known not to give him the money first, for he simply disappeared. After waiting eight hours for him to return, I knew we had been suckered and that he had taken off with our money. This moment in my life went down in history as the first and last time that I expected something for nothing. I know now that if I want something I will buy it, the honest way.

In this paragraph just one speaker is being quoted and the quotes are written as part of the text, with the proper punctuation. (For more information on punctuating quotations, see Chapter 13.) If you quote more than one speaker, begin a new paragraph with each new speaker's remarks. If the writer of the preceding had quoted his friend or himself in addition to the con man, the passage might look like this:

First he walked up to Brian and asked, "How would you like a VCR for fifty bucks?"
   Brian exclaimed, "Sure!"
   Then he turned to me and asked, "You want in too?" My eyes lit up when I heard him because I had always wanted a VCR of my own.
   "I'm in," I replied. I was overwhelmed by the deal he offered us, a VCR for fifty dollars!

ACTIVITY 4

Rewrite the following indirect statements by putting them the way they would be said if someone were being quoted directly. Put a comma before the quotation starts and quotation marks around the words the person is saying. The first one is done as an example.

1. Coach Palmer said that we just had to win this game.

   Coach Palmer said, "Team, we just have to win this game!"

2. My boss asked me if I could stay late and balance the accounts.

3. The voice on the phone informed me that there had been a serious accident in my family.

4. My friend asked me if I was still going out with Todd.

5. The history professor explained to the class that there would be a mid-term exam, a research paper, and a final exam in the course.

WRITING APPLICATIONS: Adding Dialogue to the Narrative

Read over your narrative and change some indirect conversation into dialogue to add interest to the story.

Ending a Narrative

Since the last thing readers see is your ending, you want to make certain that they understand the purpose you had for telling the story. The ending is particularly important if you decided not to begin the narrative with a topic sentence. It's risky to assume that readers will automatically get the point of your story without your specifically telling them. People sometimes draw completely different conclusions from reading the same story. For example, the story of an automobile crash could be read as a warning not to buy a certain brand of automobile, an example of the hazards of careless driving, or a reason for having stricter licensing requirements.

Even if you begin with a topic sentence, it is wise to end by emphasizing the point or by reminding the reader of your main idea in other ways. Notice that the writer of "You Get What You Pay For" ended with: "This moment in my life went down in history as the first and last time that I expected something for nothing. I know now that if I want something I will buy it, the honest way." These two sentences restate the point made in the topic sentence.

With these ideas in mind, you are now ready to write a complete rough draft of the narrative.

WRITING APPLICATIONS: Writing a Rough Draft

Using your freewriting as altered by the suggestions in the chapter, write a complete draft of your paragraph.

Revising a Narrative

Before revising your own narrative, read the following bike racer's rough draft and note the handwritten changes he made to improve the topic sentence and to leave out details that slowed the narrative or were unnecessary.

The Hard Way to Learn a Lesson

A bike race last weekend in upstate Pennsylvania taught me an important lesson about racing.

(A lesson occured for me at a road race in upstate Pennsylvania near Wil-   ~~omit~~

liamsport) (When I arived at about 8:00 in the morning, I register~~ed~~ *after* *ing* ~~along~~ with

sixty other riders, (At registration we all recived *omit* numbers and line assign-

ments. After that we returned to our coaches where we were breifed of the

course and given a massage)

~~Next~~ we all took our positions at the starting gate. With a bang the gun

sounded. All of us locked into our pedals and pushed down with all we could.

We were all shoulder to shoulder going into the first turn. I turned my head for

a second and saw one of the worst accidents of my career. A racer had leaned too far over and caught the ground with his pedal, which brought him and the rider next to him down very hard. I heard the loud snap of bones being broken. I turned, looked forward, and then looked back again to see ten more riders in a pile of flesh, blood, and aluminum. I kept riding and tried to put the whole incident behind me. I knew that I had three hours of very competitive racing, over three twenty-mile loops, through the hills and valleys of Williamsport. However, every time I passed the site of the accident, my whole body cringed from the sight of dried blood on the road. I tried to concentrate my attention on my race. By the last lap, I was leading the chase group, trying to catch the four leaders. We were about thirty seconds behind the lead group. At that point I decided now was the best time to break away from the pack and try to catch the leaders. Soon I was fifteen seconds behind and had the group in sight. My heart was pounding so hard by then I could hear it. The veins in my legs and arms were popping out all over, and my lungs were about to blow up. But my competitive spirit kept me going. At one kilometer from the finish line, I threw off my water bottles and food to get rid of extra weight. Then I made my move to sprint to victory. I passed all four racers and was out in front, when I made the biggest mistake of my race. I turned my head to see where the others were, then blam! Three riders road right by me. My jaw dropped so far down it hit the handle bars, as I remembered the number one rule in sprinting, "NEVER LOOK BACK!" After the three guys passed me, I pushed down hard on the pedals ~~and got in~~ behind the third place rider and ~~road~~ *rode* across the

finish line in fourth place.

I was so disappointed about how stupid I was, ~~and how~~ I had first place

in the bag and blew it because of a stupid mistake. (I talked it over *omit* with my

coach afterwards, and added up my points, and found out I was two points

behind from getting my racing license for the next class Amateur Pro!

Later at the party I found out the accident *omit* wasn't too bad only two peo-

ple suffered serious injuries, a broken collar bone and a broken wrist. A few

slipped by with only getting stitches.) All in all, this day ~~has~~ taught me two

important lessons: Always make a sharp turn with the inside pedal up, and

never—I mean *never*—look back when you are in the lead. (It will cost you a *omit*

race!)

ACTIVITY 5

In class discussion, answer the following questions about the preceding paper.

1. Why do you think the title was changed? What do you think of the writer's decision to tell both incidents?

2   Compare the two opening sentences (the original and the handwritten one). Which is more effective? Why?

3. Why are several sentences crossed out at the beginning and end of the paper? Do you agree with the decision to leave them out? Explain. Are there others that should be left out?

4. Are there places details need to be added?

5.   Circle transitions in the paper. Are there any other places that could use them?

6.   There is no dialogue in this narrative. Should there be? Why or why not?

7.   How effective is the ending of the paragraph?

Using a Revision Checklist

WORKING WITH PEERS

In small groups or with one other person, exchange your rough draft and ask the reader(s) to fill out the revision checklist that follows. Note that the checklist first asks questions about content and organization before calling attention to mechanical errors.

Revision Checklist

1.   How does the paragraph begin—with a topic sentence or directly with the incident? _____ What changes would you suggest for the beginning? Explain.

2.   As the story unfolds, are there any details that should be left out because they bore the reader or are simply unnecessary? Explain.

      Are there places where more details should be added because you have difficulty understanding the story? Explain.

3.   Would the paper be more interesting with directly quoted dialogue?

      _____ If the writer already uses dialogue, is it effective?

      _____

4.   Does the writer use effective transitions to help you follow the stages of the story? _____ If not, indicate which sentences could use transitions.

5.   Is the time order clear? _____ Should any parts be rearranged? Explain.

6.   How does the paper end?

      Does the ending help you understand the writer's purpose? Explain.

      Make suggestions, if any, for a more effective ending.

7.   Are the sentences free from mechanical errors? _____ If not, point out places that need to be corrected.

8.   Is the spelling correct? _____ If not, suggest words that need to be checked.

WRITING APPLICATIONS: Final Draft

Revise your rough draft after considering the suggestions from the Revision Checklist.

ADDITIONAL WRITING TOPICS: NARRATION

1.   Write an account of your most memorable moment in sports for someone who may not understand your enthusiasm for the sport. For example, someone might not understand your passion for ice-fishing, sky-diving, drag-racing, or even baseball. Let them experience one of your triumphs through your narration of an incident.

2.   Explain to a friend or business associate an incident showing how someone took advantage of your trust. In your narrative you could emphasize how foolish you were or how wily and clever the other person was. Either may serve as a valuable lesson for the reader.

Readings for Part II

Main Street America—1900
FREDERICK LEWIS ALLEN

remote: far away

expedition: journey

It is hard for us today to realize how very widely communities were separated from one another when they depended for transportation wholly on the railroad and the horse and wagon—and when telephones were still scarce, and radios nonexistent. A town which was not situated on a railroad was really remote. A farmer who lived five miles outside the county seat made something of an event of hitching up and taking the family to town for a Saturday afternoon's shopping. (His grandchildren make the run in a casual ten minutes, and think nothing of it.) A trip to see friends ten miles away was likely to be an all-day expedition, for the horse had to be given a chance to rest and be fed. No wonder that each region, each town, each farm was far more dependent upon its own resources—its own produce, social contacts, amusements—than in later years. For in terms of travel and communication the United States was a very big country indeed.

QUESTIONS
Before answering questions that focus on specific features of the writing, think about this passage and discuss in your writing journal what you thought was important and how you reacted to the reading. Then answer the following questions, if assigned.

1. What examples does Allen use in this paragraph to make the reader understand how far apart people lived in 1900?

2. What is the purpose of the sentence in parentheses? "(His grand-children make the run in a casual ten minutes and think nothing of it.)"

3. The ending of the paragraph explains the significance or importance of the communities' being widely spaced. What is the importance of that fact?

Writing Journal Suggestion: Have you ever been somewhere away from convenient transportation and modern communication (such as radios, television, telephones)? How did it make you feel?

Who's in Town in August
NEW YORK TIMES EDITORIAL

massive: large
eerily: mysteriously

On a hot August night, the massive old apartment buildings on Central Park West are eerily dark. Across the park, doormen stand idly under the awnings of Fifth Avenue. The residents are in the Hamptons, or Connecticut, or Maine—wherever the summer people go.

chaos: confusion

Just beyond this rim of wealth, though, it's business as usual. People sit on cars outside Broadway restaurants waiting for tables. Damrosch Park at Lincoln Center is chaos; the balcony of the New York State Theater is packed at intermission. The Mostly Mozart Festival is sold out.

congested: crowded

It's the same all over town. In Greenwich Village, there's hardly a seat to be found in Washington Square Park. The boards at the Chess Club on Thompson Street are busy. In Chinatown, the sidewalks are so congested people have to walk in the street.

In Paris, the long summer vacation is an institution: August off is nearly a natural law. That's not New York's style. At midnight, the galleries and poster shops on Bleecker Street are open for business. On Sixth Avenue, $5 buys a blinking headband or an African figurine.

evident: clear
destination: place to
  go
botanizing: acting like
  a plant
asphalt: tarred street

Not everyone is purposeful. Late on a hot summer night, hundreds of people walk the streets without any evident desti-nation—"botanizing on the asphalt," as the German critic Walter Benjamin once put it. The city itself is the show, even in the heat. At 1 o'clock in the morning you have to stand in line to buy a subway token at Sheridan Square. It's August and everyone's away: Says who?

QUESTIONS

Before answering questions that focus on specific features of the writing, think about this passage and discuss in your writing journal what you thought was important and how you reacted to the reading. Then answer the following questions, if assigned.

1. This newspaper editorial is written in five paragraphs but could be written as just one. What is the main point of the article?

    Is there a sentence that states this main idea? _____

    If so, which one?

2. What specific examples support the main point?

3. Why are there so many examples in this short reading?

    If the writer had used only one or two examples, what would that have done for the support for the main idea?

4. The first paragraph is a beginning or introduction to the rest of the editorial. Why does the writer begin this way?

5. What is the ending? What kind of ending is it, based on what you learned in the chapter?

6. Circle the transitions in the article.

Writing Journal Suggestion: Write about your hometown during a particular season of the year.

No Name Woman

MAXINE HONG KINGSTON

"You must not tell anyone," my mother said, "what I am about to tell you. In China your father had a sister who killed herself. She jumped into the family well. We say that your father has all brothers because it is as if she had never been born.

"In 1924 just a few days after our village celebrated seventeen hurry-up weddings—to make sure that every young man who went 'out on the road' would responsibly come home—your father and his brothers and your grandfather and his brothers and your aunt's new husband sailed for America, the Gold Mountain. It was your grandfather's last trip. Those lucky enough to get contracts waved good-bye from the decks. They fed and guarded the stowaways and helped them off in Cuba, New York, Bali, Hawaii. 'We'll meet in California next year,' they said. All of them sent money home.

protruding: sticking out

"I remember looking at your aunt one day when she and I were dressing; I had not noticed before that she had such a protruding melon of a stomach. But I did not think, 'She's pregnant,' until she began to look like other pregnant women, her shirt pulling and the white tops of her black pants showing. She could not have been pregnant, you see, because her husband had been gone for years. No one said anything. We did not discuss it. In early summer she was ready to have the child, long after the time when it could have been possible.

doubled: were reflected in

bunds: dikes

"The village had also been counting. On the night the baby was to be born the villagers raided our house. Some were crying. Like a great saw, teeth strung with lights, files of people walked zigzag across our land, tearing the rice. Their lanterns doubled in the disturbed black water, which drained away through the broken bunds. As the villagers closed in, we could see that some of them, probably men and women we knew well, wore white masks. The people with long hair hung it over their faces. Women with short hair made it stand up on end. Some had tied white bands around their forearms, arms, and legs.

flared: appeared quickly

"At first they threw mud and rocks at the house. Then they threw eggs and began slaughtering our stock. We could hear the animals scream their deaths—the roosters, the pigs, a last great roar from the ox. Familiar wild heads flared in our night windows; the villagers encircled us. Some of the faces stopped to peer at us, their eyes rushing like searchlights. The hands flattened against the panes, framed heads, and left red prints.

"The villagers broke in the front and the back doors at the same time, even though we had not locked the doors against them. Their knives dripped with the blood of our animals. They smeared blood on the doors and walls. One woman swung a chicken, whose throat she had slit, spattering blood in red arcs about her. We stood together in the middle of our house, in the family hall with the pictures and tables of the ancestors around us, and looked straight ahead.

"At that time the house had only two wings. When the men came back, we would build two more to enclose the courtyard and a third one to begin a second courtyard. The villagers rushed through both wings, even your grandparents' rooms, to find your aunt's, which was also mine until the men returned. From this room a new wing for one of the younger families would grow. They ripped up her clothes and shoes and broke her combs, grinding them underfoot. They tore her work from the loom. They scattered the cooking fire and rolled the new weaving in it. We could hear them in the kitchen breaking our bowls and banging the pots. They overturned the great waist-high earthenware jugs; duck eggs, pickled fruits, vegetables burst out and mixed in acrid torrents. The old woman from the next field swept a broom through the air and loosed the spirits-of-the-broom over our heads. 'Pig,' 'Ghost,' 'Pig,' they sobbed and scolded while they ruined our house.

"When they left, they took sugar and oranges to bless themselves. They cut pieces from the dead animals. Some of them took bowls that were not broken and clothes that were not torn. Afterward we swept up the rice and sewed it back into sacks. But the smells from the spilled preserves lasted. Your aunt gave birth in the pigsty that night. The next morning when I went for the water, I found her and the baby plugging up the family well.

started to menstruate: reached child-bearing age

humiliate: shame

"Don't let your father know that I told you. He denies her. Now that you have started to menstruate, what happened to her could happen to you. Don't humiliate us. You wouldn't like to be forgotten as if you had never been born. The villagers are watchful."

QUESTIONS

Before answering questions that focus on specific features of the writing, think about this passage and discuss in your writing journal what you thought was important and how you reacted to the reading. Then answer the following questions, if assigned.

1. The writer's mother tells her the tragic story of her aunt for a reason. What is her reason or purpose for telling the story? Where is there a statement of that purpose?

2.   The time order is not just as the story took place. What paragraph actually begins the story of the night the aunt gave birth?

Where does the narrative of that night end?

3.   What is the purpose of including the information in paragraphs 2 and 3?

4.   Are there sentences in the paragraphs telling the story that are not actually about that night? If so, where? Could they have been left out? Explain.

5.   Which details of the narrative seem especially vivid to you? Which are most frightening?

Writing Journal Suggestion: If you are female, how does this story make you feel? How does the fact that the author's mother told it to her as a lesson make you feel? What lessons from your own childhood can you recall?

If you are male, what reactions do you have to the story or to the mother's using it as a lesson? What lessons from your own childhood do you recall?

PART III

Writing an Essay from Observation and Personal Experience

To develop an idea, frequently you will combine your powers of observation with your recollections of personal experience. Your mind actively shifts between what you see, hear, smell, and taste in the present time and what you remember of past experiences. For example, think about what happened when you learned to drive a car or ride a skateboard or dance a new dance. You probably watched while someone else showed you what to do, and then you tried it yourself. Depending on talent, you may have been good the first time, or you may have had to observe once more before you tried it again. Each time, you used both your observations and your memory of past attempts to improve your performance. In Part III you will draw on what you observe and what you have experienced to explain a process to a reader and to explain in what ways two things are similar or different.

Also in Part III you will build on what you have learned so far about writing paragraphs. In this part you will write essays with more than one paragraph. While a paragraph may be enough to express some ideas, often you will need to write more than one paragraph to explain an idea in enough detail so that your reader will understand it. The paragraph is the building block for the essay, and you will learn in this part how to fit together what you know about writing paragraphs into the larger structure of the essay.

CHAPTER 5

Developing an Essay Through Process Analysis

Thinking About Explaining a Process

If you have ever followed a recipe, put together a model kit or child's toy, or assembled a piece of furniture bought in a flat carton, you appreciate the importance of clear process analysis. If your experience is like mine, there have been many times when you muttered nasty remarks under your breath (or even out loud) at the person who wrote the directions you were following, because you couldn't find "slot A," or the piece marked "front" didn't seem to fit in the front.

But process analysis involves more than putting together things or following a recipe. If science writers need to explain why the nuclear plant at Chernobyl exploded or why the space shuttle Challenger disintegrated, they use their understanding of the way things work and what went wrong to explain the process to their readers. Sportswriters may explain the way a team's defense or offense works to the fans. Doctors explain how some body system works so people can understand what they need to do to take care of themselves or what they must do to get better. It's safe to say that at some time or another everybody must write, read, or at least hear the explanation of a process.

Understanding Purpose and Audience:
Topics for a Process Analysis Essay

As has been true before, what you write will depend on your purpose for writing and your intended audience. Some processes are intended to be ones a person can follow step by step, such as recipes or model kits. Other processes are not intended to be duplicated by the reader—no one expects to construct a nuclear generating plant in the backyard or perform a triple heart bypass on the kitchen table. However, the reader may have good reasons for wanting to know about nuclear plants and heart bypasses. This is to say that processes can be divided into two main purposes:

1.   Explaining to a reader how to do something

2.   Explaining to a reader how something is done

After the purpose is decided, who the essay's intended audience is will determine how simple or technical the process explanation will be. An explanation of a heart bypass operation to a fifty-year-old patient would differ from the explanation to a medical school anatomy class or from the explanation in a national news magazine such as *Time*. The patient needs to understand the basic bypass process and also needs reassurance of its safety and necessity. The anatomy class needs to know the structures involved in such an operation. *Time* magazine readers want a clear, objective explanation, not as technical as for an anatomy class, but not as personalized as for a patient.

Think about the purpose and audience for an essay on one of the following topics. (As before, there are additional topics at the end of the chapter.)

1.   Choose something you know how to do quite well (a skill learned in a sport, hobby, craft, or job) to explain to someone of your own age and interests who does not know the process but would like to learn. Think of your explanation as the text for a booklet or manual that someone new to the skill could read. In the case of a skill learned on the job, think of your reader as a new employee whom you are training. Some examples:

How to play chess

How to change a bicycle tire

How to close a cash register at the end of a shift

How to give a bed-ridden patient a bath

How to customize a car or van

How to paint a house, hang wallpaper, build a garage or deck, or install a carpet

2. Choose a process that you know about through observation or experience to explain to a group of fifth-graders (ten-year-olds) in an elementary school class studying local government and politics, science, health, art, or some other subject. Or choose another audience such as senior citizens or high school students. You are the visiting expert and will write your script for your presentation. Drawings or pictures may accompany your script but must be explained. Some examples:

How the local school board or city council or other government body decides an issue

How local political candidates are chosen and elected

How to administer first aid or CPR

How to care for your teeth

How a battery works

How a ceramic vase is made

How a house is built or a piece of furniture is made

How a food or drink is processed from raw materials to finished product

To help you choose a topic and get started with the process essay, the following section suggests some ways to generate ideas.

Generating Ideas

Selecting a Process to Explain

To explain a process effectively to someone else, it helps to choose a topic you know a great deal about, having watched others complete the process or having completed the process yourself. You will be more confident of your ability to explain the process if you are truly an expert yourself.

Also, think of a process that really needs to be explained in order for it to be understood. You want your reader or audience to be interested in your explanation and not bored by its being too obvious—how to make a peanut butter and jelly sandwich, while practical, would probably not hold a reader's interest!

There are three strategies you have tried before that will help you select a topic and gather material to write about: writing in your journal, observing, and asking questions.

Writing in Your Journal

If you have been writing frequently in your journal, you may already have some subjects discussed that would make good process papers. If not, use your writing journal now to think about all the things you know how to do well.

WRITING APPLICATION: Listing in the Journal

Make a list entitled "I know how to _____" and fill in the blank with as many things as you can think of. To get started, look at the following list of verbs and objects:

I know how to . . . cook a turkey
build a garage
take inventory
sell sports equipment
design a landscape

Your aim is to explore as fully as you can what you can do. Don't second-guess yourself at this stage and say, "No, that's not a good idea." Just open the floodgates of your ideas.

Observing

Sometimes people have seen a process repeatedly or have done it often themselves, but if asked to explain it to someone else they may have trouble because they did it mechanically without paying attention to exactly how it was done. For example, have you ever tried to explain to a toddler how to tie his or her shoes? If so, you probably fumbled a bit for words to describe an action you do without thinking. Another more complicated example might entail giving directions to someone about how to get to your house, apartment, or dorm. If you have traveled the route often, you can probably find your way by driving or taking public transportation without thinking about all the street names, the right and left turns, or the distances involved, but someone new to the process needs all that information, or the person could get lost.

Observing and taking notes on what you observe will help you in two ways. First, you will find out whether the process is really one that needs to be explained in an essay to someone else. For example, let's say you have tentatively chosen the subject "How to Put on a Band-Aid." You observe the process the next time you do it and your notes say:

1. *Wash cut with soap and water.*
2. *Dry with clean cloth or gauze.*
3. *Apply antibiotic cream or spray.*

4. *Open wrapper of Band-Aid.*
5. *Remove paper backing.*
6. *Apply to cut.*

Given these six steps, you are probably not going to have enough to write an essay about. That is, the process is so simple it really doesn't require much expert explanation. Complex processes usually have several stages, each of which has several steps. For someone new to learn the procedure, complex processes often require the expert help of someone who has practiced the process. A second advantage to observing and note-taking is that you will begin to gather information on the concrete details of each step of the process that you will need to explain it.

WRITING APPLICATION: Observing and Note-taking

If you have tentatively selected a process to explain from your journal list that you are able to observe or do yourself, take detailed and careful notes of the process as it is being done. Note, too, any warnings of false steps or things to watch out for as you observe the process.

The following student sample takes note of the process to repair a bicycle tire.

Sample Observation—Fixing a Bicycle Tire

Turn bike over.
Loosen axle nuts of wheel with flat tire.
Deflate remaining air.
Pry tire off rim w/dull flathead.
Pull tube out.
Check for hole by inflating and holding under water or
* by inflating and feeling for air escaping large hole.*
If hole is large, buy a new tube. If hole is small, buy a
* patch kit.*
To patch: Wash off excess dirt.

Mark hole with pen.
Scrape around hole w/flathead.
Find or cut patch 1 inch larger than hole.
Apply rubber cement to patch.
Let dry for 10-20 seconds.
Put patch over hole in tube and hold firmly for
    1 minute.
Insert tube on rim.
Put tire back on rim.
Inflate tube.
Put wheel back on bike.
Engage the chain.
Tighten axle nuts.
Ready to ride again!

Asking Questions

Another strategy to help you generate ideas is to ask questions about a process from your journal list or your observations that you think your reader would ask. There is no stock list of questions, for each process generates different questions, but to get started here are some you might consider:

What materials do I need to complete this process?

Where do I find the materials?

What do I do first? second? third? etc.?

What problems should I watch out for?

What is the end result of the process?

How do I know if I or someone else did a good job?

WRITING APPLICATION: Asking Questions

Ask the questions that you think your reader might ask about the process you are explaining, and answer them as you go along. You will end up with a list of the steps of the process, the materials needed, the pitfalls to watch out for, and the like, but it will most likely not appear in its final form.

WORKING WITH PEERS

Exchange your questions and answers or your notes from your observation (or both) with classmates. Ask them if they have additional questions about the process that you did not consider. If they know something about the process, ask them if there are steps or warnings you left out of your notes on your observation. Give them the same help with their questions or notes.

Understanding Time Order in Explaining a Process

If you have read Chapter 4, you have had some experience organizing ideas in time order. Explanations of a process are also usually organized in this way. You want readers to be able to follow the steps of a process, especially if the goal is for them to be able to do the process themselves.

Basically, the idea of time order for a process is the same as that for a narrative—with a few important differences. Before you begin with the steps of the process, you may wish to tell readers what materials they will need before they begin (if it's a "how to" process) or a sense of the scope or importance of the process (if it's a "how it is done" process). That is to say that while a narrative may begin with "It was a dark and stormy night," a process may require a bit more of an introduction. You will learn about introducing a process explanation later in this chapter.

Also, it may be more likely for a process paper to stop after a particular step—to take stock, prepare for the next step, or to explain another part of the action going on at the same time. For example, if you were explaining the making of wood panels, you might need to say, "As the panel layers are being squeezed together at high pressure, the outward surface of the panel is being sanded with special sandpaper rollers. Such sanding creates the smooth surface of the finished panel."

Finally, it is very important that each of the steps of the process be reported in the proper order. Can you imagine the readers' confusion if they are told to put a cake in the oven and then told to add three eggs to the batter? If you change the order of events in a narrative, your readers might not even notice, but in a process it could mean failure instead of success. Also, people sometimes get forgetful when they explain routines they have done many times. (For example, someone giving directions might suggest several steps in the process later; "Did I tell you to turn right just after crossing the bridge?")

Just as you need transitions to signal your readers to move from one event to the next in a narrative, so do you need transitions to move from step to step in a process paper. These transitions can be single words like *next, then, first, second,* and *third* or phrases and clauses that refer to previous or subsequent steps such as "after removing the wheel," or "before inflating the tire." To give yourself some practice in using transitions, complete the following activity.

ACTIVITY 1

Read the following student draft about fixing a bicycle tire. Supply transitions (one word or several words) where there are blanks in the draft. If you find yourself using the same transitions over and over (such as "next" or "then"), try to think of alternative choices that would fit.

Draft—How to Fix a Bicycle Tire

If you ever need to fix a bicycle tire, there are some basic, easy steps that you need to follow. _____ it is necessary to take the wheel off by loosening the axle nuts and removing the chain from the sprocket and wheel. _____ you must drain the rest of the air from the tube by exerting even pressure on the tube while holding down the nozzle. The _____ step is to pry the tire off with your hands or a dull flathead screwdriver to prevent further damage to the tube. _____ it is necessary to remove the tube by slipping it out of the tire and the rim. _____ the tire is out, you must find the hole by inflating it and holding it under water to look for bubbles. If the hole is too large, you may want to buy a new tube. If the hole is small, purchase a tire patch kit. _____ wash the excess dirt off and mark the hole with a pen. Choose a patch one inch larger than the hole. _____ apply rubber cement over the hole and surrounding area. Let the cement dry for about twenty seconds. _____ put the patch on, covering the hole, and hold firmly for one minute. Replace the new or patched tube between the tire and the rim, but make sure the tire is on securely _____ inflating the tube. _____ replace the wheel on the bike, with the chain in place. Tighten the axle nuts. _____ you are ready to ride your bike again.

Note that in addition to the transitions, the writer frequently repeats a word from the last sentence in the first part of the next sentence: ". . . damage to the tube. It is necessary to remove the tube . . ." This repetition also helps carry the reader along from step to step.

Understanding Completeness in Explaining a Process

Because you are expecting your readers to follow your explanation of a process—either to do it themselves or to understand how it is done—you must explain all the steps and not leave anything out. Most people have had the experience of following someone's directions only to come to a Y in the road and have no clue whether to turn left or right, because the direction-giver had forgotten that step. Or, again using the example of the cake-baker, what would happen if you put the cake in a plain baking pan when the directions should have called for a greased pan? The cake would be difficult or impossible to remove, and the finished product would not turn out as it should.

Look at the draft of the bicycle tire repair process. Is there anything the writer left out? I would like to know, for example, how large a hole is too large to repair. How do I know when I can patch a tube and when I have to replace it? Also, is it just the tube that needs to be patched? What about the tire itself? Can you think of other questions that may need to be answered?

Writing and Revising the Process Essay

Having generated some ideas for your process paper, you will now begin to put your ideas into a form your reader will be able to understand. Since this is the first essay assignment, it may be helpful to discuss the relationship of paragraphs to essays before going on.

Building Paragraphs

Even expert writers are uncomfortable trying to define what a paragraph is or to determine exact rules for when a new paragraph is required and when it is not. As you have probably noticed, paragraph length varies widely from the very short paragraphs characteristic of newspaper columns to the long, sweeping paragraphs of 18th- and 19th-century essay writers. Modern paragraphs seem to have gotten shorter, perhaps in response to impatient readers who want information in a hurry. Just as cutting up a piece of meat makes eating easier, splitting ideas into paragraphs makes "chunks" of information more manageable for readers to "digest" or understand. If a paragraph gets too long, it may tire readers by asking them to keep too many things in mind at one time. Paragraphing, after all, does provide a kindness to the reader in the form of a rest, a convenient stopping place before the prose continues.

You have practiced writing paragraphs with a topic sentence and supporting details, examples, or incidents. Those paragraphs now become the building blocks for an essay. If you had two points you wanted to make about your hometown, in a paragraph you included both ideas in a topic sentence and developed each point in subtopic sentences supported by examples. In an essay, each of those subtopics could become a full-fledged paragraph, with the subtopic sentences becoming the topic sentences for the new paragraphs. The key here is how much detail or explanation is necessary to develop the idea—the more complicated the ideas, the more paragraphs needed to explain them to the reader.

While all this is true—it's not the whole story. Some paragraphs have special functions in an essay and may not be there to develop a subtopic idea. Frequently, for example, a paragraph may be devoted to introducing an essay in one of a variety of ways, as you will see in the following section. Also, concluding paragraphs to essays have their own special functions, which can include summarizing main ideas, emphasizing the importance of what has just been written to a reader or to society as a whole, or answering a question raised earlier in the essay.

In addition to these two rather easily distinguished special-function paragraphs, writers may indent for other reasons. Some paragraphs, for example, may act as transitions between ideas, others may divide a long explanation into more easily read parts, and still others may accommodate a writer's style, including the use of dialogue and surprise questions or statements. Usually, however, there is *some* reason for a new paragraph; effective writers do not just indent willy-nilly.

If all of this seems a little overwhelming because it is not easy to pin down and make rules about, the following discussions and activities about paragraphing the process essay and in subsequent chapters about writing other kinds of essays may make things clearer. Use your rough drafts as opportunities to experiment with different paragraph structures. In that way you gain feedback from your instructor or your peers on whether your efforts help or hinder them in understanding your ideas.

Writing an Introductory Paragraph

Some writers find it difficult to write an introduction before they write the body of the paper. "How do I know," they ask, "what to say in an introduction if I don't know what I am going to introduce?" That's a good question. If this is a problem for you, skip the introduction and write the paper, going back to look at it when you are finished to see if some introductory material would be helpful to the reader of the paper. However, a process paper is usually easier to introduce because a writer generally has a fairly clear idea of what he or she will explain. If the writer is writing about what he or she knows well, the steps of the process have been thought out and are familiar to the writer.

Giving some background before actually beginning the detailed steps of the process may help get the reader's attention and prepare him or her for what follows. An introductory paragraph can prepare readers for the process explanation by answering one or more of the following questions:

1. What materials are needed to complete the process (if I am to duplicate it)?

2. Why should I be interested in learning about the process? Is it important to me personally? Is it important to society that I know something about it?

3.   When is (or was) such a process used? Are there differences between the way something used to be done and the way it is done now?

4.   Why should I believe what the writer tells me? What background or experience makes the writer an expert?

Read the following introductory paragraph to the student paper on fixing a bicycle tire. What questions does the introduction address?

Introduction—How to Fix a Bicycle Tire

It used to be that kids gave up their bikes as soon as they could get a license to drive a car, and they never went back. But cycling for pleasure or health now attracts all ages. However, many of these cyclists have probably been sidelined by a flat tire that can't simply be reinflated with a bicycle pump. Frustrated, they may have abandoned their plans to take to their wheels. But this doesn't have to happen. As a veteran bike rider and road racer, I have had to repair many bicycle tires and am happy to share the easy steps to bicycle tire repair.

WORKING WITH PEERS

In pairs or small groups, write an introductory paragraph for one or more of the following process paper topics, drawing on the questions just suggested. While it probably helps if you know something about the process involved, by asking questions readers ask (that is, that you as a reader may want to know), you can probably write a reasonable introduction.

1.   How to make spaghetti sauce

2.   How to replace a cracked window

3.   How beef moves from field to table

4.   How a radar speed trap works

5.   How to take inventory in a clothing department

WRITING APPLICATION: Writing an Introduction to the Process Essay
Write an introductory paragraph to the process you have chosen to explain. When you decide what to include in your introduction, keep in mind your purpose and the needs of the audience.

Writing a Thesis Sentence for a Process Essay

In earlier chapters, you learned that a topic sentence for a paragraph formed a kind of contract with the reader—you promised the reader that the paragraph would discuss a certain idea. The topic sentence for an essay, often called a *thesis sentence,* does the same thing: it lets readers know what they will be reading. Frequently in a process essay, the thesis sentence is found at the end of the introductory paragraph (as in the student example about repairing a bicycle tire) or in the first sentence of the next paragraph, at the beginning of the process explanation. While in a narrative paper a writer might want to "create suspense" by delaying the thesis sentence to the end, in a process essay the writer generally wants the reader to know from the beginning what process is being explained.

Look at the following student examples of thesis sentences and then try your hand at writing some in Activity 2:

a. Lifting an elderly person from a bed to a wheelchair can be an easy task if one knows the proper techniques.

b. If you want to be a rock and roll star, you'd better learn to bend your guitar strings.

c. A printer needs the right touch to get a printing press to print to its full color potential.

Note that each of these thesis sentences states the subject of the process and suggests a reason why a reader may want to know the process—to make a task easier, to be a rock and roll star, to get good results from a printing press. Since not every reader is interested in every topic, the thesis serves as an "early warning" of subjects to avoid or as a kind of an invitation to read about subjects that interest the reader. Readers appreciate this information.

ACTIVITY 2

Write a thesis sentence for each of the following subjects, drawing on your knowledge of a process and of people who might like to know something about the process.

1. How to make something to eat, wear, or use in a house

2. How to do something connected with a sport

3. How to do something at a job

4. How to register, get a student loan, drop or add a course, or complete another procedure at your school

5. How to get a driver's license, file for unemployment, fill out a tax form, or complete some other bureaucratic process

---

WRITING APPLICATION: Writing a Thesis Sentence for Your Process Essay

Look back at the introductory paragraph you wrote for your process essay. Is there a sentence that could serve as a thesis or main idea sentence? If so, underline it. If not, write a possible thesis sentence here.

WORKING WITH PEERS

Read your introduction and thesis sentence to a small group of classmates. Is it clear to them what you will be explaining? What suggestions do they have for interesting readers or making your intentions clear? Help them with their work as well.

Organizing the Supporting Paragraphs for a Process Essay

As was said earlier, a process explanation is written in time order, and while that generally makes the task of organizing ideas easier, there are still some decisions to make in writing the body paragraphs of the process essay. If you are writing about a fairly complicated process, it is likely that you will have too much explanation to be read comfortably in one paragraph. (Remember that readers like to rest occasionally and that indented paragraphs provide brief rests.)

Where then do you begin and end your body paragraphs? One answer is to look at your observations and question-asking notes to see if the process can be divided into groups of steps or stages. For example, the bicycle tire repair process could be divided into removing the flat tire and tube from the rim, examining and patching the hole in the tube, and then replacing the tube and tire and inflating it again. Each of these stages could be a paragraph.

Another idea is to think about any materials that are needed or preparation that has to be done before the process starts, and to then set aside a paragraph for that explanation. Anyone who has wallpapered a room knows that much of the time involved in the process is spent gathering the materials and preparing the wall surfaces before the actual paper-hanging starts.

Also, if you must stop the process explanation in order to warn readers about pitfalls along the way or to explain a "process within a process" (like how to check for leaks in a bicycle tube), you might consider putting such information in a new paragraph.

WORKING WITH PEERS

Exchange your lists and notes of the process you are explaining, and discuss with classmates which steps should be grouped together to form paragraphs. Put brackets { } around related steps, and number them in what seems to be a logical order.

ACTIVITY 3

Read the following student paper, which is written without paragraphs. Answer the questions about the places new paragraphs might begin.

The Bends

Rock and roll is my life's blood. I love listening to it, and I love playing it, from Elvis Presley's "Blue Suede Shoes" to the latest by my favorite punk rock trio, Hüsker Dü. There are myriad styles in the broad classification of rock, but what gives them all this label is the guitar. The piano remains "the easiest to learn and the hardest to master," but the guitar, especially the electric guitar, will always be *the* rock and roll instrument. Learning the basics of the guitar is not difficult, but if you want to be a rock and roll star, you'd better learn to bend your guitar strings. That is the technique that produces the crying and screaming notes heard in so many songs. "What do you mean by bending the strings?" you ask, and I'm glad you did. Let me explain. A brief description of the mechanics of the instrument will be helpful. Since this technique works 100% better on an electric guitar, I'll stick to that instrument. The strings on a guitar are adjusted at the upper end, the thin end with the knobs. The strings are suspended, usually 1/8 inch or less, along the neck by running them over slightly raised bars or bridges at either end. At the lower end are the pickups. These turn the vibrations of the strings into electrical signals that can then be amplified. The frets are the lines you may have seen running across the neck. They are raised above the neck but are not high enough to interfere with a string's vibration. A properly tuned string will give off a specific note when played. The note depends on the length and tension of the string. The higher the tension and/or the shorter the string, the higher the note. The tension is set when you tune the guitar. The frets allow you to change the length of the string. When you press a string down between two frets, you shorten it by forming a new bridge. The frets are calibrated so that each one gives a higher note than the one above. Bending lets you change the tension on a string. While you are holding a string down, you push the string across the neck. This is not as easy as it sounds. The string must be held very hard against the neck to maintain the higher tension. Your fingers must be strong with tough callouses. Also you must know the note you are trying to reach and hear it when you get it. Otherwise, the sound you make will be as obnoxious to you as the right one would be to your parents! Some guitars have a whammy bar attached to the lower bridge. It lets you pivot the bridge and produce the same effect as bending. It has the advantage of letting you not only raise notes, but lower notes as well. A disadvantage is that since the lower bridge is no longer stationary, the guitar needs to be retuned more than usual. Well, there you have it. Bending's not a technique you will use in every song, but it will enhance your playing noticeably. It becomes part of your style as you mature into a true rock and roll animal.

QUESTIONS
1.   How does the writer introduce the subject?

      Does he answer any of the questions mentioned on pages 107–108? Where does the introduction end? Should the paragraph end there?

2.   What is the thesis sentence?

      Could it begin a paragraph?

3.   The writer explains the mechanics of the guitar. Should that material go in a separate paragraph? _____

      If so, where should that paragraph start and stop?

4.   Where does the writer explain the actual process of bending?

Should that begin a new paragraph? _____

5.   The writer includes an alternative process of bending strings. Should that go in the paragraph with the first process or be placed in a separate one? _____

6.   Is there a conclusion? _____

If so, should it be in a separate paragraph? _____

General questions: How difficult did you find it to read and understand an essay without paragraphs? _____ Did you differ with your classmates in figuring out where the paragraphs should go? _____ Is there one right answer to paragraphing, or are different combinations of steps and explanations possible?

WRITING APPLICATION: Planning Sheet for a Process Essay

The following planning sheet might help you organize the paragraphs for your process essay.

Suggested Process Planning Sheet

Paragraph 1.   Introduction (Rewrite your introduction here.)

Thesis Sentence at end of introduction or beginning of next paragraph

Paragraph 2.   Discuss gathering materials, preparation, or first stage of process.

Paragraphs 3, 4, 5, etc.   Discuss next stages of process or possible pitfalls or "process within a process."

Conclusion.   (See the following section before completing this part.)

Writing a Conclusion

As has been said before, readers appreciate knowing when a piece of writing ends. Conclusions are not always separate paragraphs; often they are single sentences that signal the reader that the writing is ending. Terms like *finally, in conclusion, therefore,* and *last* may signal the end. Writers may use the conclusion to "nail down" ideas discussed in the essay. Since the ending is the last thing the readers see, they may remember it best. So writers frequently summarize or highlight main points. They may emphasize the importance of the discussion for an individual or for society as a whole. Finally, writers may go back to some idea mentioned at the beginning as a way of reminding the reader of the contract they made. For example, the writer of "The Bends" reminds his readers that bending strings will make them play like a "true rock and roll animal," a promise he held out to them at the beginning of the essay.

WRITING APPLICATION: Writing a Rough Draft

Using your planning sheet, write a rough draft of your process essay. In explaining the process, remember to take into account both the intended audience for the explanation and your purpose.

Revising a Process Essay

Once you have written a draft, you can step back and look at it and its parts. You can decide whether your draft seems to achieve its purpose, whether the steps of the process are logically organized and well explained, and whether you have given readers enough information. To gain practice looking at a draft in this way, complete the following activity.

ACTIVITY 4

Below is a rough draft of a student process essay. First, decide whether it clearly explains the process. Where is the thesis sentence? Are there places that you need more information? Then look at its organization. Are the steps in a logical order? The writer could not decide where to put the paragraphs. Where would you indent? Why? What transitions help you move from step to step? Would you suggest others? What changes would you make in the introduction or conclusion? Are there any problems with sentence structure or any errors in usage? Feel free to write in the margins or between the lines.

Getting Color (Rough Draft)

One of the jobs I have had is working in a printing plant. I always thought before that printing was run by machines and was automatic. After working with color presses, however, I have learned that a printer needs the right touch to get a printing press to print to its full color potential. First, the printer starts with a plate. A plate has an image burnt on it. It will have different screens, a screen is a group of dots. The percentage of dots gets higher as the dots get closer to each other. For example, light gray being a 10% screen of Process Black ink. At 100% screen being a black solid. The full color process requires four plates: Process Black, Process Blue, Proces Red, and Process Yellow. All four plates have the same image burnt on it, but they will have different screen percentages. This will allow the different color inks to be distributed where they are needed. They will overlap in some places making different colors. The printer's job is to distribute the inks on the rollers according to the screen percentages on the plates. He or she does this by adjusting keys, opening them up to let out more ink or tightening them down to let out less ink. The right amount is determined by experience or by trial and error. Each time the printer makes changes in the ink, the feeder runs

about 200 sheets through the press to even out the flow of ink and to check

the results. It depends on the skill of the printer, but it usually takes about five

or six of these runs to get the precise color needed. Since each run uses

paper and ink and takes time, printers who can get the job done right with

fewer runs are in demand. Even in an automated printing plant there is a

need for an experienced, talented human being.

Using a Revision Checklist

WORKING WITH PEERS

In pairs or small groups, exchange your rough draft and ask your reader(s)
to complete the following revision checklist.

Revision Checklist

1.   How does the writer introduce the process?

     What changes would you suggest for the introduction?

2.   What is the thesis sentence?

     Does the thesis sentence make it clear to you what process is being discussed and why?

3.   As the process is being explained, has the writer taken into account the age, experience, and interest of the audience? _____ What further suggestions for reaching the audience would you make to the writer?

4.   Is the process clear? _____ Are the steps of the process in order? _____ What transitions are used to move from step to step?

Indicate sentences that could use transitions.

5.   Is the process complete? _____ What additional explanations should the writer make (preparation, materials, warnings, process within a process)?

6.   What is the conclusion?

What suggestions can you make for a more effective conclusion?

7.   Are sentences free from error? _____ If not, underline the sentences that need to be corrected.

8.   Is the spelling correct? _____ If not, circle words that should be checked.

WRITING APPLICATION: Final Draft

Revise your rough draft after working with the suggestions on the Revision Checklist.

ADDITIONAL WRITING TOPICS: PROCESS ANALYSIS

1.   You have been asked by the college newspaper to write an article on how to prepare for an exam, how to write a paper, or how to balance going to college and working at a job. Your audience is your fellow students. While they might appreciate some humor in your approach, they also want some practical advice.

2.   *Gourmet* magazine is running a contest for the best family-favorites recipes. They are particularly interested in recipes not generally found in cookbooks but unique to a particular family, region of the country, or ethnic group. You have such a recipe and decide to enter the contest. You must explain how to make the recipe in such a way that the reader will be able to make it too.

CHAPTER 6

Developing an Essay Through Comparison and Contrast

Thinking About Comparison and Contrast

Comparing and contrasting, another strategy people use to explain something, often depends on keen observation or personal experience or both. If you want to give a friend advice about what car to buy, you may give him or her the benefit of your experience with several cars, comparing their overall performance and repair records. Or you may have worked in a service station where you have seen many cars and are able from your observations to make comparisons. When you shop for athletic shoes or any other item, you are observing and comparing prices, and contrasting quality, style, and fit in order to decide which brand to buy. You may also have past experience with a certain brand, which helps you make your decision. After all, if you've always worn Nikes and they have served you well, chances are you will put them high on your list the next time you need sneakers.

Writers also frequently find a need to compare and contrast. Political reporters compare candidates for office, sportswriters compare athletes' abilities or accomplishments, consumer affairs writers compare makes of automobiles or brands of refrigerators, and financial writers compare stocks, bonds, and other investments. In college, students often are asked to compare historical figures, characters from a short story or novel, or theories in psychology. However, no matter what the subject is, the purpose and the audience remain important.

Understanding Purpose and Audience:
Topics for Comparison and Contrast

Frequently, the purpose for a comparison or contrast is to make a judgment:

EXAMPLES

Who is better, Michael Jordan or Larry Bird?
What jeans should I buy, Levis or Lee?
What are the advantages of one job over another?

Occasionally, the purpose is simply to explain to readers similarities or differences that exist that they might not have been aware of:

EXAMPLES

Newcomer Mario Lemieux shows some amazing similarities to the great hockey star Wayne Gretzky.
Though they look just the same, my twin friends Debbie and Jennifer are really quite different.
The traditional housewife and the working wife may have more in common than each of them realizes.

Technically, *comparing* means finding similarities, while *contrasting* means finding differences. Though sometimes people use *comparing* to mean both, you should be sure in your own mind if you are trying to explain similarities, differences, or both. As you will see, your purpose will help determine ways to organize the essay.

Your audience or reader determines, as before, the way you will write your essay. You have to take into account how much readers know or can understand about a subject and why they might want to read about your subject.

For example, comparing makes of cars for *Motor Trend* magazine might demand more technical details than such a comparison for your local newspaper. Similarly, while historians might be interested in the specific movements of each army in the Battle of Gettysburg, the casual tourist visiting the battlefield wants a more general understanding of the southern and northern armies' positions and accomplishments there.

What follows are some writing situations for you to consider. Additional topics appear at the end of the chapter.

1.   You are a movie or television reviewer for a local or campus newspaper and choose two new movies or TV shows to compare or contrast or both. You will want to be fair in choosing the items to write about: comparing

a new Clint Eastwood movie with a Goldie Hawn comedy probably won't work. Similarly, TV sitcoms are unlikely subjects for comparison with news shows like "20/20" and "60 Minutes." Your purpose here can be evaluative (which one is better?) or informational (what's new this season?).

2.　In your experience, you may have had several jobs. To help someone else choose what job to take—part-time or full-time—write an essay comparing or contrasting two jobs, paying attention to their advantages, disadvantages, or both.

Generating Ideas

Understanding Comparison and Contrast

You have probably heard the expression "You can't compare apples with oranges." Actually, you can, since both are fruits. But this saying warns of a common pitfall in comparing and contrasting: making a comparison between two things that can't logically be compared. It would be unfair (and unenlightening) to compare a bag lunch of a peanut butter and jelly sandwich, corn chips, an apple, and oatmeal cookies to lunch in one of the nation's best French restaurants. Even if you were interested in the nutritional content of both lunches, it would be better to compare two bag lunches or two lunches in French restaurants, because they share a common setting or purpose.

However, there are comparisons that take as their main purpose linking items that may at first appear extremely dissimilar. Similes, metaphors, and analogies are such comparisons frequently used in poetry or fiction to get readers to examine subjects from a fresh perspective. So "My love is like a red, red rose" expresses a connection that is not at first apparent. Similarly, "The fog comes in on little cat feet" makes a connection between heavy water vapor and an animal that may affect a reader's image of the way fog acts, but at least initially seems to be an illogical comparison. Sometimes, writers of essays who wish to explain things will use one of these techniques, such as when someone wishes to explain the nervous system in terms of electricity or likens the circulatory system to a collection of pipes linked to a pump. The point is that writers should choose with care subjects to compare, paying attention to the reason or purpose for the comparison.

Finding a Subject for the Essay: Observing, Listing, Questioning

As you think about possible topics, begin to develop information about the subjects by using some of the strategies from earlier in this text. Of course, different subjects may require different strategies. Movies or TV shows can be observed first hand, and the results of the observation can be written down for future reference. If you think you may use this topic for your essay, complete the following Writing Application.

WRITING APPLICATION: Observing and Comparing

To help you compare (or contrast) the movies or TV shows, fill in the following chart with the results of your observations. As you observe, think about the characters and their relationships to each other, the way the actors play the characters, the story or plot, the action scenes or special effects, the dialogue, the photography, the costumes, the music, or any other notable feature. Write down specific remarks about each film or show—don't just put "special effects—good," because later you may not remember what made it good or bad. Instead, write "great stunt—hero goes off building suspended by a fire hose."

After observing both films or programs, put a "+" by the things that were similar about the shows and a "−" by things that were different.

Put any additional comments below the chart.

	Title: Movie or TV show	Title: Movie or TV show	+ or −
Features			
1.			
2.			
3.			
4.			
5.			
6.			

7.

8.

9.

10.

Additional comments (including perhaps which one you preferred and why):

WRITING APPLICATION: Listing in Your Writing Journal

If you will develop your subject by referring to your experience, a list may also help you to discover similarities and differences. For example, if you are comparing two jobs, either one present and one past or two both in the past, you can list features you remember. Think about salary, working conditions, hours, people you worked with, other features. Again, be specific as you list items so that you can draw on the information when you write your paper. If you think that this might be your topic, use the following form for your list in your journal.

	Job 1	Job 2
Advantages:		

Disadvantages:

Other comments:

Asking questions is another way to develop information for both observations and experiences. You can start with the who, what, where, when, why, and how questions, or make up questions specific to your audience, purpose, and topic. For example, you might ask yourself: "What does my reader want to know about jobs? Answer it as fully as you can. If you can't answer a certain question, you may have to observe again, or in some other way get the information needed to answer the question. Use the following Writing Application to apply this strategy.

WRITING APPLICATION: Asking and Answering Questions

Ask yourself questions about your topic and answer them in the following space or in your journal. Answers can be words, lists, incomplete sentences. The goal here is to develop material for the essay.

Gathering Specific Details and Examples

After you have worked with one or more of the preceding Writing Applications, you may now have two subjects to compare or contrast and some preliminary information about them. Check your information to be sure that it is as specific as possible, because it is specific details that interest and convince a reader. For example, if you are writing about two jobs and you say one pays well while the other does not, your reader is likely to ask, "How well does it pay?" Similarly, it is not enough to say that one new movie is "boring" while another is "interesting." Readers want to know what scenes, characters, or dialogue made something boring or interesting. Above all they don't want just to take your word for it; they want evidence. As was said in earlier chapters, you need to *show* readers, not just *tell* them. The following activity gives you some practice in sorting the specific from the general.

ACTIVITY 1

Read the following list of job characteristics. Put all the general words or phrases in one column and all the specific items in another.

miserable jobs	$5.25 an hour	flexible hours
scrubbing dishes	minimum wage	convenient
washing cars	meager wages	a week's notice
cutting grass	fatter wallet	weekends off
timbering trees	reasonable pay	schedule around school work
supermarket cashier	10% increase	

General   Specific

WORKING WITH PEERS

In pairs or small groups, exchange any of the preceding Writing Applications that you did, and have classmates label your information G for general or S for specific. If you notice many more G's than S's, go back and try to supply more specific points of comparison or contrast. Some G's are fine, because you may use the more general statements to form the topic sentences of your essay.

Writing and Revising a Comparison or Contrast Essay

Writing an Introduction

An introduction to a comparison or contrast essay gives enough background to readers so that they know what the subjects are and, even more important, why the subjects are to be compared or contrasted. Readers naturally ask, "Why do I need to know this? What's in it for me?" The readers of an essay on jobs may be curious about the advantages or disadvantages of holding certain jobs because they may see themselves working at similar ones now or in the future. Readers interested in seeing films or watching television enjoy knowing about what's worthwhile to see and what's not, or are curious about new films or programs.

In addition, the introduction allows the writer to build credibility with the reader, that is, to answer the readers' questions "Why should I listen to you? What do you know about this?"

Finally, an introduction may give writers the opportunity to discuss a common aspect of two subjects before contrasting them, or, on the other hand, to point out superficial differences before focusing on essential similarities. So, for example, a writer discussing two restaurant jobs might point out that the duties of each were the same: seating customers, taking orders, and serving food. However, in every other aspect the jobs were vastly different: the pay varied, the working conditions were nowhere near the same, and attitudes of customers and workers were quite different. In another case, a writer evaluating the latest horror movies might point out that despite the fact that Jason Voorhees in "Friday the 13th" never talks, while Freddy Krueger of "Nightmare on Elm Street" fame is fond of puns and witty remarks as he dispatches his victims, the two films have much in common. Readers also welcome incidental information in the introduction that might seem off the subject once the comparison or contrast of the two subjects begins in earnest.

While an introduction serves all these useful functions, when the introduction is written may vary among individual writers. Some writers prefer to write the main body of the paper before introducing their subject to the reader. For other writers, the introduction provides a warmup for the rest of the essay and gets their ideas flowing.

The following activity presents some sample introductions for you to analyze.

ACTIVITY 2

Read the following two student introductions, and answer the questions that follow each:

Right Choice (introduction)

On the way up the financial ladder, I have put in many back-breaking hours doing all sorts of tasks for meager wages. I've done just about every-thing, from scrubbing dishes to washing cars, cutting grass to timbering trees, and digging gardens to shoveling snow. I've tried all the miserable jobs that teenagers get burdened with, so I know that the best decision I ever made was taking a job at a local supermarket. More than any other job I've had, being a cashier provides flexible hours, a chance to meet people, and, most important, reasonable pay.

QUESTIONS
1.   How does the writer build credibility with readers?

2.   What will the subject for the essay be?

Germany: Country of Contrasts (introduction)

Germany is as diverse as the fisherman of the Sylt Islands differs from the farmer of an Upper Bavarian mountain village beyond the Hintersee. Divided roughly into northern and southern areas, Germany contains almost two different countries. Travelers who go to Germany should be aware of these differences and should plan their trips so that they can get the most out of their vacation.

QUESTIONS
1.   How does this writer build credibility with the reader?

What difference do you notice in the way each of these two writers approached this task?

2.   What sentence specifically appeals to the reader's purpose for read-ing this essay?

The previous introduction had no specific appeal to the reader's need to read the essay. Did it need one? Why or why not?

3. What will the subject for this second essay be?

WRITING APPLICATION: Writing an Introduction

Write an introduction for your essay that makes use of one or more of the following options.

1. Gives readers some background

2. Gives readers a purpose for reading the essay

3. Builds the writer's credibility

4. Discusses minor similarities (if the paper will emphasize differences) or minor differences (if the paper will emphasize similarities)

5. Gives incidental information that is not directly involved with the comparison or contrast (how much money a movie made, for example, or what a TV show's ranking is)

WORKING WITH PEERS

Exchange introductions with classmates and get feedback from them as readers. Do they have suggestions for a more effective introduction?

Writing a Thesis Sentence

The thesis sentence for a comparison/contrast essay usually tells readers how the writer sees the two subjects—that is, are they alike or different? It may also tell readers why. So, for example, at the end of the first of the preceding student introductions, the writer says, "More than any other job I've had, being a cashier provides flexible hours, a chance to meet people, and, most important, reasonable pay." Readers know that the writer thinks that this job is better than others and has three reasons for this judgment. This thesis sentence leads readers to expect that the body paragraphs of the essay will cover flexible hours, meeting people, and reasonable pay. If the writer fulfills this expectation, or "contract," with the reader, the paper will be successful. Such a sentence also helps the writer stay on track, because it gives him or her a plan to follow in the rest of the essay.

At the end of the second of the preceding student introductions, the writer does not reveal an attitude toward the differences in the two parts of Germany but urges future travelers to be aware of the differences. Although this thesis does not form as binding a contract with readers because it does not tell what the differences are, the sentence may be enough to interest them in reading the rest of the essay. This second thesis sentence also does not give the writer a plan to follow in writing the rest of the essay, so the writer will need to guard against getting off the subject as he or she writes the rest of the essay.

Frequently, the thesis sentence is written at the end of the introductory paragraph, as in the previous examples, or occurs early in the next paragraph. While there may be reasons in other essays to delay the thesis sentence to the end, readers of a comparison/contrast essay may become impatient with a writer who doesn't reveal his or her thesis. You don't want your readers to think, "Why am I reading about these two things? What is the point?"

WRITING APPLICATION: Writing a Thesis Sentence

Check the introduction you wrote for your essay to see if you have already written a thesis sentence. If not, write a sentence now that expresses the similarities or differences between two things that you want to develop in an essay. If you wish, include several reasons or features explaining why you think these things are similar or different: "While there may be some minor differences, 'Nightmare on Elm Street' and 'Friday the 13th' resemble each other in plot, choice of victims, gore, and special effects."

Recognizing Methods of Organizing a Comparison/Contrast Essay

Once you have details of two subjects' similarities or differences or both and a thesis sentence, you need to know how to organize the details so that a reader will be able to understand them. A jumble of similarities and differences is as hard to sort out as a deck of playing cards tossed in the air during "52 Pickup." Readers expect the writer to do the sorting out, and there are two basic ways to do that (with a few variations).

Method A: The Point-for-Point Method
This way of organizing the essay takes each point you want to make about the topic (for instance, in the earlier example of horror films: plot, choice of

victims, gore, and special effects) and devotes a paragraph or more to each one, covering both films under each point. This can be graphically represented by alternating points XY XY XY XY.

Sample Outline

I. Introduction and thesis
II. Similar plots
 X. "Nightmare on Elm Street"
 Y. "Friday the 13th"
III. Similar choice of victims
 X. "Nightmare on Elm Street"
 Y. "Friday the 13th"
IV. Similar use of gore
 X. "Nightmare on Elm Street"
 Y. "Friday the 13th"
V. Similar kinds of special effects
 X. "Nightmare on Elm Street"
 Y. "Friday the 13th"
VI. Conclusion

The advantage of this method is that it emphasizes each point of the comparison. The disadvantage is that it may become somewhat like watching a tennis game in which the players trade shots endlessly—back and forth, back and forth. However, there are ways to develop each paragraph that minimize the disadvantages.

Method B: The Whole-Subject Method
This method discusses all features of one subject at one place and then all features of a second subject at another place. This may be graphically represented by XX XX YY YY.

Sample Outline

I. Introduction and thesis
II. "Nightmare on Elm Street"
 X. Typical plot
 X. Choice of victims
 X. Use of gore
 X. Special effects
III. "Friday the 13th"
 Y. Similar typical plot
 Y. Similar choice of victims
 Y. Similar use of gore
 Y. Similar special effects
IV. Conclusion

The advantage of this method is that it discusses the whole subject at once; and if each point is relatively short, it gives the reader a good idea of the subjects' features. The disadvantage is that the several points discussed may be hard for the reader to keep in mind when the second subject is compared, and the writer may forget to discuss the points in the same order, thereby creating confusion for the reader.

It is very important in both methods to use the same points of comparison in the same order so that readers will be able to follow the discussion.

If you want to discuss *both* similarities and differences of two subjects, a variation of these methods will help you organize your thoughts.

Sample Outline

I.   Introduction and thesis
II. Ways two films are similar
   A.   Feature 1
      a.   Film X
      b.   Film Y
   B.   Feature 2
      a.   Film X
      b.   Film Y
III. Ways two films are different
   A.   Feature 3
      a.   Film X
      b.   Film Y
   B.   Feature 4
      a.   Film X
      b.   Film Y
IV. Conclusion

If your purpose is to evaluate the two subjects, put last the subject you like better or think is more important. That way you will have the opportunity in your comments to show its superiority over the first subject, and your conclusion will reemphasize your position.

To see these organizational techniques at work in students' papers, read the following examples in the next Activity, and answer the questions following them.

ACTIVITY 3

Read the following two student papers and answer the questions that follow each.

Right Choice

On the way up the financial ladder, I have put in many back-breaking hours doing all sorts of tasks for meager wages. I've done just about everything, from scrubbing dishes to washing cars, from cutting grass to timbering trees, and from digging gardens to shoveling snow. I've tried all the miserable jobs that teenagers get burdened with, so I know that the best decision I ever made was taking a job at the local supermarket. More than any other job, being a cashier provides flexible hours, a chance to meet people, and, most important, reasonable pay.

For one thing, the hours are convenient and flexible to my work schedule. Working at the grocery store gives me the chance to take nights off that might conflict with school work. If a major exam comes up, or a big football game rolls into town, I can usually schedule the day off. This is very different from my previous job at a restaurant where I was always working weekends and I had to let the manager know two weeks ahead of time when I would need time off. Generally, at the store I need only a week's notice, and sometimes I can even work out something just a day in advance.

Another advantage of this job at the supermarket, besides the convenient hours, is that I have a chance to meet people. I have already met some neighbors that I didn't even know were my neighbors. As a matter of fact, I just met a neighbor who works for the Marriott Restaurant Corporation doing managerial groundskeeping. Since I'm interested in a career in landscape architecture, I was interested to hear about his job. After we had talked a while, he offered to take me out on his job for a day. In my last job as a dishwasher in a restaurant, I had no contact with the public and would never have had this opportunity to further my career goals.

Because I am a poor college student, I find the wages I earn at the supermarket even more important than the potential contacts. My starting wage was $5.50 an hour, compared with minimum wage at the other jobs. Furthermore, the supermarket offers more frequent pay increases. I now earn $6.50 an hour after one year, and I would probably still be getting minimum wage as a dishwasher.

All in all, my decision to take this job has given me more freedom in my work schedule, new acquaintances, and a fatter wallet. This job has truly been the best thing I have done for myself in a long time.

QUESTIONS
1.   Is this paper organized by the point-by-point method or the whole-

subject method? _____

2.   Fill in the following outline based on the paper.

Thesis Sentence: _____

Point 1: _____

New job _____

Old job _____

Point 2: _____

New job _____

Old job _____

Point 3: _____

New job _____

Old job _____

Conclusion: _____

3.　Would it have been as effective for the writer to have discussed all about his old job first and then all about his new job? Why or why not?

4.　What does the conclusion of this paper do for a reader?

West Germany: Country of Contrasts

West Germany is as diverse as the fisherman of the Sylt Islands differs from the farmer of an Upper Bavarian mountain village beyond the Hintersee. Divided roughly into northern and southern areas, West Germany contains almost two different countries. Travelers who go to Germany should be aware of these differences and should plan their trips so they can get the most from their vacations.

Northern West Germany presents a rather bleak landscape, and most of the population lives in large, modern cities. The land is flat, with large areas of moors and bogs. Even the many islands on the North Sea and the Baltic are barren of trees. Travelers looking for picturesque scenery will be disappointed if they visit only the north. However, the cities of northern Germany are large industrial centers, which were rebuilt following World War II in modern styles. For example, Hamburg and Bremen are big shipping centers where life is fastpaced. The people in the north tend to be impatient and hard for the traveler to get to know.

In contrast, southern West Germany is hilly and mountainous, with most of the population living on small farms or in villages nestled in large wooded areas. The Black Forest is an ancient forest where the tourist can still find endangered species of mushrooms growing. The majestic Alps rise to dizzying heights. Cable cars take tourists to the top of the mountains for skiing and mountain climbing. The countryside is dotted with lakes for swimming and fishing. This is the Germany pictured on the travel posters. The traditional clothes and costumes are still worn in many villages. The picture of the German in his lederhosen with a stein of beer in his hand comes from southern Germany. The towns and cities have preserved their medieval charm, and many beautiful baroque churches shine like jewels in the countryside. Mountain villages like Berchtesgaden, Garmisch-Partenkirchen, and Lauterbach charm the visitor. Munich, the largest city in the southern part of Germany and beer capital of the world, is a beautiful city. In keeping with the smaller-sized towns and the slower-paced life, the people of southern Germany are warm-hearted, generous, and easier to get to know.

The traveler who has enough time should try to visit all of West Germany. However, if one has little time and wants the scenic and charming experience of traditional Germany, then he or she is advised to see as much of southern Germany as possible.

QUESTIONS

1.   Is this paper organized by the point-by-point method or the whole-subject method of development? _____

2.   Fill in the following outline.

Thesis Sentence: _____

Subject 1: _____

        point 1 _____

        point 2 _____

        point 3 _____

Subject 2: _____

        point 1 _____

        point 2 _____

        point 3 _____

Conclusion: _____

3. Would this paper have been better organized in another way? Why or why not?

4. How does the conclusion help the reader?

WORKING WITH PEERS

Discuss your subject with another classmate or in a small group. Which method of organizing your material seems to make sense to you? What does your classmate think?

Writing a Conclusion

The concluding sentences or paragraph of a comparison/contrast essay reminds readers of the purpose for making the comparison in the first place: One thing was better than the other, two things appear to be the same on the surface but are really different, or two things appear to be different at first glance but are really the same. Without a conclusion, readers may forget why they have been reading these details about two subjects—they may, as the expression goes, not be able to see the forest for the trees. The writer's job at the end of this essay is to get readers to see the overall picture—the forest, as it were.

WRITING APPLICATION: Writing a Rough Draft

Use the lists and other ideas you have generated to write a rough draft of your essay. The previous outlines may guide you in organizing your essay point for point or by one subject first and then the other. Include a conclusion at the end of your draft.

Revising a Comparison/Contrast Essay

As you read your rough draft, focus on two potential problem areas: the organization of the paragraphs, and the transitions between points of comparison or contrast.

First, as you read make sure you compared or contrasted the two subjects on the same points and in the same order. That is, if you were comparing two houses and mentioned size, style, and location for one, you would also discuss size, style, and location of the other.

Second, as you moved from one subject to another or another point to another, be sure you signaled the move to the reader by using a transition such as *however, in contrast, on the other hand,* or *similarly, furthermore,* and *moreover.* Another way to signal the reader is to use words like *comparable, similar, similarity, different, difference, advantage,* and *disadvantage.* If you used the point-for-point method, you probably will need more transitional words, because you are asking the reader to switch from one subject to another more often.

Using a Revision Checklist

After you have had time to reconsider your draft, have one or more of your peers read it and complete the following checklist.

WORKING WITH PEERS

In pairs or small groups, exchange your drafts and fill out the following checklist for each other.

Revision Checklist

1. How does the writer introduce comparison or contrast?

    What changes would you suggest for the introduction?

2. What is the thesis sentence?

    Is the purpose of the comparison or contrast clear to you as a reader?

    _____ Write what you understand the purpose to be.

3. Are you convinced after reading the draft that the two subjects really are similar or different or that one subject really is better than the other?
    _____ If not, what information or details need to be supplied? (Explain by referring to specific paragraphs you find weakly supported.)

4. Could you follow the comparison or contrast? _____

Was it organized point for point or by whole subject?

Locate sentences or paragraphs that puzzled you or that could use better transitions.

5.   What is the conclusion?

What suggestions can you make for a more effective conclusion?

6.   Are sentences free from error? _____ If not, underline sentences that need to be corrected.

7.   Is the spelling correct? _____ If not, circle words that should be checked.

WRITING APPLICATION: Final Draft

Revise your rough draft after working with the suggestions made on the Revision Checklist.

ADDITIONAL WRITING TOPICS: COMPARISON/CONTRAST

1.   Your boss asks you to prepare a short report comparing two brands of items that your company needs to buy: two computers, two printers, two copiers, two desks or chairs, two delivery vans, two new styles of uniforms, or two brands of anything that might be used at work. You research each brand and write a report comparing the two and recommending one.

2.   You visited a place or person recently that you haven't seen for quite some time and were surprised (even shocked) at the changes you saw. Write a letter to a friend contrasting what you observed on your recent visit with the way the place or person used to be.

Readings for Part III

Oranges: Florida and California

JOHN McPHEE

hyperboles:
  exaggerations
arid: dry

An orange grown in Florida usually has a thin and tightly fitting
skin, and it is also heavy with juice. Californians say that if you
want to eat a Florida orange you have to get into a bathtub first.
California oranges are light in weight and have thick skins that
break easily and come off in hunks. The flesh inside is marvel-
ously sweet, and the segments almost separate themselves. In
Florida, it is said that you can run over a California orange with
a ten-ton truck and not even wet the pavement. The differences
from which these hyperboles arise will prevail in the two states
even if the type of orange is the same. In arid climates, like
California's, oranges develop a thick albedo, which is the white
part of the skin. Florida is one of the two or three most rained-
upon states in the United States. California uses the Colorado
River and similarly impressive sources to irrigate its oranges, but
of course irrigation can only do so much. The annual difference
in rainfall between the Florida and California orange-growing
areas is one million one hundred and forty thousand gallons per
acre. For years, California was the leading orange state, but Florida surpassed California in 1942, and grows three times as many
oranges now. California oranges, for their part, can be safely
called three times as beautiful.

QUESTIONS
Before answering these questions that focus on specific features of the
writing. think about what you have read and discuss in your writing journal

what you thought was important and how you reacted to what you read.
Then answer the questions.

1. This paragraph contrasting two kinds of oranges is organized by
    which method, whole subject or point for point? _____

2. List the details that show the differences in the oranges:

    Florida   California
    _____

3. What is the purpose of the remarks made by Floridians against Cal-
    ifornia oranges and the Californians against Florida oranges?

    Are both right in a way? _____

4. After all the technical remarks, why does McPhee end with a state-
    ment that California oranges are "three times as beautiful"?

5. What descriptive details seem particularly vivid (those you can see,
    touch, taste, smell, or hear)?

Writing Journal Suggestion: Think about two places you have visited, or
the same place during different seasons of the year, or the same place in
the past and in the present. Write about the differences you remember.

They Sing, They Dance, They're Utterly Different
JON PARELES

When Prince started a two-night stand at Madison Square Garden on Oct. 2, and Michael Jackson arrived at the New Jersey
Meadowlands the next day for his first of three shows, it shaped
up as a trans-Hudson battle of the bands.

icons: images
flamboyantly: showy,
    dramatic
eccentric: unusual,
    individual

        The 30-year-old Mr. Jackson and the 28-year-old Prince are
the two biggest stars (and icons) in pop, the two best song-and-
dance men of their generation and easily the most flamboyantly
eccentric superstars of the 1980's. They have been promoted as
each other's opposites, updating the old Beatles-versus-the-Roll-
ing Stones contrast with Mr. Jackson (who owns the Beatles' song
copyrights) as the goody-goody pop singer and Prince as the

raunchy rocker. The characterizations are partly true, but after seeing them on successive nights, it was obvious that they are not polar opposites—they are two different species.

species: types or kinds

Both shows are choreographed arena spectacles intended to dazzle, and both do just that, with dancing, lights, costumes and stage effects that draw as much response as the music. Some details also overlap; both shows use a flag with a peace symbol, both include a number with simulated shootings (Mr. Jackson's "Smooth Criminal" and a song from Prince's unreleased "Black Album"), and both use the sound of drums, bass and synthesizers at full rumble—Mr. Jackson to begin the show and various songs, Prince to suggest an apocalypse at the conclusion of "1999." Both concerts are showcases for showoffs, enthralling audiences with the multifarious talents and sheer stamina of the performers.

simulated: pretended

apocalypse: disaster

multifarious: of great variety, many

stamina: strength

The two tours are hopscotching across the United States into November, with stops at arenas in or near Washington (last night and tonight for Prince and Thursday, Monday, next Tuesday and Oct. 19 for Mr. Jackson), Detroit (Oct. 24 through 26 for Mr. Jackson and Oct. 30 and 31 for Prince, after an Oct. 24 stop in the Nassau Coliseum on Long Island) and Los Angeles (Nov. 5, 7 and 8 for Prince and Nov. 13, 14, 15, 20, 21 and 22 for Mr. Jackson).

But in everything from physical layout to overall spirit, they are very different events.

Mr. Jackson's show includes nothing that would be out of place in a G-rated movie. It is the culmination of the old-fashioned, straight-forward celebrity extravaganza or Broadway revue, with one set piece per song. The Prince tour, with sexy bump-and-grind antics and rude expletives, kicks the revue-extravaganza into the non-linear film and video age, chopping up and reshuffling songs in a dizzying (and sometimes frustrating) suite of free associations. Where Mr. Jackson sticks to various styles of modern pop songs, from Motown to ballads, Prince romps through jazz and rock, leaping from blues, swing and be-bop to James Brown funk to guitar-heavy rock to electronic hip-hop.

expletives: swear words

The Jackson tour places the stage at one end of the arena, with the band in a pit behind Mr. Jackson and dancers flanking him on stage, as video screens magnify his every move. Mr. Jackson is the sole center of attention; even when he sings a duet with a backup singer, he is illuminated by two spotlights while she gets none. It is a centralized show, all eyes on the star.

Prince, by contrast, performs in the round on a stage whose sections move up and down, and the band members use wireless microphones to dance all over it; there is no video. Where Mr. Jackson uses specialists, Prince's band, dancers and backup singers are the same people—and on purely musical grounds, it is a much snappier, more flexible band than Mr. Jackson's. Although Prince keeps busy, another band member is always working the part of the crowd he isn't facing, and Prince invites the audience to chant the names of Sheila E., the drummer and occasional dancer, and Cat, the dancer and occasional rapper. He is clearly in charge, but he shares the spotlight; the show is decentralized, a miniature circus.

juxtapose: contrast

The setup and the programs reinforce very different messages. Mr. Jackson's songs juxtapose images of terror and loneliness with affirmations of love, but what comes across most on stage is the effort he is making. His face, blown up on the video screens, is unsmiling, yearning, straining, suffering; his body is a sculpture of gravity-defying tension, frozen in pose after pose. He seems to be saying, "Look at me, love me because I'm working so hard." (The most obscure song in the set, from Mr. Jackson's two-decade recording career, is called "Working Day and Night.")

While Mr. Jackson cues the audience for brief sing-alongs, most of the audience participation he wants is applause; every few songs, he stops the music in the middle, stands utterly still and waits for the screams and applause to flow over him, to reanimate him. (His in-concert video clips on MTV intercut bits of performance with shots of ecstatic crowds, as if the music were only incidental to the hysteria.) The image is of someone desperate for approval and applause, yet too ravenous ever to be satisfied. If this is Mr. Jackson's farewell tour, as his manager has said, it is hard to imagine how he will get enough adulation to sustain him. (It would also be a commercial mistake, a large part of what has made Mr. Jackson's recordings so successful is that fans know of his brilliance onstage, where there is no possibility of retakes or video trickery.)

ravenous: hungry

adulation: praise

Prince, by contrast, is as confident as they come. He struts, he teases, he shreds his songs, he even mocks an audience after a weak sing-along. He does not wait for applause; his two sets hurtle from song to song with barely a break. What he wants, instead, is the kind of call-and-response a gospel preacher shares with his congregation—the crowd shouting song titles, trading wordless phrases, completing the music. Prince even preaches that "God is love," a "love" that encompasses everything from ending wars to bouncing on a brass bed. It is a message that, while devout and apparently sincere, bears little connection to any established religion, unless there is a Tantric branch of Christianity; it is also unconnected to Prince-worship.

Tantric: magical or mysterious

Where Mr. Jackson's dancing is a series of geometric, freeze-frame poses—on his toes, in a robot crouch, miming—Prince is always in motion, undulating, leaping, even crawling on his belly. Mr. Jackson's show, too, seems frozen; his concert on Oct. 3 was a virtual replay of the ones he did in February, down to the few sentences he spoke. The Prince show, despite its fixed routines, has already changed since its Minneapolis opening last month, dumping a ballad medley in favor of a funk workout. And Prince's preaching retains its themes, but varies the script at whim.

In the end, Mr. Jackson's show speaks of confinement. One song ends with him in a cage of laser beams; at one point in every concert, he asks, timidly, "Can I go over there?" (Sure he can; it's his show.) An official tour T-shirt shows Mr. Jackson seated in what looks like a prison cell, with bars high overhead. His celebrity seems to have trapped him, forcing him to delight his audiences or else, and he dare not deviate from the script that has worked so far. For Prince, meanwhile, popularity means possibilities. He can mix-and-match musical styles, he can shimmy with Cat and then sing about "The Cross," he can mock his own celebrity (with a blues, "If I Had a Harem"), he can tear apart his own songs, he can fool around and then get serious.

Both shows celebrate hard work, ingenuity and remarkable talent. But where Mr. Jackson asks for the simple exchange of his efforts for the audience's approval, Prince's show exults in joyful, risky freedom. His hard work pays off in fun—for Prince as much as for his audience.

QUESTIONS

Before answering these questions that focus on specific features of the writing, think about what you have read and discuss in your writing journal what you thought was important and how you reacted to what you read. Then answer the questions.

1. This contrast between Michael Jackson and Prince was written for what kind of audience and for what purpose?

2. Can you find a sentence early in the essay that states the writer's point of view—a thesis sentence? _____ If so, which one?

3. What basic similarities does the writer discuss before discussing the singer's differences?

Why does he discuss their similarities at all?

4. Does Jon Pareles organize his essay by whole subject or point for point? _____

5. Looking at the beginning of each paragraph from #6 on, list the points used to contrast the two stars:

	Michael Jackson	Prince
#6		
#7		
#8		
#9		
#10		
#11		
#12		
#13		

6. How does the writer end his essay?

Do you agree with his point of view?

7. Circle transitions that introduce contrasts between the two singers. Underline other transitions that indicate the end of the essay or other examples of the writer's points.

Writing Journal Suggestion: Choose two other musicians who have some similarities and differences and explore their characteristics.

How I Learned to Read and Write [editor's title]

MALCOLM X

It was because of my letters that I happened to stumble upon starting to acquire some kind of homemade education.

I became increasingly frustrated at not being able to express what I wanted to convey in letters that I wrote, especially those to Mr. Elijah Muhammad. In the street, I had been the most articulate hustler out there—I had commanded attention when I said something. But now, trying to write simple English, I not only wasn't articulate, I wasn't even functional. How would I sound writing in slang, the way I would *say* it, something such as, "Look, daddy, let me pull your coat about a cat, Elijah Muhammad—"

Many who today hear me somewhere in person, or on television, or those who read something I've said, will think I went to school far beyond the eighth grade. This impression is due entirely to my prison studies.

It had really begun back in the Charlestown Prison, where Bimbi first made me feel envy of his stock of knowledge. Bimbi had always taken charge of any conversations he was in, and I had tried to emulate him. But every book I picked up had few sentences which didn't contain anywhere from one to nearly all of the words that might as well have been in Chinese. When I just skipped those words, of course, I really ended up with little idea of what the book said. So I had come to the Norfolk Prison Colony still going through only book-reading motions. Pretty soon, I would have quit even these motions, unless I had received the motivation that I did.

emulate: imitate

I saw that the best thing I could do was to get hold of a dictionary—to study, to learn some words. I was lucky enough to reason also that I should try to improve my penmanship. It was sad. I couldn't even write in a straight line. It was both ideas together that moved me to request a dictionary along with some tablets and pencils from the Norfolk Prison Colony school.

I spent two days just riffling uncertainly through the dictionary's pages. I'd never realized so many words existed! I didn't know *which* words I needed to learn. Finally, just to start some kind of action, I began copying.

riffling: paging

In my slow, painstaking, ragged handwriting, I copied into my tablet everything printed on that first page, down to the punctuation marks.

I believe it took me a day. Then, aloud, I read back, to myself, everything I'd written on the tablet. Over and over, aloud, to myself, I read my own handwriting.

I woke up the next morning, thinking about those words—immensely proud to realize that not only had I written so much at one time, but I'd written words that I never knew were in the world. Moreover, with a little effort, I also could remember what many of these words meant. I reviewed the words whose meanings I didn't remember. Funny thing, from the dictionary first page right now, that "aardvark" springs to my mind. The dictionary had a picture of it, a long-tailed, long-eared, burrowing African mammal, which lives off termites caught by sticking out its tongue as an anteater does for ants.

I was so fascinated that I went on—I copied the dictionary's next page. And the same experience came when I studied that. With every succeeding page, I also learned of people and places and events from history. Actually the dictionary is like a miniature encyclopedia. Finally the dictionary's A section had filled a whole tablet—and I went on into the B's. That was the way I started copying what eventually became the entire dictionary. It went a lot faster after so much practice helped me to pick up handwriting speed. Between what I wrote in my tablet, and writing letters, during the rest of my time in prison I would guess I wrote a million words.

I suppose it was inevitable that as my word-base broadened, I could for the first time pick up a book and read and now begin to understand what the book was saying. Anyone who has read a great deal can imagine the new world that opened. Let me tell you something: from then until I left that prison, in every free moment I had, if I was not reading in the library, I was reading on my bunk. You couldn't have gotten me out of books with a wedge. . . .

QUESTIONS

Before answering these questions that focus on specific features of the writing, think about what you have read and discuss in your writing journal what you thought was important and how you reacted to what you read. Then answer the questions.

1. What is Malcolm X's purpose in explaining the process he followed in learning to read and write better?

2. What is the function of the first two paragraphs?

3. In which paragraph does the actual step-by-step process begin? _
   Where does it end? _____

4. Could any of the paragraphs be combined? _____
   What effect would combining them have?

5. What details does Malcolm X use that seem especially vivid to you?

Writing Journal Suggestion: How successful do you feel your education so far has been? What might have improved it? What plans do you have for your education now?

PART IV

Bringing Authority to Your Writing: Writing an Essay Using Information

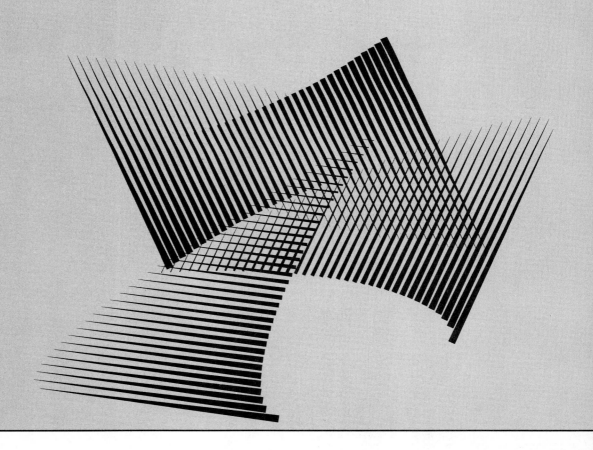

While observation and personal experience are valuable sources for writing, there is a limit to their usefulness. Writers need to be able to draw on other writers' observations and personal experiences in order to understand many complex ideas and to communicate these ideas to their readers. If everyone were limited only to what he or she experienced, there would be little progress made, because each person or small group would have to reinvent everything. However, because people can share experiments, discoveries, opinions, and analysis through reading others' works and writing their own thoughts, they can become more informed and be more informative to others. Furthermore, by supporting your ideas with other writers' evidence, you can also be more persuasive to your readers. How many times have you been in an argument and had somebody say, "What do you know? It's only your opinion."? If you can cite others who agree with you, you are more likely to be believed.

In Part IV you will bring authority to your writing by using other writers' information in addition to your own keen observations and experience. The essays you will write will define a word or idea, analyze information by classifying it into understandable groups, and examine evidence to determine the cause or effect of some situation. As you write these essays you will most likely draw on what you have already learned about describing, narrating, giving examples, explaining a process, and comparing and contrasting. In addition, you will learn how to incorporate other writers' ideas into your own writing effectively and responsibly.

CHAPTER 7

Developing an Essay by Explaining a Word or Idea: Defining

Thinking About Definition

Writers frequently face the task of explaining what a word or idea means so that a reader who is new to the subject will be able to understand it. Any student taking the first courses in sociology, psychology, anthropology, or just about any other subject soon realizes that he or she is learning many new words and phrases. Ideas such as *behavior, ethnocentrism, social class,* and *acculturation* have to be defined and learned. Indeed, one of the reasons the first two years in college are often difficult is that so many new courses and new vocabularies are being introduced that the knowledge can overwhelm students. I can remember sitting mystified through a lecture in an introduction to literature class while the professor talked about literary "genres." I did not know at the time that the word meant various types of literature, such as plays, novels, and short stories. As a result, I got very little out of that particular lecture. If the professor had defined the term, it would have made what he was discussing clearer to me and probably to many of my classmates. What this anecdote shows, once again, is that knowing your audience and meeting its needs is an essential part of communication.

Understanding Purpose and Audience: Topics for a Definition Essay

Definitions can be as short as providing a synonym for the word: *grisly* (terrifying). Frequently, however, a sentence, a paragraph, or an essay may be necessary to define a word so that the reader understands it fully. Writers need to define words in several situations:

1.   When a word represents an abstract thought that may be difficult for readers to understand or that different people may define in different ways. *Examples:* love, hate, democracy, freedom, discrimination, courage.

2.   When a common word is being used in an unusual way, perhaps peculiar to a particular occupation. *Examples:* closing (a cash register or part of a sales pitch), cleanup (in baseball), reconcile (in accounting).

3.   When the word is important for a reader new to a subject to know. *Examples:* cardiopulmonary resuscitation (to someone learning first aid), anticline/syncline (for the geology student), post pattern (for the football running back).

As you can see from these situations, the audience's need to know a definition helps to determine the writer's purpose. Writers have to ask themselves, "Will my reader understand what I am talking about?" Keeping the audience in mind will also help you choose the details and examples to explain the word.

Read the following topic suggestions and choose one to to define. Additional suggestions appear at the end of the chapter.

1.   An instructor in one of your college courses has asked you to write a definition of a term used in the course. As sources of information, you may use your course textbook, dictionaries and encyclopedias, other reference books, and, if appropriate, your own experience. The instructor may choose the best essays and make copies for class members to review before the exam.

2.   Support groups for people suffering from various conditions help victims of the disorder understand and cope with their conditions. For example, some groups help people with various *phobias* (fears). Common among these are *acrophobia* (fear of high places) and *claustrophobia* (fear of enclosed places). Other groups help people with anorexia, bulimia, psoriasis, and many other conditions. As a victim or relative or friend of a victim of one of these conditions (or of some other disorder), write a definition essay explaining what the disorder is, to help people in the support group understand their condition better. Use expert sources as well as any first-hand information.

Generating Ideas

Reading and Understanding Terms: Formal Definition

You may wish to start with a formal definition of the word you have chosen. A formal definition is usually at least one complete sentence that has three parts: the word, the class or type of objects to which it belongs, and the distinguishing features of the object or idea. So, for example, the word *balloon* could be defined as follows: A balloon is a bag that can be inflated with air or a lighter-than-air gas such as helium. Small ones are used as toys, while much larger ones may be used to carry people or goods.

Dictionaries and glossaries in textbooks are frequent sources for formal definitions, which you can use to write such a sentence. Try the following activity.

ACTIVITY 1

Write a formal definition of the words in the chart, following the example. Make the last one the word you have tentatively chosen to define in your essay.

	Word		Class or Type	Distinguishing Features
Ex.	A robin	is *a*	*bird*	*that has a red breast.*
1.	A thief	is		
2.	Honesty	is		
3.	A fever	is		
4.	A dermatologist	is		
5.	The sun	is		
6.	(Your word)	is		

Freewriting

Another way to generate ideas for a definition essay is to freewrite your associations to the word in question. Exploring your own feelings about what a word means may give you some ideas that later can be developed in your essay. Words have *denotations*, which are the meanings given in dictionaries and glossaries. But perhaps just as important are their *connotations*, that is, the positive or negative emotions attached to certain words. For example, the word *courage* means "facing something dangerous, difficult, or painful, rather than backing away from it." For some people that represents physical courage such as shown by soldiers in combat. Others know people who have shown courage in the face of their grief over the death of a loved one. Still others think of someone who showed moral courage by questioning a policy of a government or other authority. Some people might go so far as to say that anyone who sticks his or her neck out is being not courageous but foolhardy. What connotations do the words have in the following activity?

WORKING WITH PEERS

Look up the meaning(s) or denotation(s) of each word. Then discuss any emotional associations or connotations you or others have about the word. Note that the words may have more than one meaning and have different meanings for different people. People of different backgrounds, different genders, different races may react differently to words.

politician
    denotation:
    connotation:

loyalty
    denotation:
    connotation:

brother
    denotation:
    connotation:

radical
    denotation:
    connotation:

landlord
    denotation:
    connotation:

boss
    denotation:
    connotation:

drugs
    denotation:
    connotation:

lady
    denotation:
    connotation:

dude
    denotation:
    connotation:

cat
    denotation:
    connotation:

WRITING APPLICATION: Freewriting

Write for ten minutes, without stopping, about the word you have chosen to define. Explore all the feelings and experiences you have had that relate to the word.

Asking Questions

When seeking to gather information about a subject, you may not know where to begin. Many people start reading about a subject and writing down information as they read. While that may work for some, others find this process confusing, because the facts have no order and one idea runs into another. If this has been your experience, then you may want to ask questions *before* you begin your search for information. Then, as you read, you can put the facts that answer the questions under the appropriate question. Of course, as you read you may think of more questions than at first, and that is fine. Having some place to start often gives you something to build on.

What kinds of questions can you ask about a word? Although the who, what, where, when, why, and how questions are always serviceable, there are some other specific questions you can ask about words:

1. What is the word's history? When did it enter the language? Where did it come from? Has its meaning changed from the time it was first introduced?

2. Can it be compared with other words? What are its similarities to or differences from other words?

3. How do others use the word? Does everybody use it in the same way? Are there any controversies connected with the word?

The word you have chosen to define might raise other questions in your mind that would give you ideas for gathering information. Dictionaries are a good source of information to begin with, but don't overlook encyclopedias, atlases, and other reference works. In addition, you may need to look at magazine articles and books to explore a word's meaning.

WRITING APPLICATION: Asking and Answering Questions

Ask yourself at least five questions about the word you are writing about, and then look up the answers and write down your findings.

1.

2.

3.

4.

5.

Citing Sources

This essay is the first one that has asked you to gather information other than from your own experience or observations. That is, you will be using other people's writing, in dictionaries or other sources, as at least part of the information in your essay. You need to know how to use these sources in a way that your reader can understand and that is in keeping with accepted methods of citing sources.

First, every statement you take word for word from a source must have quotation marks at the beginning and the end. Frequently, you will introduce such a statement by mentioning the source, as in the following example:

John Naisbitt, in *Megatrends,* explains that "whenever new technology is introduced into society, there must be a counterbalancing human response—that is, high touch—or the technology is rejected. The more high tech, the more high touch."

Note that, as in this example, the quote may fit into the sentence pattern of the introduction, and if it does, it need not be set off with a comma or start with a capital letter.

Once you start quoting someone's sentence, you must either include all that the writer said or indicate where some words were left out by using three spaced periods (. . .) called *ellipsis marks:*

> John Naisbitt, in *Megatrends,* explains that "whenever new technology is introduced into society, there must be a counterbalancing human response . . . or the technology is rejected."

Of course, a quote may stand alone as its own sentence and begin with a capital letter:

> Fanny Farmer said, "My passion is chocolate."

You may put the source citation at the beginning, as in the previous example, in the middle:

> "My passion," Fanny Farmer said, "is chocolate."

or at the end:

> "My passion is chocolate," Fanny Farmer said.

Notice the placement of commas in each of the examples. For more examples and practice on punctuating quotations, see page 254. Following are common phrases used to link the quotation and its source.

Mrs. Smith said, stated, declared, yelled, whispered, exclaimed, repeated . . .

Mr. D'Angelo wrote, scribbled, inscribed . . .

According to Mr. Brown, . . .

As Ms. Romero remarked, . . .

The following activity gives you practice in linking quotations with their sources.

ACTIVITY 2

Here are several quotations and their sources. Put the two together in a sentence using an appropriate word or phrase to join the two. Try to use several different ways of joining the source and quotation, not just "Mr. Smith said."

1.   "As for me, give me liberty or give me death!"   *Patrick Henry*

2.   "It ain't over until it's over." *Yogi Berra*

3.   "When in doubt, tell the truth." *Mark Twain*

4.   "There can be no perfect democracy curtailed by color, race or poverty." *W. E. B. DuBois*

5.   "Come up and see me some time." *Mae West*

Another way to handle information from sources is to *paraphrase,* that is, put someone's definition or other information into your own words. If you paraphrase, you don't need quotation marks, *but you do need to cite the source:*

EXAMPLE

John Naisbitt in *Megatrends* says that he sees personal reactions developing to the introduction of new scientific or electronic devices like computers in which people attempt to make such devices serve human needs better.

If you paraphrase, be sure to take the basic idea or gist of the quote and use your own words. Don't just "translate" one set of words into another, and don't mix some of the author's words with some of your own. Generally, you will find that your paraphrase is longer than the quotation, because it seems to take more words to explain what someone else said.

ACTIVITY 3

Write paraphrases of each of the quotations in Activity 2. Be sure to name the source in your paraphrase.

1.

2.

3.

4.

5.

WORKING WITH PEERS

In small groups write a paraphrase of one of the paragraphs from any one of the reading selections read so far. Remember to indicate the author of the original as the source of the paraphrased idea.

Writing and Revising a Definition Essay

Having gathered information on the word or term to be defined, you are now ready to begin writing the essay. The basic ingredients of introductory paragraph, thesis and supporting paragraphs, and concluding paragraph are the same as before, but each part of the definition essay may have its own distinctive character, which bears discussing.

Writing an Introductory Paragraph

You may want to skip this section for now and come back to it when you have decided how to define the word you have chosen. But if you are one of those writers who like to warm up by writing an introduction, the following will help you get started.

An introduction to a definition essay can serve one or more purposes:

1.   To explore common meanings of the word before you define a more unusual meaning. *Courage,* for example, often is used to describe acts of physical bravery. Certainly, dramatic rescues or acts of bravery in wars are courageous. However, *courage* may mean standing up for what you believe in or quietly bearing the pain of grief.

2.   To present one or more examples of situations in which understanding the meaning of the word would help someone understand people or events better. Newspapers frequently begin the discussion of a difficult idea such as *tax reform* by telling a story about or giving an example of how such laws will affect one particular person.

3.   To give the reader a reason for wanting to read the rest of the essay by explaining the importance of the word's meaning to the reader. Does his grade in a course depend on his knowing the word? Does her life depend on knowing what something means?

4.   To provide enough history, background, or context for your later discussion so that the reader will understand your definition. If you were

defining the Compromise of 1850, for example, you would need to explain the background of fugitive slave laws, the threatened upset of the balance of power between the slave and free states, and the desire by many to avert civil war.

Note that none of these insist that you begin with a book or dictionary definition. In fact, it is best not to. Think of why your reader wants to know or should know this word, and concentrate on that purpose. If you need to refer to a formal definition from a source, work such a reference into the introduction. Don't start off with it, however. See how the following student introduction to the paper on lasers handles this task.

ACTIVITY 4

Read the following student introductory paragraph to see how one person introduces a concept from a course. Answer the questions that follow.

Lasers (student introduction)

What do you think of when someone says *laser*? Star Wars? Light shows? Death rays? You may know that lasers are beams of light, but unless you have read about them before, you probably can't define what a laser is or how it differs from regular light. A l.a.s.e.r., according to the *Columbia Encyclopedia,* stands for "light amplification by stimulated emission of radiation" that produces a very special kind of light. You could think of a laser as a super flashlight. However, the beam that comes out of a laser differs from the light that comes out of a flashlight in four basic ways: intensity, direction, color, and coherence.

QUESTIONS
1. What is the purpose of the questions at the beginning?

2. What important difference is the writer trying to explain to the reader?

3. Is there a sentence that serves as a focus or thesis for the rest of the paragraph? _____ If so, which one? _____

WORKING WITH PEERS

With one or more of your classmates, discuss possible tactics to introduce your definition.

> **WRITING APPLICATION:** Introductory Paragraph
>
> Write an introductory paragraph for your definition essay, using one or more of the strategies mentioned earlier.

Writing the Thesis Sentence: Selecting a Strategy for the Definition

The thesis sentence, as you know, makes a contract between the writer and the reader that the essay will be about a particular subject. Furthermore, the thesis sentence may often indicate the organization of the rest of the essay. In the preceding student introduction, you probably identified the last sentence as a possible thesis sentence. It says that lasers differ from light from a flashlight in four ways: intensity, direction, color, and coherence. The reader now expects a discussion of each of these four ways in the order presented in the thesis. That is, the thesis sets forth a plan to be followed.

In definition essays there are many possible plans—many ways to develop the definition of a word. In fact, you can use any of the organizational strategies you have learned so far:

1. You can write a description of the word's qualities.
    Example: Pointillism is a style of painting that creates an image with tiny dots of color.

2. You can illustrate a word's meaning by using examples.
    Example: To understand the meaning of courage, a person can look at the child braving treatment of a serious illness, an employee blowing the whistle on a company's illegal actions, a single parent raising and supporting children, as well as the hero on the battlefield.

3. You can tell a story that will help a reader understand a word.
    Example: The memory of my fear of heights, or acrophobia, extends to age 5, when my brothers challenged me to climb into their treehouse high up in our backyard oak tree.

4. You can explain what a word means by explaining a process.
    Example: To understand the artist's achievement in painting a fresco, one must appreciate the difficult process of painting with watercolors on fresh plaster.

5. You can compare or contrast the word you wish to explain with another word.
    Example: A laser differs from the kind of light that we are used to seeing.

These five strategies do not exhaust the possibilities, but these are familiar to you from your work in previous chapters. If you have another idea in mind for the word you will define, ask your instructor for help in organizing your essay.

WRITING APPLICATION: Writing the Thesis Sentence

Choose a strategy to develop your definition and write a thesis sentence that sets forth a plan for the essay.

Supporting the Thesis

How you present the definition of a word or idea will depend, of course, on which strategy you decide will be most effective in getting across your ideas. As you have learned in previous chapters, each strategy (description, illustration or example, narration, process analysis, or comparison/contrast) has its own characteristics. However, remember that narration and process strategies depend on clear chronological (time) order, that examples are frequently arranged from least to most important (emphatic order), and that comparison/contrast may be point for point or by wholes.

Each supporting paragraph needs to lead the reader from one aspect of the definition to another through the use of transitions or repetition of key words (usually the word being defined).

WORKING WITH PEERS

Read the student paper on lasers that follows and analyze it in pairs or small groups. Now that you see the whole essay, what do you think of the writer's introduction to the subject? What is the definition of the laser? What source did the writer use? What organizational strategy did the writer use to define lasers? What words does the writer repeat frequently? Why? What other transitions are there?

Lasers, A Special Kind of Light (student paper)

What do you think of when someone says *laser*? Star Wars? Light shows? Death rays? You may know that lasers are beams of light, but unless you have read about them before, you probably can't define what a laser is or how it differs from regular light. A l.a.s.e.r., according to the *Columbia Encyclopedia,* stands for "light amplification by stimulated emission of radiation" that produces a very special kind of light. You could think of a laser as a super flashlight. However, the beam that comes out of a laser differs from the light that comes out of a flashlight in four basic ways, as the encyclopedia explains: intensity, direction, color, and coherence.

First, laser light is *intense.* Yet only a few lasers are powerful. That's not the contradiction you might think. Intensity, according to physics, is a measure of power per unit area, and even a laser that emits only a few milliwatts (0.001 watts) can produce a lot of intensity in a beam that's only a millimeter in diameter. In fact, according to David Macaulay, it can produce an intensity equal to that of sunlight. An ordinary light bulb emits more light than a small laser, but that light spreads out all over the room.

Laser beams are also narrow. This quality is called *directionality.* You know that even the most powerful flashlight beam will not travel far. Aim one at the sky, and its beam seems to disappear quickly. On the other hand, *Columbia Encyclopedia* reports, beams from lasers with only a few watts of power were bounced off the moon, and the light was still able to be seen back on Earth, not bad when you consider that it had traveled a quarter of a million miles!

Next, lasers produce light of only one color. Or, to say it in a more technical way, the light is *monochromatic.* Ordinary light combines all colors of light you can see (for instance, the colors in a rainbow). When mixed together, they appear white. Laser beams have been produced in all the colors of the rainbow, red being the most common, but each laser can emit one color and one color only.

Finally, laser light is *coherent,* which means that all the light waves coming out of a laser are lined up with each other. An ordinary light source, such as a light bulb, generates light waves that start at different times and head in different directions. As my physics instructor says, it's like throwing a handful of pebbles into a lake. You cause some tiny splashes and a few ripples, but that's about all. However, if you could take the pebbles and throw them one by one, at exactly the right rate, at exactly the same spot, you could generate a more sizeable wave in the water. Put another way, a light bulb or a flashlight is like a shotgun; a laser is like a machine gun.

Practical applications of the laser seem unlimited, according to *Newsweek* magazine. Lasers have been used to transmit up to two billion bits (units of information) per second—the equivalent of 40,000 telephone calls—through a single optical fiber the diameter of a human hair. Lasers can write too. Laser-equipped printers can produce 20,000 lines of print in a single minute. Perhaps the most interesting application of the laser is in medicine. Lasers are used to perform delicate surgery within the human eye, welding a detached retina to the back of the eyeball without having to cut the eye. Considering its various applications, the laser may prove to be as important a technological breakthrough as the light bulb itself.

Concluding the Definition Essay

The conclusion to your essay may restate the definition, explain the word's importance, end with a human interest point of view, or suggest further opportunities for research. You want the reader to have a sense of "closure," that is, a sense that the definition was complete and has ended. Furthermore, you want the reader to feel that what was read was worthwhile—no writer wants a reader to say, "so what!"

WRITING APPLICATION: Rough Draft

Using your draft of an introduction, your thesis sentence, your freewriting, and other material, write a draft of your definition, including a conclusion at the end.

Using a Revision Checklist

WORKING WITH PEERS

Exchange your draft with one or more of your classmates and help each other revise your papers using the following checklist.

Revision Checklist

1. What strategy does the writer use in the introduction?

    Is this effective? _____ What changes would you suggest?

2. What is the thesis sentence?

    Does the thesis give you as a reader a plan to follow the definition?

    _____ What is the plan or strategy to be followed?

3. List the points of the supporting paragraphs.

    Do the supporting paragraphs follow the plan of the thesis?

    _____ If not, where do they go off the track?

Do the supporting paragraphs give you enough details and information to help you understand the word? _____ If not, put an asterisk (*) next to spots in the paper that need more support.

4.   What transitions are used to help you read from one idea to another?

Any suggestions for additional transitions? Changes in ones that exist?

5.   How does the writer end the paper?

Any suggestions for changing the conclusion?

6.   Does the paper use sources of information? _____ Are the direct quotations properly punctuated and the sources identified? _____ Do the paraphrases seem to be in the writer's own words? _____ Are sources indicated for the paraphrases? _____

7.   Are sentences free from error: _____ Circle any errors in spelling and usage so that the writer may revise the paper.

WRITING APPLICATION: Final Draft

After considering the comments made on the checklist, revise your rough draft.

ADDITIONAL WRITING TOPICS: DEFINITION

1.   Many brand names have crept into our language and become so common we don't even think about where they came from or how they started. Try to find out how Kodak, Xerox, Coke, Pepsi, Kleenex, Scotch tape, Betty Crocker, McDonald's, Wendy's, or any other brand name came to be and write an essay explaining its origins. Assume the essay will become part of the company history.

2.   An essay contest sponsored by your state will give a college scholarship to the winner. You can choose to define *freedom, responsibility, integrity,* or *courage.* You may use a combination of outside sources and your own observation and experience.

CHAPTER 8

Developing an Essay by Analyzing Information: Classifying

Thinking About Classification

Anyone who has shopped at a supermarket, department store, or large drugstore appreciates the principle of *classification,* that is, the process of putting related things together in groups. Certainly, when you want to buy carrots, you look for them where all the other vegetables are, not in the dairy section. Similarly, if you want men's shirts, you look for them in a men's department and not among women's sportswear or in housewares. Can you imagine the chaos if a drugstore unloaded each carton, as it arrived, onto the nearest empty shelf, putting the baby formula next to the shampoo next to the aspirin next to the toothpaste? Once I lived in a small town where the local hardware store was not organized in any particular way. Each customer had to ask the owner where to find the nails or the doorknobs, because everything was jumbled on the shelves. The owner had no trouble locating his stock, but I often wondered what would happen if he ever got sick and couldn't make it to the store. No one else, including his clerks, knew where anything was.

Writers sometimes have the same task when confronted with a large amount of information. Let's say, for example, that the U.S. Census has just been completed. Thousands of census takers have gathered information from millions of citizens on their place of birth, education, occupation, and even ownership of cars, television sets, and radios. The Census takes all the individual reports and puts the information in categories, so that anyone can see how many Americans own cars, etc. Writers interested in trends may look at the data for 1990 and compare it to the data for 1980 or even earlier decades

165

in order to draw conclusions about the life-styles of Americans. Without some way of classifying data, the Census would be a meaningless jumble of numbers.

Understanding Purpose and Audience: Topics for a Classification Essay

How writers classify information depends in large part on their purpose. Let's take the familiar example of students at a college. The registrar might classify students into groups depending on how many credits they had accumulated: first term, second term, etc. The college might classify according to their major: accounting, psychology, English, biology, forestry, nursing, etc. The dean of students might be interested in gender (male, female), race, or ethnic status (African-American, Asian-American, Hispanic, etc.), place of residence (commuters from home, dorm residents, off-campus apartment residents, fraternity or sorority residents, etc.). Students might group fellow students according to activities they participate in: athletics, politics, campus newspaper, theater guild, music or art buffs, club members, the uninvolved. The data base remains the same—students—but that large complex group is made up of many different subgroups that can be identified for one of several purposes.

The needs of the audience will help you determine your purpose. You can ask yourself what is it that my audience needs or wants to know about this subject? As you have just seen, students need different information about other students than do administrators, and administrators in one department need information that differs from that needed by another department. Remember that classifying items is a way of imposing order on a large amount of information that may be just too confusing to understand otherwise.

Here are some topics for a classification essay.

1.   Analysis of what Americans watch on television can reveal what our society values. Analyze *one* of the following to determine the kinds of entertainment we are seeing:

Soap-opera characters
Situation comedies
Saturday morning children's programs
Game shows

What does your analysis tell you about us as viewers? What do we learn about ourselves by looking at the kinds of heroes or villains on soap operas? What do messy children's shows like "Double Dare" tell us about the needs of American children? Assume your essay may be considered for a panel discussion on popular culture. (You may need to read other peoples' analysis of TV in addition to your own observation. Remember to keep accurate note of quotes and facts taken from the TV shows as well as of opinions from your sources so that you will be able to use the material responsibly in your essay.)

2.   Read all you can about an occupation such as accounting, nursing, computer programming or any other field that you would like to investigate, to determine what kinds of jobs exist in that occupation. In an essay written for a prospective major, explain the different job classifications, mentioning qualifications, duties, and any other information someone interested in the field should know.

Generating Ideas

As you have seen, writers use many techniques to generate ideas: journal writing, observing, freewriting, listing, and asking questions, to name a few. In addition to these, getting ideas for a classification essay may be helped by looking for groups within the data base (or body of information).

Grouping Information

To classify, you need to look for patterns or subgroups within the larger body of information. For example, if you are analyzing prime-time TV shows, you could first look at all the shows listed in that time period (usually 7–11 p.m. EST) on the three major networks. Copying a list from a guide for just one Monday yields the following shows (excluding specials):

7:00 p.m.	7:30 p.m.	8:00 p.m.
Entertainment Tonight	Evening Magazine	Fresh Prince of Bel Air
Jeopardy!	Wheel of Fortune	MacGyver
Family Feud	Inside Edition	Evening Shade

8:30	9:00	9:30
Blossom	Murphy Brown	Designing Women
Major Dad		

10:00
Northern Exposure

Looking at this list, you can now begin to classify the shows on TV by assigning each program to a group: popular information shows, game shows, situation comedies, and adventure shows. As you look at shows for the rest of the week, you may add categories or even split categories into smaller groups. For example, situation comedies might be split into those oriented toward family life, like "The Cosby Show" and "The Wonder Years," and those based on other situations, like "Cheers" and "Night Court." When you have a list of shows in classes or groups, you may then be able to see patterns. For example, how many are situation comedies, how many are adventure programs? Next, you may want to watch all the programs in a particular group to begin to analyze their characteristics so that you will find something to write about each type of show.

WRITING APPLICATION: Grouping Information

Make a list of TV shows or jobs within a certain occupation, depending on your chosen topic. Then group similar items together.

Avoiding Faulty Classifying

Sometimes the process of grouping information can be flawed. Groups can sometimes overlap, which will only create confusion. For example, if you decided to group TV shows into funny shows, serious shows, and game shows, the groups would overlap. Can't a game show like "Family Feud" be funny? Isn't "Jeopardy!" serious for the contestant? In the example of college students (at the beginning of this chapter), there were several classification schemes suggested, depending on the purpose. It is very important, however, that the groups be based on the same principle of classification. For example, while students can be classified according to major or according to activities, those two shouldn't be mixed. A classification that listed accounting majors, biology majors, athletes, and student government leaders would be flawed, because a student could belong to more than one group. One student could be an accounting major, an athlete, and a student leader.

Another consideration is to try to account for all the entries in your data base (students, people at an event, TV shows) in the various groups. If your categories don't add up to 100 percent, then your reader may not be convinced that your analysis of the information is worthwhile.

Finally, try to avoid stereotyping when you are observing and classifying people. All of us have heard others classify people according to the way they look and dress (dumb jock, typical beach bum), but such classifications don't contribute much to our understanding of human beings or their behavior.

Instead, look at the actual behavior of individuals in the group you are studying to see if you can find meaningful classifications that will help readers understand the situation. For example, what are some typical reactions of people witnessing an emergency? What kinds of behavior are evident at a professional football game?

ACTIVITY 1

Examine each of the following classification schemes, and decide if any items overlap each other in a particular pattern. That is, could one item fit in more than one group? Cross out any that overlap.

1. *College students:*
   Dorm residents
   Commuters
   Freshmen

2. *Movies:*
   G   General Audience
   PG   Parental Guidance
   PG-13   Parental Guidance for those under 13
   Adventure movies
   R   Restricted for those under 17
   NC-17   Children not admitted

3. *Baseball players:*
   Pitchers
   Catchers
   Home run hitters
   Infield players
   Outfield players

4. *Fast-food workers:*
   Counterpeople
   Grill workers
   Managers
   Drive-thru window attendants
   Teenagers

5. *Cars:*
   Full-size sedans
   Station wagons
   Compact sedans
   Sports cars
   Expensive cars

6. *Teachers:*
   Elementary school
   Biology
   Middle school
   High school
   Community College

WORKING WITH PEERS

Exchange your preliminary list of categories with one or more of your classmates. Let them check it for accuracy, completeness, and nonstereotyping.

Writing and Revising a Classification Essay

Once you have gathered your information and classified it into the groups that you wish to explain to your reader, you are ready to begin planning your essay. At this point you have actually accomplished the classification task—that of taking all the data and assigning it to certain subcategories. Now you have to explain the groups to a reader in a way that can help him or her understand the information. To explain each group you may use many strategies. You may describe each group, illustrate your discussion with examples, compare or contrast each group with the others, or differentiate each group from the others by definition.

One student who decided to try to explain the different kinds of skiers he observed at a ski resort came up with four groups:

1.   Those who "Go for it"

2.   Those who "Check it out"

3.   Those who "Look the part"

4.   Those who are "Just learning"

Now that he had the groups, he had to decide how to explain them and in what order. Writing a thesis sentence would help him and his readers focus on the point he wanted to make about these groups.

Deciding on a Thesis Sentence

To help you decide on a thesis sentence, think about your attitude toward the subject and toward the groups you have discovered in your data base. Are you surprised to find so many game shows in prime time? Are you offended by the behavior of the fans at a football game? Are you bored by the similar programming offered at prime time during the week? Your attitude toward your subject may be an important key to an effective thesis sentence. What you want to avoid is a sentence that simply announces, "Football fans can be classified into three groups" or "Prime-time TV shows fall into four categories." Such announcements mean that readers have to wait to discover the purpose of the classification. They invite a "so what" response, or a question in the reader's mind, "Why am I reading this?"

The student classifying skiers decided that one of the four groups served as a model while the others were amusing in different ways. He thought that readers would be entertained if he described some of the funny things three groups did on the slopes and contrasted their behavior with that of the model group. To accomplish this purpose, he thought he needed a different order to his discussion of the groups. He decided first to tell about the amusing groups in order of their silliness and then to show the model group on the slopes. The groups now were organized as follows:

1.   Those who are "Just learning"

2.   Those who "Look the part"

3.   Those who "Go for it"

4.   Those who "Check it out"

The student's thesis sentence and first paragraph are as follows:

Skiers—A Motley Crew! (Student's first paragraph)

Skiing is a sport for everyone, something you realize soon after you have arrived at a ski resort. While people look normal in the parking lot or in the lodge, they begin to show their true colors on the slopes. Only one group of skiers should serve as an example to others, but other groups are entertaining to watch from the lifts or on the ski trails.

ACTIVITY 2

For each of the following groups think of a possible thesis sentence, exploring the given attitude toward the subject.

1.   *Professional shoplifters:*
      Boosters
      Tag switchers
      Diversion pairs
      Attitude: Awareness needed to apprehend

      Possible thesis sentence:

2.   *Litterers:*
      Careless campers
      Unconcerned urbanites
      Too-busy beachgoers
      Attitude: Disgust with lazy litterers

      Possible thesis sentence:

3.   *VCR film rentals:*
      Comedy
      Horror
      Adventure
      Romance
      Issue drama
      Attitude: What's popular in film today

      Possible thesis sentence:

WRITING APPLICATION: Thesis Sentence

Look over your categories, and write a thesis sentence that expresses your attitude or main purpose for discussing the categories with the reader.

WORKING WITH PEERS

Exchange your list of categories and your thesis sentence with one or more of your classmates. Have the reader(s) answer the following questions:

1.   What do you expect this essay to be about after reading the list of categories and the thesis sentence?

2.   What suggestions do you have to make the thesis sentence clearer to you as reader(s)?

Selecting Strategies for Developing the Classification

As already mentioned, once you have analyzed the information and grouped it into manageable categories, you have completed the task of classifying. Furthermore, you have a thesis that provides a focus or direction for your discussion. Now you need to write the essay in sentences and paragraphs that clearly explain your ideas to the reader.

Often, the classification categories form a kind of outline, with a paragraph being allotted each category. Each paragraph is then developed using one of the strategies you have already practiced: description, narration, illustration, comparison or contrast, process analysis, or definition.

Transitions between paragraphs are just as important in a classification essay as they have been in other writing you have done. Readers can lose sight of a writer's purpose as each new category or group is discussed. Be sure to remind readers as you go along of your purpose: that this is another group of lazy litterers or that another type of professional shoplifter should be watched for. Readers appreciate knowing if one group is more common, more important, different from the other groups, or is the last group to be discussed. The kinds of transitions you use will probably depend on the strategies you select. As you have seen, comparison/contrast invites certain transitions such as "but" or "in contrast," and illustration leads to transitions such as "for example."

Read the following student paper on skiers as an example of how one person decided to discuss each of the categories of skiers. Questions follow the selection.

Skiers—A Motley Crew! (Student's draft)

Skiing is a sport for everyone, something you realize soon after you have arrived at a ski resort. While people look normal in the parking lot or in the lodge, they begin to show their true colors on the slopes. Only one group of skiers should serve as an example to others, but other groups are entertaining to watch from the lifts or on the ski trails.

The first-time skiers, those who are just learning, are amusing to everyone except themselves. They try so hard to keep their balance getting off the bunny lift, but usually lose the battle with slippery snow and gravity and end up sprawling on their rears. If they make it to the slope, you may see a loose ski flying down the hill by itself, followed by a person on one ski trying to get to the bottom without taking it off!

Another entertaining type of skier may fool you at first. These are the ones that look the part. That is, in the parking lot or lodge, they look great, dressed in the latest boots and parkas, right up to their "I Ski" glasses. However, they are only intermediate skiers at best, and when they lean too far on a turn and mess up, they invariably turn around to see who saw them. If they notice you looking, they turn redder than their brand new ski boots! It's funny how fast they lose their "I'm the only snowflake on the mountain" attitude.

The "Go for it" group tends to be the craziest and usually the funniest. These people just fly down the mountain at great speeds but have not developed any control. As you ride up the chair lift, you may see one of these skiers heading for a tree on the side of the trail. Another may have made it to the bottom but can't figure out how to stop without plowing into the crowd waiting for the lift. It's this group that keeps the doctors busy at the ski clinic!

There is one sensible group at most ski areas that should serve as a model for most skiers. These people check out a new area carefully, taking the first few runs slowly and easily while getting to know the trail. They are experienced skiers in turns, stopping, and other forms of control, but they are not necessarily expert skiers. They just want to enjoy their day and be able to leave the area as they came in—on their own two (unbroken) legs!

QUESTIONS
1. What strategies did the writer use to discuss each group?

2. What transitions between paragraphs signaled to the reader that a new group was going to be discussed?

3. What suggestions would you make to the writer about the discussion of each type of skier?

Was there enough evidence? _____ Was the evidence well chosen to illustrate the funny skiers and the model skiers? _____

4.   What does the introductory paragraph do besides contain the thesis?

5.   Does this essay need a separate conclusion? _____ Why or why not?

The strategies you use to develop your essay will depend on your purpose as expressed in your thesis. Description and illustration (giving examples) are used frequently to inform readers about different groups. If one group is more important than another, then comparison and contrast are useful strategies. If there are new or difficult terms used to label groups, then definition also becomes important. Remember that these strategies can be used in combination, so that one supporting paragraph may have a definition followed by several examples. In your rough draft, experiment with strategies to explain your classification to your readers.

WRITING APPLICATION: Writing the Rough Draft of the Classification Essay

Write a rough draft of your essay, using your thesis sentence and your list of categories to organize your essay. Discuss each group, using one or more of the strategies you have already practiced.

Using a Revision Checklist

WORKING WITH PEERS

Help your classmates revise their papers with the help of the following checklist.

Revision Checklist

1.   What is the purpose of the classification?

Write the sentence or sentences that express this purpose.

2. What categories does the writer use to analyze the information?

3. Are the categories accurate? _____ If not, what changes should be made?

4. Are the categories complete? _____ If not, what ones should be added?

5. What strategies are used to discuss each category?

6. Is there enough information given on each category to be convincing to the reader? _____ Put an asterisk (∗) next to any areas that should have more examples or details.

7. Are there clear transitions between paragraphs? _____ If not, make suggestions for better transitions.

8. How does the writer end the paper?

   Suggestions for changing the ending?

9. Does the paper use sources of information outside his or her own observation? _____ If so, are the sources identified and quotes properly punctuated? _____ If paraphrases are used, do they seem to be in the writer's own words? _____

10. Are sentences free from errors? _____ Circle any errors in spelling and usage so that the writer may revise them.

WRITING APPLICATION: Final Draft

After receiving your rough draft and the checklist from your classmate(s), revise your paper.

ADDITIONAL WRITING TOPICS: CLASSIFICATION

Foreign students on your campus are trying to learn about American sports but find themselves puzzled by all the different players and their positions. Help them understand baseball, football, basketball, or hockey by explaining the players' positions and duties. Refer to specific players as outstanding examples of skill at various positions.

CHAPTER 9

Developing an Essay by Analyzing Evidence: Cause and Effect

Thinking About Cause and Effect

If you think about events you read about in the newspaper or hear on a TV news report, you probably ask the question," Why did this happen?" Finding out the answer is finding the cause of something. Causes can be relatively easy to determine—my car got a flat tire because I picked up a nail on the road—or very complex—the Space Shuttle *Challenger* exploded when the "O" rings failed to seal off the hot gases generated by the rockets because they had become too cold to stay flexible. Doctors look for the causes of a patient's symptoms by conducting tests, by examining the patient, or by ordering x-rays. In the case of *Challenger* or the sick patient, much evidence has to be gathered and analyzed before the cause can be found. Many times people can only make a guess about the cause of something because the evidence is confusing or not available. For example, people have been studying the assassination of President Kennedy for over twenty-five years trying to determine who, if anyone, was involved besides Lee Harvey Oswald.

Sometimes people make rash judgments, without enough evidence, about causes of events. Superstitions arise from such quick judgments: A black cat crossed my path, causing me to have bad luck; or, I spilled some salt this morning, which caused me to fall and break my leg. It is important to gather evidence carefully and not leap to conclusions.

Sometimes the cause is known and what interests the writer is the result, also known as *the effect*. Effects, too, can be either simple or quite complex and long-lasting. For example, the effects of the stock market crash of 1929 lasted for at least ten years and, in turn, led to lasting changes in the way the U.S. government operates. Such programs as Social Security, Unemployment Compensation, federally insured bank deposits, and other protections for the economic well-being of citizens are effects of the economic upheaval caused by the crash.

You may notice that a cause may lead to an effect, which in turn may be a cause that leads to another effect—in a sort of chain reaction. For example, if your tire picks up a nail (cause), the tire may go flat (effect). Having a flat tire (cause) may make you late for work (effect). Being late for work (cause) may make your boss angry (effect). Having an angry boss (cause) may make your stomach upset (effect). As you can see, this causal chain could continue on and on, with one cause leading to an effect that in turn could be the cause of something else.

Understanding Purpose and Audience: Topics for a Cause/Effect Essay

Whether you investigate causes or effects or both depends once again on your intended reader and on your purpose for writing. Many times writers analyze causes or effects to give their readers information. College courses frequently investigate causes of political events such as World War II and the Vietnam War, of economic events such as the Great Depression, of human behavior such as drug addiction and juvenile delinquency. Students are often asked in examinations and papers to write accounts of the evidence that show why something took place.

On the other hand, an instructor may specify a situation in which the cause is known, such as using steroids, and ask students to write about the effects of the drugs on the body.

Writers may have another purpose besides conveying information when they look for causes and effects. Frequently, such a discussion leads to a recommendation for a change in laws or policies. For example, newspaper reporters may investigate the causes of bank failures for their readers or report the effects of toxic wastes on residents of nearby communities. But in either of these cases they may have as their purpose arousing readers to demand changes in financial policies to prevent bank failures or changes in environmental laws to prevent toxic waste dumping.

Whether the purpose is purely informational or also persuasive, writers have to explain unfamiliar terms and processes, and provide enough details and examples so readers will understand the articles. Sometimes evidence may be classified into groups or compared and contrasted so that it can be understood more readily.

Consider the following topics and choose one about which to write an essay. Additional topics appear at the end of the chapter.

1.   Investigate the causes of an event that interests you and might interest other students on your campus. Cite any sources you use in your article, and punctuate direct quotations correctly. If you paraphrase someone else's ideas (i.e., put them in your own words), give credit in the article to the original author. Subjects may be drawn from events in your community, or you may consider the following events:

   a.   The explosion of the nuclear power plant at Chernobyl
   b.   The near-meltdown of the nuclear power plant at Three Mile Island (Pennsylvania)
   c.   The banning of DDT, cyclamates, ALAR, or some other chemical
   d.   The explosion of the Space Shuttle *Challenger*
   e.   The cause of some major crime (such as an insider trading scandal, a controversial murder case, or a corruption case)

2.   Learn about the health effects of certain drugs, vitamins, or foods, and present them as you would in a lecture to a high school or college health class. Cite your sources carefully, and punctuate quotations properly. Some possibilities include the following (or choose some other topic that interests you):

   a.   Steroids for bodybuilding
   b.   Cocaine/crack
   c.   Marijuana
   d.   Aspartame (Nutrasweet®)
   e.   Saturated and unsaturated fats
   f.   Fruits, vegetables, fiber, red meat, or dairy products in the diet
   g.   Vitamin or mineral supplements, particularly vitamin C or calcium

Generating Ideas

Gathering Evidence

If you are trying to determine why something happened or what resulted from it, you will need to find out as much about the topic as you can. If the topic is a community issue or one you have been involved with, you may be able to go to the scene, interview eyewitnesses or experts, observe effects firsthand in people or in controlled laboratory experiments, and generally conduct what is called *primary research*. Topics that involve past events in distant places or that require expert knowledge are necessarily researched by reading what others have said about them, which is called *secondary research*.

Considering Several Points of View

Whether you are observing or reading, you will want to get several points of view from sources as reliable as possible. Several points of view ensure more complete analysis of evidence. The old saying "Two heads are better than one" is true here. Also, having more points of view avoids the problem of relying on one possibly biased source. If all your information on aspartame came from the makers of the product (Nutrasweet® by Searle Corp.), your readers would be right to question your information about the product's effects. See the student paper on aspartame (page 190) as an example of including several points of view.

Listing Sources

Readers often appreciate a list of your sources at the end of an essay. This list may be called a *Bibliography* or *Works Cited* or, simply, *Sources*. Use a separate page for your list, and place it at the end of your essay. Sources are listed alphabetically by person's last name in the case of interviews or author's last name for printed sources. If there is no stated author, the item is alphabetized by the title. While forms for the bibliography may differ (check with your employer or instructor for the form to follow), one generally accepted form for books and articles is as follows:

Books: Author's last name, first name. Title of book (underlined). Place of publication: Publisher, Date of publication.

Example: McPhee, John. Oranges. New York: Farrar, Straus and Giroux, 1966.

Articles: Author's last name, first name. Title of article (in quotation marks). Name of magazine or newspaper (underlined and no period) Date of publication, including month and day if known: magazine page numbers. (For newspaper articles, after the date put a comma, then the newspaper section number followed by a colon and then the page or pages.)

Examples: Pareles, Jon. "They Sing, They Dance, They're Utterly Different." The New York Times 11 Oct. 1988, sec. C: 15.
Quinn, Jane Bryant. "Down-and-Out Investing." Newsweek 3 July 1989: 46.

WRITING APPLICATION: Listing Sources

List the sources you have found for your topic (in the form just shown or as your instructor directs), whether primary (firsthand) or secondary (printed materials). Indicate if the sources have a vested interest in the topic (victim, suspect, prosecutor, producer of a product, etc.) or are neutral.

Thinking Clearly About Cause and Effect

As you begin to find information about your topic, you need to keep in mind some tips for clear thinking about cause and efffect:

1.   Look for all the possible causes of an event, not just the one that may have been closest in time to the event. You may find out that the causes are more complex and important than at first appeared. For example, some investigators say that car accidents initially thought to be caused by carelessness may be caused by depression and subconscious thoughts of suicide. Remember that an event may be at the end of a chain of cause and effect that you may wish to trace back to a "root" cause.

2.   Be aware that just because one event happens after another doesn't mean that one caused the other. The two events could simply be a coincidence. Superstitions are based on believing such coincidences: I wore my lucky jacket, and that's why I hit the home run.

3.   Evaluate the evidence before you conclude that it supports the cause or the effect of something. Sometimes just one piece of evidence is enough if it is clear and not open to interpretation: a shoplifter is arrested in the act of putting a radio under his or her coat. Some evidence, however, may seem clear but still be open to question. Fingerprints on a gun may not always belong to the killer; a videotape of a bank robbery may be hazy and lead to mistaken identity; eyewitnesses may have been too frightened to identify the criminal. To increase your chances of being right about a cause or effect, seek out many pieces of evidence. Even if you think you have enough evidence, you may wish to qualify your statements to guard against the outside chance that something elso was the cause. Words like *seem, appear, likely,* and *probably* signal the reader that you believe what you say is true but are being cautious not to overstate your case.

The following activities may help sharpen your thinking about cause and effect.

ACTIVITY 1

Read each list of actions and put them in the order in which they seem to have happened. After each one, indicate whether it is cause, effect, or both, if one effect becomes the cause of the next action (causal chain). Cross out any statements that seem irrelevant or coincidental.

1.   I caught my foot on the stair carpet.
      I walked down the stairs in the dark.
      I needed to get a letter from downstairs.

I bent my toe under my foot and sprained it.
I was in pain.
My horoscope said not to write anything that day.
I could only wear a sneaker on the injured foot for three days.
I felt silly wearing sneakers at work.

2. Martin, my boss is a compulsive gambler.
He is sure he will win, even while he is losing.
He loses on lotteries.
He loses on horseracing.
He loses on sports events.
He loses on slots and blackjack in Atlantic City.
He is a very nice person and an understanding boss.
His business is in trouble and is in danger of bankruptcy.
I am afraid that I will lose my job.

3. While camping, the patient saw a small black insect on his leg.
The patient had recently been on a camping trip.
The patient had not seen a doctor for two years.
After returning home, the patient noticed a ring-shaped rash on his leg.
Then the patient developed a fever and flulike symptoms with some aching of joints.
The patient had a positive blood test for Lyme disease.

ACTIVITY 2

Read each of the following statements and decide if they (a) represent clear thinking or (b) could be just coincidence or (c) could be subject to interpretation and need more evidence to be sure of the cause or effect.

1. I get better grades on tests when I study the night before.

2. Marion broke a mirror and has had seven years of bad luck.

3. The butler's fingerprints were on the murder weapon, so he must have done it.

4. Joan saw her friend Anne talking to Joan's boyfriend, Brian, and accused Brian of being disloyal.

5. The golfer wears the same clothes in every tournament since he won his first championship.

6. The woman thought that she had a brain tumor because she had a severe headache.

7. The geologist looking for oil located a rock formation similar to one in an oil field nearby and ordered a test well to be drilled.

8. If you give tomato plants water, sunlight, and good soil, they have a good chance of growing and producing tomatoes.

9. If you give tomato plants water, sunlight, and good soil, they are guaranteed to grow and produce tomatoes.

10. Carol was born on Madonna's birthday, so she will be a great rock star too.

WORKING WITH PEERS

The following list of evidence is some of what is known about the assassination of President John F. Kennedy on November 22, 1963. Sort through the list and place the item numbers in two columns as appropriate: evidence that supports the one-assassin (Oswald) theory, and evidence that supports the multiple-assassin theory. Any evidence that doesn't fit either theory leave in the list. Is either list convincing to you? What questions, if any, still remain in your minds?

1. Witnesses heard three shots fired from sixth floor of Texas Book Depository.

2. Malcolm Summers, a witness standing on the grassy knoll in front of the motorcade as shots were fired, said he heard two shots far away and one shot "real close."

3. An analysis of sounds recorded by an open mike on a policeman's motorcycle revealed "95% certainty that a shot came from the grassy knoll."

4. The tape of the sounds also has talk recorded after the assassination, and time sequence is unclear.

5. Lee Harvey Oswald said, "I didn't shoot anybody, no sir."

6. While in custody, Oswald was killed himself a few days later by Jack Ruby, a bar owner with Mafia ties.

7. The Warren Commission in 1964 concluded that a lone person shot the president.

8. The House Select Committee in 1977 concluded that Lee Harvey Oswald had an accomplice who fired and missed.

9. Lee Harvey Oswald worked in the Texas Book Depository.

10. Behind some book cartons on the sixth floor were three spent cartridges, and a bolt-action rifle with Oswald's palm print on it.

11. A mail order for the rifle was found in Oswald's handwriting but under another name.

12. One whole bullet found on a stretcher at the hospital was traced to Oswald's rifle, and bullet fragments found in Governor Connally (also shot while sitting in the same car with Kennedy) were chemically similar to the whole bullet.

13. Rifle experts doubt Oswald could get off three shots, given the movement of the motorcade and the time it took to work the bolt-action rifle.

14. Oswald had spent some time in Russia and had married a Russian woman.

15. The autopsy on the president was conducted by a doctor inexperienced with gunshot wounds. He did not trace the path of the bullet. His autopsy notes were burned.

16. Dallas doctors attempting to save the president's life were under the impression that the wounds came from above and behind the president.

17. Governor Connally remembers hearing a shot and turning from the front seat to see the president slumped over in the back when he himself was hit "almost simultaneously."

Evidence for Single Assassin	Evidence for Multiple Assassins

WRITING APPLICATION: Sifting Evidence for Cause and Effect

Write down what you have found to be the causes or effects of the topic you are working on, along with the evidence that supports your conclusions.

WORKING WITH PEERS

Exchange your lists of causes and effects and evidence with your classmates, preferably with ones who are working on the same topic. Check evidence to see if it supports their conclusions. Point out any coincidences or matters subject to interpretation. Suggest areas that need more or better evidence to be convincing.

Writing and Revising a Cause/Effect Essay

One of the problems some people have in writing a cause/effect essay is knowing where to start in the causal chain. After all, if you are investigating an accident or crime, you could go all the way back to the subject's childhood and look at all the forces and events that made the person the way he or she was. Some writers, believing some traits are inherited, have even examined the subject's family tree for similar behavior. There is no absolute rule for where to start, but the farther back you go in the causal chain or the broader the subject you choose, the longer the essay will be due to the need to use evidence to support your conclusions. One way to "put a fence around your topic" is by writing a clearly focused thesis sentence that indicates to the reader what you will be discussing.

Writing a Thesis Sentence

To appreciate the problem of having a thesis sentence that is too broad or not clearly focused, please read the following rough draft of a paper on pollution.

Pollution's Dangerous Effects (Unfocused student draft)

Pollution exists in the world today for very definite reasons. The main reason it exists is due to the fact that people have wants and needs. To satisfy these needs, society produces products, but it also turns out waste. This waste takes the form of smoke from factories, exhaust from cars, noise from aircraft, trash from anything packaged, and so on. There are literally millions of sources for pollution.

Many undesirable things are happening because of this problem. Water supplies are becoming contaminated. The Earth only has a given amount of water that can be consumed. Wildlife is threatened. Fish are dying in toxic waters. Birds die in oil spills. Serious as these are, the most tragic is the effect on humans. Pollution creates many illnesses for millions. Smog keeps people inside. Smoke causes many breathing problems. Noise causes deafness. Scientists have a name for one outcome of pollution that may affect all of us in a relatively short time. The Greenhouse Effect is caused by pollution in the atmosphere trapping the sun's rays and causing an increase in heat. This heat, given enough time, causes the Earth's temperature to rise. This, in turn, causes melting of the polar ice caps, which raises the ocean levels beyond normal. Because the majority of Earth's population is on or near water, many lives and properties are threatened.

Even though the causes and consequences of pollution are known, little is being done. We must find solutions or make compromises in our standard of living, or we may face very serious consequences.

This student chose the subject of pollution, which is too broad to discuss in a short essay. Notice how water pollution, air pollution, and noise pollution are mentioned but not discussed in any depth. Since the student ends with a bit longer discussion of the Greenhouse Effect, it may be that this is the subject she really wants to focus on. If so, she could focus on the Greenhouse Effect from the beginning, explaining its cause and then detailing the effects that scientists fear and why these effects would be so devastating. Rather than just listing all the problems in general (which readers already know, so they would learn little from her draft), she then could focus on one subject and offer readers real information and insight into the problem. The following is a revision of just the first paragraph, to show the student's new focus:

The Dangerous Greenhouse Effect (Revised first paragraph)

Scientists theorize that one of the most dangerous effects of air pollution may be what they call the "Greenhouse Effect." In their theory, the layer of pollutants from burning oil, gasoline, coal, and other fossil fuels can trap the sun's rays and prevent heat from radiating from the Earth back into space. As this happens, temperatures on the Earth gradually rise, having potentially serious effects on weather patterns, food production, and even on the Earth's geography.

As you begin to think about a thesis sentence, think again about your purpose in writing and your audience. Are you going to concentrate on the causes of a situation or its effects? What does your reader want to know about the subject? Try to give your reader the main ideas "in a nutshell," a kind of capsule summary that forecasts what you will discuss in some detail. In the preceding student revision, the summary of effects includes weather patterns, food production, and Earth's geography. An attitude word also can help provide a direction for the reader to follow in your essay. In the same revised paragraph, note that the word *serious* applied to *effects* helps to give readers some perspective.

ACTIVITY 3

In each of the following thesis sentences for a cause/effect essay, circle the attitude word, if one is present, and underline the "nutshell" or summary of ideas.

1. Bulimia, a condition of overeating and then purging the body of food, has severe medical and psychological consequences.

2. Analysis of the explosion at Chernobyl shows that the main causes of the disaster were faulty design of the plant and human error.

3. Contributing factors to the recent scandal of judges on the take were simple human greed and the political system of electing judges.

4. The effects of China's brutal reaction to the students' quest for increased freedom are loss of international trade, decreased political influence, and, very possibly, internal instability

5. Steroid users illegally take the drug to enhance their image of their bodies, to gain an edge athletically, and ultimately to satisfy a developed craving for the drug.

6. The personal computer has revolutionized the way many writers compose and revise text.

7. My sister's illness taught me patience and respect for her determination.

8. The effects of divorce on children may not be evident for many years.

9. Although still poorly understood, hurricanes and tornadoes stem from the enormous energy created by differences in air pressure and temperature.

10. Bad weather, equipment malfunction, and pilot error contributed to the crash of Delta Flight 104.

WRITING APPLICATION: Writing a Thesis Sentence

Using your list of causes or effects and the evidence you have gathered, write a thesis sentence that expresses your ideas in a nutshell.

Writing an Introduction

The first paragraph of a cause/effect essay usually performs a very important function. If you intend to discuss the cause of an event, such as an explosion or a crash, the event itself is explained in the first paragraph, so the reader will understand both what the situation was and why finding out the cause is important. If the effects are the main focus of the essay, then the first paragraph usually tells the reader the cause. For example, in the student's revised paragraph on the Greenhouse Effect, the cause—air pollution caused by burning fossil fuels—was explained before the serious effects were listed. If a paper will discuss a chain of events, the first paragraph "gets the ball rolling," with whatever the writer has determined to be the starting point.

Read the following introduction to an essay on aspartame (Nutrasweet) and note how it sets up the discussion of effects. Which sentence serves as the thesis? What attitude is expressed toward aspartame's effects?

Aspartame: The Perfect Sweetener? (Student introduction)

To be able to eat sweets free from worries of calories and cavities is the dream of nearly every American. Unfortunately, all sugar substitutes until recently have carried the dreaded warning: Causes cancer in laboratory animals. Now enter aspartame! Has the perfect sweetener been found? The food industry seems to think so. The tremendous sales of aspartame (Nutrasweet® brand) have been an enormous financial boost for manufacturer G. D. Searle and Company. Searle grossed $600 million from aspartame sales in 1984, an increase of more than 800% over 1982, according to reporter Jane Brody. Not everyone is as enthused as Searle, however. Leading scientists have raised questions over aspartame's safety, citing possible side effects of brain damage, tumors, toxic levels of poisons, and behavioral changes.

ACTIVITY 4

Choose three of the thesis sentences in Activity 3 (pp. 186–187) and write an introduction leading to the thesis. You may need to make up details in your introduction.

1.

2.

3.

WRITING APPLICATION: Writing an Introduction

Write an introductory paragraph for your topic that will lead the reader to your thesis sentence. Provide the background of either cause or effect so that your reader will be able to understand the main focus of your essay.

Organizing the Supporting Paragraphs

The paragraphs that support your thesis sentence may be organized in one of several ways. Following are three common patterns—but other patterns are surely possible:

Pattern A: para. 1   Introduction, including cause; thesis explaining effects

para. 2   Effect #1, described, illustrated, narrated, or defined

para. 3   Effect #2, compared with effect #1, or described, illustrated, narrated, or defined

para. 4+   Other effects, if any, similarly developed

last para.   Conclusion, showing importance of the effects and perhaps suggesting ways to change the situation that caused them

Pattern B: para. 1   Introduction, including effects; thesis suggesting causes

para. 2   Cause #1, described, illustrated, narrated, or defined

para. 3   Cause #2, compared with cause #1, or described, illustrated, narrated, or defined

para. 4+   Other causes, if any, similarly developed

last para.   Conclusion, summarizing the causes and perhaps raising any implications for changes in policies, attitudes, or behavior

Pattern C: para. 1   Introduction of situation; thesis pointing out chain of events

para. 2   Cause #1 leading to effect #1

para. 3   Effect #1 becomes cause #2 leading to effect #2

para. 4+   Further discussion of cause/effect chain if any

last para.   Conclusion, making clear the implications of the chain of events

Useful transitions that serve to help readers sort out causes and effects include terms such as *because, therefore, subsequently, so, since,* and *as a result.*

WORKING WITH PEERS

Read the following student paper on the effects of aspartame (Nutrasweet®) as an example of one way to organize the supporting paragraphs. Discuss the questions that follow the selection with your classmates and write down answers.

Aspartame: The Perfect Sweetener? (Student paper)

To be able to eat sweets free from worries of calories and cavities is the dream of nearly every American. Unfortunately, all sugar substitutes until recently have carried the dreaded warning: Causes cancer in laboratory animals. Now enter aspartame! Has the perfect sweetener been found? The food industry seems to think so. The tremendous sales of aspartame (Nutrasweet® brand) have been an enormous financial boost for manufacturer G. D. Searle and Company. Searle grossed $600 million from aspartame sales in 1984, an increase of more than 800% over 1982, according to reporter Jane Brody. Not everyone is as enthused as Searle, however. Leading scientists have raised questions over aspartame's safety, citing possible side effects of brain damage, tumors, toxic levels of poisons, and behavioral changes.

Arguing that aspartame is safe are, of course, Searle's scientists and the Federal Food and Drug Administration, which reviewed Searle's extensive tests of the product. Searle points out, according to William Allman, that aspartame is a compound of two amino acids that are among the twenty or so used by the body to make protein. Since the body uses it like protein, not like sugar, aspartame is safe for diabetics. The only people at risk are the 1 in 10,000 people born with a genetic disorder called PKU, which makes them unable to use a breakdown product of aspartame, phenylalanine. Gurney Williams reports that Searle tested 12,000 animals and 600 people over seventeen months and at doses from normal to over 550 times normal human intake without medical problems. Normal human intake was projected to be 8–10 mg per kilogram of body weight. Based on this information, it appears that aspartame is safe except for the small number of people with PKU, who are identified at birth. So where is the controversy?

Other scientists are concerned about effects caused by the combination of aspartame with other food additives, the breakdown of aspartame contained in soft drinks into other substances, and the danger of consuming aspartame in amounts way above the 8–10 mg predicted. As Jane Brody reports, Dr. John Olney of Washington University found aspartame combines with additives like monosodium glutamate to affect nerve cells and cause possible brain damage, particularly in young animals. Further evidence of aspartame's effect on the brain comes from Dr. Richard Wurtman, at M.I.T., who, according to Brody and Allman, has found evidence that some people suffer from headaches, depression, sleeping problems, and even seizures caused by the sudden rise in the blood of phenylalanine, one of the breakdown products of aspartame. These people, while not PKU sufferers, may be more sensitive to the chemical than others. He also found that many people were consuming 30–50 mg per kilogram of body weight, far over the 8–10 mg amount predicted. Soft drinks were cited as a particular problem because of the amount consumed and because of the varying temperatures at which they are stored. Aspartame in drinks breaks down more readily at 86 degrees than at 68 degrees, according to *Consumer's Research.*

Whom are we to believe? Based on the evidence I have gathered, I believe that aspartame by itself in limited quantities is probably not a health risk. However, I will generally avoid it because I may be consuming it with other food additives unknowingly and because it is too recent a discovery to know its long-term effects. Furthermore, I would like to ask, who needs artificial sweeteners? If I watch my diet, I should be able to eat naturally sweetened foods and avoid the problem altogether.

Works Cited

Allman, William F. "Aspartame: Some Bitter with the Sweet?" *Science '84* July/ Aug. 1984: 14.

"Aspartame: Pro and Con." *Consumer's Research* 3 Sept. 1983: 11–14.

Brody, Jane E. "Sweetener Worries Some Scientists." *The New York Times* 5 Feb. 1985, sec. C: 1+.

Williams, Gurney, III. "The Search for the Perfect Sweetener." *Science Digest* Aug. 1975: 41–45.

QUESTIONS

1. What is the purpose of the second paragraph?

   How does it relate to the subject as explained in the first paragraph?

2. What details or examples does the student use to show that aspartame is safe?

3. What is the purpose of the third paragraph?

   How does it relate to the subject as explained in the first paragraph?

4. What details or examples does the student use to show that aspartame is not safe?

5.   Note that the two paragraphs show a contrast in the effects of the sweetener. Does it follow the whole method or the alternating method of contrast, as discussed in Chapter 6? _____

6.   Would you have drawn the same conclusion from the discussion as the student did? _____ Why or why not?

Writing a Conclusion

The conclusion of a cause/effect paper usually summarizes for the reader the points raised about causes or effects in the essay, and frequently goes beyond a summary to evaluate the discussion, as in the student paper on aspartame, to suggest changes in policies to prevent further situations, or to make the reader aware of the importance of the overall subject.

WRITING APPLICATION: Writing a Rough Draft

Write a rough draft of your cause/effect topic using all the information you have gathered, your list of causes or effects, your introduction, and your thesis sentence. If you find working with outlines helpful, try using one of the three patterns from page 189 as a guide for your organization.

Using a Revision Checklist

WORKING WITH PEERS

In groups or pairs, exchange your draft and get some advice based on the others' answers to the following revision checklist.

Revision Checklist

1.   Is this paper primarily about the cause(s) of a situation, its effect(s), or both? _____

2. Does the writer examine enough causes or effects? _____ If not, indicate other analysis that should be done.

3. Does the writer rely on coincidence to make the connection between cause and effect? _____ Are there irrelevant issues included? _____ If so, circle places that should be questioned for unclear thinking.

4. How does the writer begin the paper?

    Do you have any suggestions for improving the beginning?

5. What evidence convinces you as a reader that the writer is correct? (Briefly list main points.)

    Mark any places where you would like to see more evidence.

6. Are transitions adequate so that you can follow the logic of the paper? _____ If not, indicate where other transitions should be.

7. Are the sources of information identified and quotes properly punctuated? _____ Point out any problems. Note also if paraphrases are in the writer's own words or seem too close to the printed source.

8. Is the list of sources properly prepared? _____

9. How does the writer end the paper?

    Do you have any suggestions for changing the ending?

10. Are sentences free from errors? _____ Circle any problems in spelling and usage so that the writer may correct them.

ADDITIONAL WRITING TOPICS: CAUSE/EFFECT ESSAY

1. One day you or a member of your family may be famous enough to have a biography written. Assume you are the biographer assigned to write about a major event in your life or in the life of someone you know quite well.

Explain either the causes of the event or its effects or both so that readers of the biography will understand the personality of the subject.

2.   Social issues such as crime, poverty, alcoholism, drug addiction, illiteracy, child abuse, pornography, and compulsive gambling are very difficult to understand. Experts have conflicting views on what causes any of these social problems. In order to gain a perspective on one of these issues, investigate what experts say cause them and present all the causes in an informative report. Do not attempt to decide which expert or point of view is correct. Don't try to suggest solutions to the problems. Just try to present what is known or thought about the causes of the problem.

Readings for Part IV

Bulimia: Binge-Eating Cycles Followed by Purges and Guilt

JANE E. BRODY

Suzanne: I have a problem with food I eat. I mean I eat disgusting amounts of food. You can't imagine how much I eat. I go on binges. Then I start thinking about all those calories— and I make myself throw up. I can't stop myself. I hate myself, and I don't believe I'm telling you this.

The slender, attractive 19-year-old speaking to the therapist at her university's health service was describing an increasingly common phenomenon known as bulimia or bulimarexis, an out-of-control cycle of binge-eating followed by purges to get rid of the thousands of calories that may have been consumed in just half an hour.

phenomenon: occurrence

Suzanne had been voted "most likely to succeed" at her small-town high school. Now at college her high school A's had dwindled to C's and she was riddled with guilt about spending so much of her parents' money on food. At the time of her confession Suzanne had been bingeing and purging three or four times a day for six years, careful to keep her behavior a secret from family and friends and her present therapist. Now she was desperate for help.

According to her new therapist, Dr. Marlene Boskind-White, Suzanne was the first of hundreds of bulimics to seek help at Cornell University's health service in recent years. Dr. Boskind-White, along with her husband, Dr. William C. White, Jr., are authors of an illuminating book, "Bulimarexia: The Binge/Purge Cycle." The book, both realistic and hopeful, is designed to counter many bulimics' fear of disclosure and resistance to treatment.

Doctors often do not take these patients' problem seriously or sympathetically. Family and friends may try to ignore it, if they know about it at all. Strangers usually react with disbelief and disgust. But to bulimics, most of whom feel horribly guilty and frighteningly out of control, the vicious cycle of binges and purges in which they are caught is very serious, very disabling and very much in need of treatment—the sooner the better.

The extent of the problem is unknown. Some estimates say 15 to 30 percent of young women occasionally binge and purge while 1 to 4 percent do it all the time, ostensibly to maintain a normal body weight. About 5 percent of bulimics are male. Most are white and come from middle and upper-class families. Their ages range from 8 to 72 years, with the vast majority in their teens and 20's. Some have been bulimic for more than 10 years and may be suffering serious health consequences yet cannot stop their abnormal behavior. For many, the bulimia takes over their lives and they have time for nothing but working, sleeping, bingeing and purging.

Bulimics may consume 10,000 to 20,000 calories at one time, then make themselves vomit, or take hundreds of laxatives and diuretics, or do an abusive amount of exercise to unload the excess before it turns to body fat. A typical binge may begin with two packages of cookies, a loaf of bread, a gallon of milk and half a gallon of ice cream, followed by a basket of fried chicken and fistfuls of candy and pastries. The emphasis is on "forbidden foods" high in calories, fats and simple carbohydrates.

A few bulimics ingest as many as 50,000 calories a day and support their habit by taking second jobs, stealing or even becoming prostitutes. To disguise their abnormal food purchases, they may shop at a different store each day, pretend they are buying for a party, order food from catalogues or charge it on credit cards.

Experts debate how to characterize the problem. Some (the Drs. White among them) call it a habit or learned behavior; others consider it an addiction, compulsion or form of substance abuse; still others think of it as an emotional disorder or illness. But there is little disagreement about how bulimia usually begins, what perpetuates it and what must be done to overcome it. There is also general agreement that bulimia is often hidden behind a facade of normalcy and that it is more difficult to treat than its more obvious sister problem, anorexia nervosa (self-induced starvation).

ostensibly: apparently

diuretics: drugs to reduce water in body tissues

ingest: eat

facade: front, face

precipitating:
beginning

Most cases of bulimia that have been studied have started with strenuous dieting, perhaps coupled with some precipitating event, such as loss of a loved person, rejection by a sweetheart or leaving home to go to college. After a period of deprivation and hunger, the dieter may lose control and go on a binge.

Terrified of the consequences, the dieter may then seek a way to undo the damage. The purge is seen as the perfect dieting technique, a means, as bulimics put it, of "eating your cake without having to pay the price."

Some victims say they first got the idea to purge from an article or television program about bulimia. But many thousands discovered it on their own or took a cue from friends or relatives long before there was any publicity about bulimia. At first, purges may be done only occasionally, but they may soon become increasingly frequent.

Most bulimics also share a number of psychological and social characteristics that seem to predispose them to bingeing and purging. They are usually perfectionists with high expectations who present an impressive image. Yet they feel ineffective, lack self-esteem and have a very strong need for approval from other people.

nurturing: taking care
of

They become "bewildered when their perfect presentation does not result in the acceptance or care they are looking for," said Dr. Ellen Schor, a New York bulimia therapist. "They then turn to food as a means of nurturing themselves, turning from the outer world in anger or disappointment."

Though initially the binge may be a source of pleasure or comfort, it soon becomes associated with fear, shame, guilt, remorse and a feeling of lost control. The purge restores their sense of self-control and represents a renewed drive for perfection. Dr. Craig Johnson, who studies and treats bulimics at the Michael Reese Hospital in Chicago, examined the feelings of bulimics before, during and after binges and purges. He found that during binges, the women felt less in control, more inadequate, angrier and guiltier than usual. The purge, however, re-established a

dissipated: got rid of

sense of control and adequacy, dissipated the anger and enhanced alertness.

"We must suspect, then, that the purge is the most important, most gratifying part of the sequence," Dr. Johnson concluded. "Clearly, it's some kind of cathartic, reinforcing experi-

cathartic: emotional
release

ence that restores their sense of reality orientation and allows them to feel in control."

Janice M. Cauwels, author of the new book "Bulimia: The Binge-Purge Compulsion," says about 90 percent of bulimics who purge do so by vomiting, although many use more than one method. Dr. Johnson says, "Through some transformation, the bingeing becomes only a means to the vomiting, which is more important to them. We've had women tell us that they binge beyond their satiation points to make it easier to vomit and that they select foods that are easiest to bring up."

The medical consequences of frequent purges can be severe. Bulimics may suffer terrible damage to teeth and gums from the repeated exposure to acidic vomit. Other hazards of bingeing and purging include esophageal irritation, persistent sore throat, dangerous stretching of the stomach, infection of the salivary glands, hiatal hernia, dehydration, electrolyte imbalance (which can result in abnormal heart rhythm and possible sudden death), loss of normal intestinal muscle action from laxative abuse, intestinal inflammation, loss of menstrual periods, urinary difficulties and kidney failure.

esophageal: throat

electrolyte: chemicals in body fluids

Group therapy has been cited as the most effective means of changing bulimic behavior. It helps victims realize they are not alone, it gives them access to supportive friends, and it counters their isolation. In many groups, a "buddy" system is established and a "contract" of goals is signed to help members control their bulimia.

The first step in treatment, most therapists believe, is to stop purging, since the purges seem to intensify the binges. At the University of Vermont, Dr. James Rosen helps bulimics learn to live through the anxiety induced by a binge by preventing them from purging. He says patients learn to eat large amounts of food without precipitating a desire to purge. As the fear of eating diminishes, the normalcy of eating habits increases, he reports. And, interestingly, few victims gain much weight after treatment.

With bingeing and purging under control, it becomes possible to begin work on underlying problems in individual or group therapy. Victims must learn more effective ways of relieving stress, how to say "no," how to express anger without losing control, how to face pain. Perfectionist notions must be abandoned, and normal means of enhancing self-esteem appreciated.

intimate: close, personal

affirmation: praise

Many bulimics have trouble with intimate relationships. Bulimic women often depend too much on men for affirmation for their femininity and self-worth, going to abnormal lengths to please men who may treat them badly. Thus, assertiveness training is often a crucial aspect of effective treatment. As bulimics learn to trust themselves and others more, self-esteem increases and they come to realize that they have a *choice* about eating habits.

QUESTIONS

Before answering these questions that focus on specific features of the writing, think about what you have read and discuss in your writing journal what you thought was important and how you reacted to what you read. Then answer the questions.

1. What is the purpose of beginning the essay with the case study of Suzanne?

2. Where does Jane Brody give a formal definition of bulimia?

3. What examples does she use to illustrate a typical binge?

4. This extended definition also explains the causes and effects of bulimia so that the reader will fully understand the condition. What paragraphs discuss causes?

    What paragraphs discuss effects?

5. Brody ends her essay on the treatment of bulimia. What are the steps to treating bulimia successfully?

6. Notice how Brody integrates her sources within her text. Underline each reference to an outside source. Put an asterisk (*) in front of quotations and circle the paraphrases.

Writing Journal Suggestion: Have you or anyone you have known had an obsession or addiction? Discuss the problem of being compelled to do something which is self-destructive. What were the causes or reasons for it? What were the effects? How did you or the other person end the addiction, if it was ended?

Science Fiction Films: The Imagination of Disaster

SUSAN SONTAG

The typical science fiction film has a form as predictable as a Western, and is made up of elements which, to a practiced eye, are as classic as the saloon brawl, the blonde schoolteacher from the East, and the gun duel on the deserted main street.

scenario: plot outline

One model scenario proceeds through five phases.

(1)   The arrival of the thing. (Emergence of the monsters, landing of the alien spaceship, etc.) This is usually witnessed or suspected by just one person, a young scientist on a field trip. Nobody, neither his neighbors nor his colleagues, will believe him for some time. The hero is not married, but has a sympathetic though also incredulous girl friend.

incredulous: unbelieving

parley: talk

(2)   Confirmation of the hero's report by a host of witnesses to a great act of destruction. (If the invaders are beings from another planet, a fruitless attempt to parley with them and get them to leave peacefully.) The local police are summoned to deal with the situation and massacred.

(3)   In the capital of the country, conferences between scientists and the military take place, with the hero lecturing before a chart, map, or blackboard. A national emergency is declared. Reports of further destruction. Authorities from other countries arrive in black limousines. All international tensions are suspended in view of the planetary emergency. This stage often includes a rapid montage of news broadcasts in various languages, a meeting at the UN, and more conferences between the military and the scientists. Plans are made for destroying the enemy.

montage: collection of pictures

atrocities: crimes or terrible acts

(4)   Further atrocities. At some point the hero's girl friend is in grave danger. Massive counter-attacks by international forces, with brilliant displays of rocketry, rays, and other advanced weapons are all unsuccessful. Enormous military casualties, usually by incineration. Cities are destroyed and/or evacuated. There is an obligatory scene here of panicked crowds stampeding along a highway or a big bridge, being waved on by numerous policemen who, if the film is Japanese, are immaculately white-gloved, preternaturally calm, and call out in dubbed English, "Keep moving. There is no need to be alarmed."

obligatory: required

preternaturally: more than is normal or natural

(5)   More conferences, whose motif is: "They must be vulnerable to something." Throughout the hero has been working in his lab to this end. The final strategy, upon which all hopes depend, is drawn up; the ultimate weapon—often a superpowerful, as yet untested, nuclear device—is mounted. Countdown. Final repulse of the monster or invaders. Mutual congratulations, while the hero and girl friend embrace cheek to cheek and scan the skies sturdily. "But have we seen the last of them?"

The film I have just described should be in color and on a wide screen. Another typical scenario, which follows, is simpler and suited to black-and-white films with a lower budget. It has four phases.

(1)   The hero (usually, but not always, a scientist) and his girl friend, or his wife and two children, are disporting themselves in some innocent ultra-normal middle-class surroundings—their house in a small town, or on vacation (camping, boating). Suddenly, someone starts behaving strangely; or some innocent form of vegetation becomes monstrously enlarged and ambulatory. If a character is pictured driving an automobile, something gruesome looms up in the middle of the road. If it is night, strange lights hurtle across the sky.

ambulatory: moving, walking

(2)   After following the thing's tracks, or determining that It is radioactive, or poking around a huge crater—in short, conducting some sort of crude investigation—the hero tries to warn the local authorities, without effect; nobody believes anything is amiss. The hero knows better. If the thing is tangible, the house is elaborately barricaded. If the invading alien is an invisible parasite, a doctor or friend is called in, who is himself rather quickly killed or "taken possession of" by the thing.

amiss: wrong

(3)   The advice of whoever further is consulted proves useless. Meanwhile, It continues to claim other victims in the town, which remains implausibly isolated from the rest of the world. General helplessness.

(4)   One of two possibilities. Either the hero prepares to do battle alone, accidentally discovers the thing's one vulnerable point, and destroys it. Or, he somehow manages to get out of town and succeeds in laying his case before competent authorities. They, along the lines of the first script but abridged, deploy a complex technology which (after initial setbacks) finally prevails against the invaders.

vulnerable: weak

abridged: shortened

Another version of the second script opens with the scientist-hero in his laboratory, which is located in the basement or on the grounds of his tasteful, prosperous house. Through his experiments, he unwittingly causes a frightful metamorphosis in some class of plants or animals which turn carnivorous and go on a rampage. Or else, his experiments have caused him to be injured (sometimes irrevocably) or "invaded" himself. Perhaps

metamorphosis: change
carnivorous: meat-eating
irrevocably: unable to be changed

he has been experimenting with radiation, or has built a machine to communicate with beings from other planets or transport him to other places or times.

Another version of the first script involves the discovery of some fundamental alteration in the conditions of existence of our planet, brought about by nuclear testing, which will lead to the extinction in a few months of all human life. For example: the temperature of the earth is becoming too high or too low to support life, or the earth is cracking in two, or it is gradually being blanketed by lethal fallout.

lethal: deadly

A third script, somewhat but not altogether different from the first two, concerns a journey through space—to the moon, or some other planet. What the space-voyagers discover commonly is that the alien terrain is in a state of dire emergency, itself threatened by extra-planetary invaders or nearing extinction through the practice of nuclear warfare. The terminal dramas of the first and second scripts are played out there, to which is added the problem of getting away from the doomed and/or hostile planet and back to Earth.

QUESTIONS

Before answering these questions that focus on specific features of the writing, think about what you have read and discuss in your writing journal what you thought was important and how you reacted to what you read. Then answer the questions.

1.   This excerpt from Susan Sontag's essay classifies science fiction films into three basic types. List them.

Can you think of types she does not mention (which might have become popular after she wrote this essay)?

2.   What is Sontag's purpose in classifying the films?

3.   Each type of film is discussed using primarily what strategy?

Writing Journal Suggestion: Can you think of a similar classification of horror movies, rock star movies or any other type? Are they equally predictable?

Snarling Cars

PAUL BLUMBERG

LINCOLN-MERCURY COUGAR SLAIN

PITTSBURGH (UPI)—*The cougar that served as the Lincoln-Mercury advertising trademark was shot and killed today after it attacked a 9-year-old boy at an automobile show.*—News item.

macabre: strange, nightmarish

In this macabre incident, the cougar seized the boy by the neck, pinned him to the ground, resisted all efforts by the trainer to pull him from his prey, and was finally shot to death by an off-duty policeman. The boy, suffering severe neck wounds, was rushed to the hospital in serious condition. He has since recovered. The health of the American automobile industry, however, still hangs in the balance.

For decades, one of Detroit's major advertising ploys was to market its products as instruments of violence. During the entire postwar period, in fact, Detroit's marketing strategy was not to sell automobiles as sensible family transportation, as one might expect in a reasonably civilized society, but as vehicles of *mayhem: violence* mayhem and destruction.

What's in a name? In Detroit's case, plenty. Because over the years, as an auto writer once observed, the very names Detroit managers gave to their cars reveal quite plainly the industry's appeal to motives of violence and aggression. Consider the Oldsmobile *Cutlass,* the Buick *Le Sabre,* the Plymouth *Fury,* the Plymouth *Barracuda,* the Chevrolet Corvette *Stingray,* the Ford Mustang *Cobra,* the American Motors *Matador,* the Mercury *Lynx,* Mercury *Bobcat,* and Mercury *Cougar*—killers all, the last one, this time, almost literally. The theme of violence in these names *cunning: clever* has a cunning economic logic behind it. As we now know, Detroit management's guiding theology during the postwar era was: big car, big profit; small car, small profit. And what better way to sell big, powerful cars than to link them in the public's mind with the *libidinal: subconscious, emotional* libidinal release of destructive impulses?

In the postwar auto industry, as the horsepower race heated up, the managers of each company dropped ever-larger and hungrier engines into ever-bigger, heavier, and more option-laden automobiles. As late as 1970, 85 percent of U.S. cars were sold with V-8 engines. Consequently, as one sage assessed the peculiar logic of the American automobile industry, Detroit sold a 5,000-pound car to a 100-pound woman so she could drive one block to buy a one-pound loaf of bread. When Marx wrote of the *anarchy: without rules* anarchy of production under capitalism, he knew whereof he spoke, though he lived before Detroit management had honed the principle to perfection.

Of all the gadgets on the Road Locomotives (as Consumers Union called these American behemoths thirty years ago), none so clearly opens a window into the mind of the Detroit executive as the design of the speedometer. In keeping with management's appeal to raw power rather than sensible transportation, the speedometer had to show speeds of 120, 140, or 150 miles per hour—far faster, of course, than was safe, legal, or even possible for most cars. But when you scale up a small gauge with speeds to 150 m.p.h., the numbers must all be crammed so close together that it's difficult to read any of them. Here in a nutshell (or a dial) were management's values: style and libido over engineering logic. And while Detroit managers were busy refining these priorities with tail fins and sleek but dangerous hardtop convertibles (whose roofs, lacking a center pillar, might collapse if the car rolled over), foreign manufacturers were making disc brakes and radial tires.

libido: emotion

When Detroit's managers are accused of foisting the Road Locomotives on the American public and thus being unprepared for the small-car revolution, they neatly shift the blame to the public. The postwar dinosaurs weren't their idea, they protest, they were simply giving their customers what they wanted. This, the consumer sovereignty argument, overlooks the fact that consumer taste does not develop in a vacuum but is shaped by manufacturers through massive advertising. In one recent year, the auto industry spent $700 million on TV ads, $340 million more on newspaper ads, and $225 million for magazine advertising—well over $1 billion in just one year (not counting the money spent on radio, billboards, and other forms of advertising). Throughout the postwar years Detroit spent comparable billions fashioning public taste for the gas guzzlers, and then proceeded to satisfy that taste.

foisting: pushing

sovereignty: ruling group

Of course, public taste cannot be totally programmed by advertising. Ford failed to generate much interest in the Edsel, and some new and highly promoted products do occasionally fail. Nonetheless, though massive advertising cannot guarantee demand for individual products, there is no question that the billions Detroit spent after World War II pushing the big, heavy, powerful V-8s did in fact create the taste and habit for these cars. Because of postwar affluence, which allowed an ethic of conspicuous waste, and because of the underlying macho element in American culture, there was a basic public receptivity to the marketing strategy of selling murder on wheels. But if the ground was fertile, Detroit management sowed the seeds and carefully tended the fields.

ethic: value
conspicuous: obvious

In 1949 The U.A.W.'s research and engineering people

published an article, "A Motor Car Named Desire," that called on Detroit to build a small, light, affordable car, suitable for postwar urban America. They cited a contemporary opinion survey taken by the Society of Automotive Engineers, which showed that 60 percent of Americans wanted the U.S. auto industry to produce a small car. Specifically, the U.A.W. proposed a car about 170 inches in length, weighing about 2,000 pounds, with a small six- or four-cylinder engine that would get more than 25 miles to the gallon. In other words, the U.A.W. proposed a car almost identical in conception to the Datsuns, Toyotas, and Hondas now inundating America. Had Detroit heeded the U.A.W.'s advice then, it would now have the experience to meet and beat the small-car competition from abroad, rather than belatedly struggling to catch up. But it ignored the suggestion; in fact, it responded to Walter Reuther's presumption with a bold assertion of executive power meant to keep the union in its place and to protect the principle of managerial prerogative. In its contract with the U.A.W. in 1950, and in every contract thereafter, G.M. inserted a clause stipulating the "Rights of Management." It provided that "the products to be manufactured, the location of plants, the schedules of production, the methods, processes and means of manufacturing are solely and exclusively the responsibility of the Corporation."

When sensible, small-car transportation became necessary after the 1973 OPEC oil embargo, Detroit was unprepared. By hooking the American consumer on far bigger and more powerful cars than were rational or necessary, Detroit became the victim of its own shortsightedness and masterminded its own collapse. Until 1955 Detroit had the U.S. auto market all to itself; foreign imports comprised less than 1 percent of sales. But in the late 1950s the U.S. was invaded by a horde of insects—the Volkswagen beetles. And between 1955 and 1960, foreign auto imports rose to nearly 7 percent of sales. Though opposed in principle to building small, inexpensive cars, Detroit management realized that it had to offer the American public something to offset the growing popularity of the Volkswagen, the other small European cars, and the initial flow of Japanese cars. So at the end of the 1950s Detroit introduced its own compact cars— the Plymouth Valiant, Ford Falcon, Chevrolet Corvair, and the like.

These practical American compacts sold well, and the foreign car tide began to recede. By 1965 imports accounted for a smaller share of the U.S. market than they had in 1960. But Detroit executives were so hooked on the big-is-beautiful formula that they said, in effect, "Well, we'll build these compacts if we have to, but they're going to be the biggest, widest, heaviest, most powerful, most expensive compacts the world has ever seen." Each year U.S. compacts got bigger, more powerful, more loaded with options, and more costly. The U.S. auto industry was so successful in building the world's biggest compacts that it eventually abandoned the small-car field altogether. Into this vacuum came the European cars again, and with them the Japanese— this time for keeps. Foreign imports rose from just 5.5 percent of sales in 1965 to 23 percent in 1970. With that kind of a foothold the imports now could not be dislodged. But if Detroit management had stayed with the compacts in the 1960s and redirected its advertising to wean Americans from the gospel of speed, power, and mayhem, the U.S. industry could have overcome or at least minimized the foreign car challenge, perhaps forestalled the protectionist tide, and might even have started exporting significant numbers of cars itself.

Friends of the U.S. auto industry like to argue that protectionism would never have become an issue if the working men and women who build the cars weren't so greedy. Detroit cannot compete with the Japanese, it is alleged, because American workers earn $8 an hour more than Japanese workers. Most objective observers agree, however, that the presumed $8-an-hour wage difference has been exaggerated and omits such things as the substantial housing subsidies Japanese companies provide for their workers. Although U.S. workers are more highly paid, wage differences between the U.S. and Japan probably amount to less than $500 per car, which is virtually offset by duty and cost of shipping from Japan to the U.S.

Moreover, low price is not the reason foreign cars are selling here. In fact, foreign cars sold in the U.S., which years ago were cheaper than American cars, are now on the average more expensive than American cars. Commerce Department figures show that in the last quarter of 1981 the average selling price of an American car was $9,012, and the average selling price of a foreign car sold here was $9,318. Japanese companies are selling cars in this country primarily because they have the product, and they have the product because they've had long experience making it. American companies don't.

The lesson of Detroit's decline is clear: just as war is too important to leave to the generals, business is too important to leave to the managers. Detroit management has failed; their marketing strategy has been cynical and antisocial for at least a generation; their world view is obsolete. Until recently the idea of economic democracy—the participation of workers, consumers,

cynical: calculating
antisocial: against
society

paradox:
   contradiction

and the public in corporate decisionmaking—was a radical, utopian dream. Today it may be an economic necessity.

The paradox of all this is that Detroit management's prime concern with the bottom line by selling big cars for big profits proved in the long run to be extremely unprofitable. Had saner voices among workers, consumers, and the public prevailed, a sensible automobile for urban America would probably have been produced decades ago, which might have saved the U.S. auto industry from its present debacle. Ironically, production for use would have been more profitable than production for profit.

A final note: recently Dodge management introduced a new small truck. They call it the Dodge *Rampage*. These guys will never change.

QUESTIONS

Before answering these questions that focus on specific features of the writing, think about what you have read and discuss in your writing journal what you thought was important and how you reacted to what you read. Then answer the questions.

1.   This complicated cause/effect essay says that the problems of the auto industry were caused by its commitment to the big, powerful car. What evidence does Blumberg use to support his idea?

What evidence seem convincing?

Of what evidence are you suspicious, and why?

2.   When the U.S. auto industry had to compete with Volkswagen and began to make compacts, why didn't this experience help them keep the small-car market?

3.   What does Blumberg say the lesson is?

Do you agree? _____

4.   What is the purpose of Blumberg's last sentence?

To what other part of the essay does it refer?

How does the title fit his thesis?

Writing Journal Suggestion: Where do you see the American auto industry headed? Will it be swallowed up by foreign-based car makers? Will it become a cooperative venture with foreign car makers?

PART V

Understanding Grammar and Usage

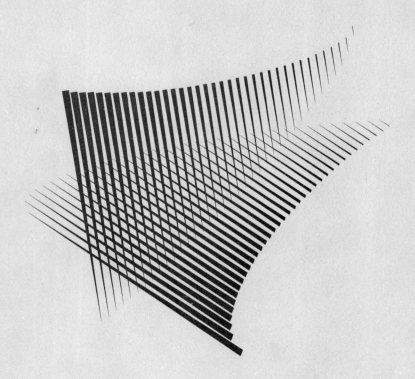

Though the basic principles of Standard English grammar and usage may not be your favorite subject, applying these principles in your written work will enable you to communicate more effectively with instructors at school and employers and colleagues on the job. Writing effectively, which includes writing correct standard forms, is often cited as a requirement for success in college and in a career. Fortunately, you probably know more about grammar than you realize. If you are a native speaker of English, you already know the basic structure of English. If you are learning English as a second language, your study and everyday practice are helping you to understand the principles of English grammar.

However, the demands of written English are very different from those of spoken English. When we talk to people directly, we can use body language to help express our ideas and feelings. We can wave our arms, point, shrug our shoulders, smile, frown, or stand on our heads, if necessary, to illustrate our points. We can raise or lower our voices or pause frequently to clarify an idea. And we can adjust our explanation to our listeners' feedback. We are able to respond immediately to questions, blank stares, or shrugs. Writers rarely have the same opportunity to supplement, correct, or clarify their material after it has been given to their readers. Your written work must do the job the first time, and it must do it effectively on its own.

In order to talk about language, you may need to know specific terms to refer to parts of sentences or to word choices. Sometimes you may feel that the study of English gets bogged down with such terms. While it is true that most writers may not know or think of all the terms as they write, nevertheless, knowing some of the terms will make it easier for your instructor to talk with you and your classmates about revising your writing. Also, knowing what options you have in constructing effective sentences may help you revise your written work. If you have ever fumbled over terms for the parts of your car's engine when you were describing some problem to a garage mechanic, you have an idea of the importance of a specific vocabulary. More than one of us has wished we had known a carburetor or an intake manifold or an alternator instead of a whatchamacallit.

Although past experience in speaking and writing will help you make many correct grammatical choices, learning some rules of standard written English and applying them may help you improve your writing skill.

CHAPTER 10

Writing Complete Sentences

When people speak to others, they rarely pay attention to the way their sentences are put together. It isn't necessary. If they give their listeners too little information, listeners can stop them to ask for more detail. If they give their listeners too much information without pausing enough, those listening can say "Slow down," or "What was that again?" Writers don't get that kind of feedback most of the time. Their readers have only the words on the printed page to communicate the writers' ideas. If writers want their ideas understood and taken seriously by readers, they must use complete, grammatically correct sentences to express their thoughts.

A few reminders about sentence structure may help you check your own sentences for completeness.

WHAT IS A SENTENCE?

1. A sentence expresses a complete thought.

2. A sentence usually makes sense when it is standing alone.

3. A sentence usually contains a complete subject-verb combination.

4. A sentence begins with a capital letter and ends with a period, an exclamation point, or a question mark.

Let's briefly review some points about sentences. While sentences can relate to ideas that come before or after them in a paragraph, a sentence should be able to be understood as a complete thought, and on its own. So if you say, "The weather was warm," people understand an idea about weather. However, if you say, "Was warm" or "Because the weather was warm," you do not have a complete thought—something has been left out. In the middle example readers don't know what "was warm"—there is no subject. In the last example, readers wait to see what happened "because the weather was warm"— the word *because* introduces a dependent idea and there needs to be a sentence to complete the thought.

To see whether sentences are complete, you need to find their subjects and verbs.

Finding Subjects and Verbs

Test 1.   It is usually easier to find the verb in a sentence before locating the subject. Ask yourself the following questions about the sentence:

What word is the action word?

What word shows that something exists?

The answer to each question will be a verb.

EXAMPLES:

Dogs bark.

What word is the action word? *bark. Bark* is the verb.

John ate pizza.

What word is the action word? *ate. Ate* is the verb.

Susan is my neighbor.

What word shows that something exists? *is. Is* is the verb.

Test 2.   Another test for a verb is to put the words *he, she,* or *they* before the word you are testing to see if it makes a sentence (no matter how short!).

EXAMPLES:

They bark.   He ate.   She is.

Once you have found the verb, ask, "Who or what is doing the action or existing?" The answer will be the subject of the sentence.

EXAMPLES:

The horses ran swiftly toward the finish line.

What word is the action word? *ran.* Test: They ran. *Ran* is the verb. Who or what ran? *horses. Horses* is the subject.

My sister is an expert skier.

What word is the action word or shows something that exists? *is.* Test: She is. *Is* is the verb. Who or what is? *sister. Sister* is the subject. (Note: "Skier" doesn't pass the test as an action word: She skier?)

Sometimes a verb will need more than one word to be complete and pass the test. An -*ing* word such as *swimming* will not pass the test alone: "They swimming" is not complete in Standard English usage. However, if you add *are* ("They are swimming"), it does pass. The word *are* is a helper, or auxiliary, which makes an -*ing* verb form such as *swimming* complete. Another example of the need for a helper is a word ending in -*en*, such as *stolen* or *spoken.* Let's apply the test: "He spoken" doesn't pass. But if you add a helper to the verb, "He *has* spoken," it does.

Other helpers are *is, am, was, were, has been, have been,* and **will be.** When you are asked to "find the verb," that means find any helpers too.

Another tricky form is the word *to* plus the verb, as in *to swim* or *to run.* This form is called an *infinitive* and can't serve as the verb. Try the test: "They to swim." It doesn't pass. You need to add a verb, such as *like* or *hate,* or *prefer:* "They hate to swim."

Try your hand at completing sentences by filling in the missing word in the following word groups so that each makes a sentence. Then indicate if the word you filled in is a subject or a verb.

☞ Exercise 1

1. Movies _are_____ one of my favorite things. (subject or <u>verb)</u>

2. As a child, I ___went_____ to the movies every Saturday afternoon. (subject or <u>verb)</u>

3. Sometimes the __Movie_____ included five cartoons, a continuing story called a serial, and the main feature. (su<u>bject</u> or verb)

4. Even as an adult, I ___wanted__ to see movies frequently. (subject or verb)__

5. ___Action___ is the kind of movie I like best. (subject or verb)

Now read the following sentences, and find the subject and verb in each one.

☞ Exercise 2

Underline the verb twice and the subject once in each of the following sentences.

1. David rode his motorcycle across the country.

2. Shana is my roommate and my best friend.

3. Justin drove his neighbor's car to the service station.

4. The expensive speakers in his television set are broken.

5. Gary asked to borrow my history notes.

6. A woman at work will be married next month.

7. School opened two hours late because of the snow storm.

8. The candidates cancelled their debate.

9. The diner's false teeth dropped into his soup.

10. The curious chicken crossed the road.

Good writers avoid the three major sentence errors: fragments, run-ons, and comma splices. Readers notice these errors more readily than just about any other error except misspelling. We will take up each of these problems in turn.

Eliminating Fragments

A *fragment* is a part of a sentence that is written and punctuated as if it were a complete sentence. A fragment cannot stand alone, because it lacks a subject, a verb, or both, *or* because it begins with a subordinating word such as *after, because, which,* or *that. Subordinating words* make an idea incomplete or dependent so that another idea has to be added to the first idea to make a complete thought. Thus, our earlier example, "The weather was warm," is complete, but "Because the weather was warm" is a fragment. You want to know what happened "Because the weather was warm"? So you could add an idea: "Because the weather was warm, we ate our lunch outside by the duck pond." Here is a partial list of subordinating words:

after	if	unless
although	since	until
as	than	when
because	that	where
before	though	while

Let's look now at some examples of different kinds of fragments and ways to correct them.

Missing Subject-and-Verb Fragments

EXAMPLE

Whistling in the dark hallway.

This is a fragment that has a verb form "whistling" but no complete verb that passes the *he, she, they* test. "They whistling" is not a sentence.

To correct such a fragment you can add it to a complete sentence:

CORRECTION

The guests could hear the monster whistling in the dark hallway.

Or you can make it into a complete sentence:

CORRECTION

The monster was whistling in the dark hallway.

CORRECTION

Whistling in the dark hallway *gave the child courage.*

Missing Verb Fragments

EXAMPLE

At one point in the semester, the chemistry professor along with several of his colleagues and students.

Although this fragment is very long and looks like a sentence, it lacks a verb, so we don't know what the chemistry professor did.

To correct such a fragment, add a verb:

CORRECTION

At one point in the semester, the chemistry professor along with several of his colleagues and students *discovered a formula for unbreakable pencil points.*

FRAGMENT

The moon rising over the trees and shining on the lake.

Note the *-ing* verb forms do not pass the *he, she, they* test: "She rising"? We need to add a helper.

CORRECTION

The moon *was* rising over the trees and *was* shining on the lake.

Missing Subject Fragments

EXAMPLE

And invited hundreds of guests to their dormitory after the football game.

This fragment sounds like a continuation of another idea, perhaps from the previous sentence. Even if two sentences make sense when read together, each one needs a subject if it is going to stand alone with a capital letter and a period.

CORRECTION

The dorm council got together and invited hundreds of guests to their dormitory after the football game.

FRAGMENT

The cafeteria was noisy. Filled with the voices of impatient students.

CORRECTION

The cafeteria was noisy, filled with the voices of impatient students.

Note that in this case the two parts could simply be joined, with the fragment now becoming part of the sentence.

FRAGMENT

Made me promise not to tell her parents.

CORRECTION

My roommate made me promise not to tell her parents.

FRAGMENT

The young-looking movie star with the big eyes.

CORRECTION

The young-looking movie star with the big eyes *is actually forty-four years old.*

Dependent Clause Fragments

EXAMPLE

Because Jeffrey had forgotten two of their dates.

This word group is a fragment because of the word *because*. That word, a subordinator, makes a reader think that another idea will follow. To fix the fragment, the subordinator may be dropped, or another complete sentence *(independent clause)* may be added:

CORRECTION

Jeffrey had forgotten two of their dates.

CORRECTION

Because Jeffrey had forgotten two of their dates, *Charlene refused to go out with him again.*

FRAGMENT

Whose brother is a famous rock star.

Note that with a question mark this sentence would be complete: "Whose brother is a famous rock star?"

CORRECTION

I am going to spend the weekend with my roommate, whose brother is a famous rock star.

☞   Exercise 3

In the following word groups, put capital letters and end punctuation on those that are complete sentences. Rewrite the fragments.

1.   speaking into the microphone as clearly as possible *the disc jockey began his* when we opened the oven the pizza *show*

2.   burned to a crisp and shriveled into small pieces

3.   Because he had always believed if he tried hard enough to succeed, *he would*

4.   that I ordered from a catalogue that the postal courier delivered last Thursday

5.   my sister watches soap operas every afternoon after school

6.   although he promised that he should never let unimportant little things like flat tires bother him again

7.   after the test, they went to the student lounge to compare answers

8.   who stood beside me when the rest of the world doubted my honesty

9.   the car that had been parked beside the fire hydrant for three days

10.   the television set that was stolen by the gang that had been working in the neighborhood for seven months

11.   once he had made up his mind to do it, the informant told all he knew about the robbery.

12.   while Rome burned to the ground

13.   beside the tree in the garden near the flower beds under a stone marker

14.   before lunch, the professor must grade two sets of papers

15.   the race car driver, being afraid to approach the sharp turn at high speed.

☞   Exercise 4

In the following paragraph, all word groups are punctuated as if they are complete sentences, although some are fragments. Read each word group carefully to see if it is a complete sentence. Correct the fragments you find in one of the ways we have discussed.

My favorite possession, my stereo system, is the source of constant conflict in my house. My parents always complain about my choice of music. Saying it sounds like noise. They also say I spend too much money on things like amplifiers and turntables. Which is really none of their business because I have a job, and I earn the money to pay for everything I buy. Besides my parents complaining. My sister is always telling me to turn the volume down. Claiming that I turn it up too high just to annoy her. And then, after complaining all the time, she has the nerve to ask me to borrow it whenever she has friends coming to visit. My little brother is even worse. Always whining that I keep playing the same songs over and over. Which is definitely not true. I have more than three hundred albums and tapes. The best collection in the neighborhood if you want to know the truth. My parents, my sister, and my brother, some group. Sometimes I think that they're all just jealous.

WORKING WITH PEERS

In pairs or groups, write five sentences more than eight words long. Check each one to see that it is a complete sentence. You should be able to answer "yes" to the following questions:

1.   Does the word group contain a complete verb that passes the *he, she, they* test?

2.   Does the word group contain a subject?

3.   If the word group begins with a subordinator such as *because, since, while, when,* or *that,* is there an independent clause (a complete sentence) attached to the word group to make it a complete thought?

4.   Does the word group express a complete thought?

Eliminating Run-Ons

A *run-on,* or fused, sentence occurs when two complete sentences are written as one without the proper punctuation.

EXAMPLE

Arthur always sleeps late he never gets to class on time.

Note that "Arthur always sleeps late" is the first sentence and "he never gets to class on time" is the second.Even though the ideas are related, they are independent thoughts and have to be punctuated correctly.

There are several methods to correct run-ons. The method you choose depends on the way you wish the ideas to be joined. Of the many methods for correcting run-ons, these are the most common:

1. Make two separate sentences by adding a period at the end of the first sentence (independent clause) and capitalizing the first word of the second sentence.

    CORRECTION

    Arthur always sleeps late. He never gets to class on time.

2. Add a coordinating conjunction (*and, but, or, nor, for, so,* or *yet*) between the two sentences *and* put a comma before the conjunction unless the sentences are very short.

    CORRECTION

    Arthur always sleeps late, so he never gets to class on time.

3. Join the sentences by leaving out the second subject.

    CORRECTION

    Arthur always sleeps late and never gets to class on time.

We now have one subject with two verbs (a simple sentence with a compound predicate). We don't need a comma before the *and* in that case.

4. If the two sentences are closely related, put a semicolon between them. As a general rule, do not use a semicolon with *and, but, or, nor, for, so,* or *yet.*

    CORRECTION

    Arthur always sleeps late; he never gets to class on time.

5. You may use a transition word after the semicolon, such as *however, moreover, therefore,* or *indeed.* If you do, use a comma after the transition word.

    CORRECTION

    Arthur always sleeps late; therefore, he never gets to class on time.

Note: Sometimes we use a transition word in the middle of one sentence ("He is, however, a miser"). In order to justify using a semicolon, we need to have two independent clauses: a sentence structure of "subject-verb; subject-verb."

6.   Turn one of the sentences into a dependent clause, using a subordinator like *because, since, while,* or *after.*

CORRECTION

Because Arthur always sleeps late, he never gets to class on time.

It may seem odd to you that there are so many ways to correct run-ons, but the choices give you several ways to express your ideas and vary your sentence structure. Just as you tired of the simple sentences in your reading primer ("See Dick run. Run, Spot. Run, Jane"), your reader tires of the same sentence structures. Also, each way of connecting two sentences may change the relationship slightly between the two sentences. In the next exercise you will be experimenting with these choices. Discuss how connecting ideas in different ways changes the meaning of the sentences.

☞ Exercise 5

In the following word groups, correct the run-on sentences in at least two different ways. Try to use all the options just discussed by the time you have finished the exercise. Be prepared to discuss how connecting the sentences in different ways affects meaning. Note: Some sentences are already correct.

1.   Andrew tried out for the school hockey team he wanted to be the goalie.

2.   Even though he tried his best, the coach was not impressed with his skating ability or with his courage.

3.   Every day after school, Andrew went to the local rink to practice skating his best friend went also.

4.   One afternoon, as they were chasing each other around the rink, a scout happened to wander in several other people gathered also.

5.   Before the boys realized what had happened, they were putting on a show the spectators loved it.

6.   The scout offered Andrew and his friend a contract with a professional hockey team the offer sounded very good.

7.   When Andrew told his parents about wanting to accept the offer and

drop out of school, his mother became hysterical his sister fell on the floor laughing in disbelief.

8. Andrew's friend wasn't any more successful at his house his parents refused to discuss the matter.

9. The boys considered leaving home but decided that it would be a foolish thing to do since neither of them had any money or knew how to do laundry.

10. In anger, Andrew broke his hockey stick later he regretted acting in haste.

☞ Exercise 6

Some of the word groups in the following paragraph are run-ons. Revise them by properly punctuating them or by rewriting.

Maryann did not enjoy working in the local record store. Parking her car nearby was always a problem there was never enough space. Her boss was nasty he always expected everyone to work extra hours for no additional salary.The customers were always impatient and often were rude. When Maryann would ask them politely to wait their turn, some dropped their packages on the counter and walked out of the store in anger. In addition to waiting on customers, she was expected to stock new merchandise on the shelves.She had to stay late to sweep and lock up the store her boss never thanked her. Finally, she decided to quit then she felt much better.

WORKING WITH PEERS

With other classmates, write five sentences of your own that contain two independent clauses, then connect each of them in two different ways.

Eliminating Comma Splices

Comma splices are similar to run-ons, in that two sentences are put together incorrectly. A *comma splice* occurs when two sentences are separated only by a comma.

EXAMPLE

Heavy snow fell for three days, the students were trapped in their dorm.

A comma is not strong enough to separate two sentences. You must use one of the methods already discussed for correcting run-ons:

1. Use a period and capital letter.

   A _____. T_____.

2. Use a comma *with* a coordinating conjunction:

   A _____, and _____.

3. Use a semicolon:

   A _____; _____.

4. Use a semicolon with a transitional word:

   A _____; therefore, _____.

5. Rewrite the sentence, making one clause subordinate:

   The students were trapped in their dorm after heavy snow fell for three days.

☞ Exercise 7

Correct the following sentences, which all contain comma splices. Try to vary your choice of correction.

1. Arthur and Marilyn eloped, later they were sorry.

2. Arthur had trouble finding a job, Marilyn resented supporting both of them.

3. Marilyn began to want more freedom, she started staying after work to talk with her friends.

4. Arthur got frustrated looking for work, he began hanging out with guys at the corner gas station.

5. Neither Arthur nor Marilyn talked about their feelings, they pretended that everything was all right between them.

6. One day Marilyn was asked to take a sales manager position at another store, she really wanted the chance to advance.

7. The new position was two hours from where Marilyn and Arthur lived, and they would have to move in order for Marilyn to accept the job.

8. Arthur did not want to move, he would not have his buddies to talk to.

9. Marilyn suggested that they look in the new area for a job for Arthur, Arthur agreed to the idea.

10.   Arthur found more job openings in the new area, he doesn't have a job
       yet, he is hopeful that he will find something soon.

☞   Exercise 8

Revise the following paragraph to eliminate the sentence errors.

Last summer, Maria, Karen, and Tysha rented a cottage at the seashore,
it was near their jobs on the boardwalk. Their parents did not like the idea.
Because they were only freshmen. Their parents thought they were too young
to stay away from home for two months. Taking care of themselves without
any adult supervision. The girls insisted that they were old enough to take
care of themselves, so their parents agreed to let them go. After moving into
the cottage, the girls discovered that there were mice in the kitchen and the
roof leaked, the landlord never returned their calls. In fact, they learned that
he had gone to Canada and wouldn't be back until winter. Which left them in
a mess. Water dripping in from the ceilings and mice scurrying in the kitchen.
After holding a meeting and considering all of their choices, the three girls
decided to stick it out at the seashore. They placed buckets under the leaks
when it rained. And bought mouse traps that trapped the mice in a maze but
didn't kill them. They told the real estate office of their problems they refused
to pay the full amount of the rent. Soon the real estate office contacted the
landlord. Who authorized repairs to the roof. Although the girls could have
given up when the cottage was not as they had expected it to be. They were
proud that they had found solutions to their problems. The girls learned
something about being on their own.

AVOIDING SENTENCE ERRORS

Type of Error	Example	Correction
Fragment		
Missing verb	the horse with a long mane	The horse with the long mane runs swiftly.
Incomplete verb	the horse running in the third race	The horse is running in the third race.
Missing subject	runs every day	The horse runs every day.
Missing subject and verb	in all kinds of weather	The horse runs every day in all kinds of weather.
Dependent clause	because the horse likes exercise	Because the horse likes exercise, the trainer takes it out every day.
	who rides the horse	The groom who rides the horse enjoys the work.

AVOIDING SENTENCE ERRORS

Type of Error	Example	Correction
Run-on	Horses are expensive to feed and groom they also run up huge veterinary bills.	Horses are expensive to feed and groom, and they also run up huge veterinary bills.
Comma splice	Some people will always enjoy watching horses, they are such graceful runners.	Some people will always enjoy watching horses, for they are such graceful runners.

CHAPTER 11

Writing Varied Sentences

Learning how to vary your sentence structure will give you more choices when you write sentences. In addition, writing that contains a variety of sentences generally is easier for a reader to understand. Short, choppy sentences make readers feel as if they are marching, rather than strolling, through your ideas. At the other extreme, long, complicated sentences make readers feel as if they are plodding, rather than walking, through your material. What you want to strive for is a balance of different types of sentences.

As was discussed in Chapter 10, all complete sentences contain a subject-verb combination that can stand alone. That is, all complete sentences contain at least one independent clause. However, that is not the only way a complete sentence can be written. Nearby is a chart showing the four basic sentence patterns you will study in this chapter. These patterns give writers many choices when they are trying to express their ideas. You will study each one in turn.

FOUR BASIC SENTENCE PATTERNS

Simple Sentence
A simple sentence contains one independent (or main) clause. That is, it has a subject-verb combination that can stand alone.

EXAMPLE

According to the latest survey, pizza is everyone's favorite food.

Compound Sentence

A compound sentence contains at least two independent (or main) clauses connected by *and, but, or, nor, for, so,* or *yet.*

EXAMPLE

According to the latest survey, pizza is everyone's favorite food, but hamburgers are probably in second place.

Complex Sentence

A complex sentence has one independent (or main) clause *and* at least one dependent clause that could not stand alone. The dependent clause usually begins with a subordinating word such as *because, since, while, when, after,* or *until.*

EXAMPLE

According to the latest survey, pizza is everyone's favorite food, which accounts for the large number of pizza restaurants.

Compound-Complex Sentence

A compound-complex sentence has at least two independent (or main) clauses connected by *and, but, or, nor, for, so,* or *yet,* plus at least one dependent clause.

EXAMPLE

According to the latest survey, pizza is everyone's favorite food, but people don't eat it every day because it is very filling and often expensive.

Using Simple Sentences

Simple sentences contain only one independent clause. They do not have any dependent clauses. Simple sentences are often short, but they do not have to be. They can be lengthened by adding phrases, such as the phrase in the chart "According to the latest survey." Regardless of their length, simple sentences have only one noun-verb combination. Generally, no commas are used to separate the subject(s) from the verb(s) in a simple sentence.

All of the following sentences are simple sentences:

                                                   phrase

s   v

The student jogged (to the pizza parlor).

       phrase

(After studying for a test), the student jogged

                                s   v

               phrases

(to the pizza parlor) (in the shopping mall) (near his home).

      s   s   v   phrases

The student and his friends jogged (to the pizza parlor) (in the shopping
    phrase

mall) (near his home). NOTE: Two subjects and one verb but still a simple
sentence.

      s   s   v   phrases

The student and his friends jogged (to the pizza parlor) (in the shopping

                      phrases

mall) (near his home) and ordered six pies (with pepperoni and mushrooms).
NOTE: Even though this is a long sentence, it is still considered a simple
sentence because it has the subjects together and the verbs together in one
combination: s and s   v and v

Sometimes, sentences are constructed with the subject and verb in reverse
order. Don't let this confuse you. Words like *there* and or *where* are not subjects.
Remember to find the verb first in the sentence and then ask who or what is
doing the action. Then you will find the true subject.

         v   s   v

There were seven swans swimming in their bathtub.

         v   s v

Where did I put my term paper?

The following exercises ask you to write some simple sentences, applying
what you have learned.

☞ Exercise 1

Write a simple sentence using the information given. Label each of your subjects and verbs. The first one is done as an example.

EXAMPLE

1. a zookeeper—two duties

   A zookeeper feeds the animals and keeps them healthy.

2. two friends—one action.

3. one athlete—one accomplishment

4. thousands of college students—two actions

5. one subject—mumbled under his/her breath

6. much to their surprise, James and Elroy—one action

7. one subject—shouted at the jury

8. two friends—two actions

9. after losing the election, the disappointed candidate—one action

10. to prepare for final exams—one subject, two actions

☞ Exercise 2

In this exercise there are some short, simple sentences that you are to combine into one by joining the two subjects or the two verbs or both. The first one is done as an example.

1. Debra shouted at the top of her lungs. Debra frightened the robber away.

COMBINED

Debra shouted at the top of her lungs and frightened the robber away.

2. George likes to sail and play tennis. Jill likes to sail and play tennis.

3. The police officer argued with the motorist about the parking ticket. The motorist argued with the police officer about the parking ticket.

4. The nervous student mumbled. The nervous student stared at the floor. The nervous student stuttered during a speech.

5. Larry, Moe, and Curly were The Three Stooges. They pretended to be plumbers, tore up a bathroom, and finally destroyed a house.

Using Compound Sentences

Compound sentences are two or more simple sentences joined together. They can be split apart where they are joined, and both halves remain as independent sentences.

EXAMPLE

s   v   s   v
Mary takes algebra, **/** and Joan takes calculus.

Note that a comma and a coordinating conjunction (*and, but, or, nor, for, so, yet*) join the two.

Another way to join the two sentences into one is by using a semicolon (;).

EXAMPLE

s   v   v   s   v   v
Today we are going to have a test; **/** tomorrow we will start a new chapter in the text.

Sometimes after the semicolon a writer will use a transition before the next sentence. The sentence can still be split into two independent parts.

EXAMPLE

                           s   v   s   v
On Wednesday it rained; / therefore, we cancelled the picnic.

Other transitions include *however, moreover, nevertheless, subsequently, for example,* and *as a result.* We use a comma after the transition, before the start of the next sentence. Remember to use *either* the comma and the coordinating conjunction *or* the semicolon to join two simple sentences into a compound sentence.

☞ Exercise 3

Combine the following simple sentences into *one compound* sentence. Use the conjunction or transition in parenthesis at the end of the sentences to join them. Use commas with the conjunctions; use semicolons with the transitions or if there is no joining word. Label the subjects and verbs. The first one is an example.

1. My twin sister is majoring in education. I am enrolled in liberal arts. (but)

    COMBINED

              s   v   v   s   v   v
    My twin sister is majoring in education, but I am enrolled in liberal arts.

2. I enjoyed the movie very much. The book was even better. (however)

3. After the storm, the electric company repaired the power lines. The fire fighters evacuated the elderly residents from their homes. (and)

4. Agatha continued to refuse Harold's phone calls. He quit calling. (finally)

5. John could use his birthday money to buy a new battery for his car. He could use it to buy a new stereo system. (or)

☞   Exercise 4

Make each of the following sentences a compound sentence by writing another
sentence and joining it to the first one. Be sure to join the two with a comma
and a coordinating conjunction (*and, but, or, nor, for, so, yet*) or with a semicolon.
Use transitions with the semicolons as you think necessary. The first one is an
example.

1.   After dinner, Andrew took the dog for a walk.

     NEW COMPOUND SENTENCE:

     After dinner, Andrew took the dog for a walk; later,
     they both lay curled up in front of the fireplace.

2.   The bank lowered the interest rate on home mortgage loans.

3.   The prosecutor asked the judge to give the convicted robber a ten-year
     sentence.

4.   Harold agreed to take his cousin to a school party.

5.   Torrential downpours flooded the coastal regions.

6.   David would like to watch football games all weekend.

7.   Drought in the South ruined the crops.

8.   The salesman quit his job at Acme Vacuum Company.

9.   Movie makers never seem to tire of sequels.

10. My brother kept snakes and tarantulas as pets.

Using Complex Sentences

What we have studied so far are sentences that present ideas that are equal in rank. That is, we have written a simple sentence, or we have simply joined together two sentences that each claim equal attention from the reader. Sometimes, however, we want to present two ideas that are not equal. Perhaps some event occurred *before* another event, or perhaps something was going on *while* an event was occurring, or perhaps one thing occurred *because of* another event. Complex sentences allow us to present ideas that are unequal in rank. Read the examples that follow:

EXAMPLE

sub.   s   v   *dependent clause*   s   v   *independent clause*
(Before we could go on our trip,) we had to arrange for the cat to be fed

and the mail to be brought in.

EXAMPLE

s   v   sub. s   v
Mark thought of his family every day (while he was away.)
    independent clause   *dependent clause*

EXAMPLE

s   v   sub.   s   v
Joan decided to take an insurance course at night (because it would help
        independent clause   *dependent clause*

her get a promotion at work.)

As you can see, each of these sentences has an independent clause and a dependent clause that begins with a subordinator like *before, while,* or *because.* Sometimes writers will leave out the subordinator *that* in speech and in writing, although it is clearer to use it:

EXAMPLE

                    (that)

s   v   v   s   v
Maria couldn't believe (she had won the lottery.) OR
    independent clause   *dependent clause*

<blockquote>
s   v   v   sub.   s   v   v

Maria couldn't believe (that she had won the lottery.)

independent clause   *dependent clause*
</blockquote>

Dependent clauses may occur anywhere in a sentence, but you punctuate them differently depending on where they occur. If the dependent clause begins the sentence, we put a comma after it and before the main clause:

EXAMPLE

<blockquote>
sub.   s   v   v   s   v   v

(Although Jim had studied fro the test), he was not prepared for the

dependent clause   *independent clause*

difficult questions.
</blockquote>

However, if the dependent clause goes at the end of the sentence, no punctuation is used unless needed for clarity or contrast:

EXAMPLE

<blockquote>
s   v   v   sub.   s   v   v

Jim was not prepared for the difficult questions (although he had studied

independent clause   *dependent clause*

for the test.)
</blockquote>

Finally, when the dependent clause comes in the middle of the sentence, we put commas around it if it interrupts the main sentence:

EXAMPLE

<blockquote>
s   sub/s   v   v   v

Jim, (who studied for the test), was not prepared for the difficult questions.

dependent clause
</blockquote>

(NOTE: In this example, the dependent clause begins with a word that acts as a subordinator AND the subject of the clause. Words like who, whom, which, and that serve these two functions.)

(For more discussion of punctuating dependent clauses, see Chapter 12.)

☞ Exercise 5

Here are some dependent clauses you are to use as part of a complex sentence. You will need to write an independent clause and attach the dependent clause at the beginning, middle, or end. Try to punctuate correctly. The first one serves as an example.

1. after the rain stopped.

    COMPLEX SENTENCE

    After the rain stopped, the baseball team ran back onto the field.

2. although Jerry apologized

3. which was cancelled

4. since Kate was a college freshman

5. although I felt my meal at Luigi's was tasty and well-prepared

6. who must commute to campus

7. because it was two o'clock in the morning

8. that they had wasted their money

9. while they were riding on the bus

10. who are among my heroes

WORKING WITH PEERS

Combine the following simple sentences to form complex sentences. Use subordinators like *because, after, when, that, who,* or *while* to make logical connections between the ideas. Try to punctuate correctly. Underline the dependent clause. The first one is an example.

1. The mother waited for her child Tanya. Tanya was putting on her boots.

COMPLEX SENTENCE

The mother waited <u>while her child Tanya put on her boots</u>.

2. Joe moved into a new apartment. The apartment was closer to his work.

3. My friend borrows my clothes. She is five inches taller than I am. She looks foolish in them.

4. The rain finally stopped after two days. The expedition continued its search for rare birds.

5. The company was fined for dumping raw sewage in a local stream. It changed its method of waste disposal.

6. The toddler was frightened. The German shepherd growled at him.

7. Helga heard a loud noise at night. She decided to investigate. The hamster had made his escape.

8. Seventeen inches of snow fell in Wellsboro last winter. There are large potholes in all the roads.

9. Trash collectors organized a strike for better pay. Trash began to pile up in the streets and on the sidewalks.

10. The manager criticizes new employees. The department has a large turn-over in salespeople.

Using Compound-Complex Sentences

The last pattern is the most complicated, and allows writers to combine ideas in two ways. First, they can join two ideas together in a compound sentence made up of two independent clauses; and second, they can include other ideas in dependent clauses within the main sentences. Study the following example. The independent clauses are underlined and the dependent ones are in brackets:

Some of the families [who left the cities a few years ago] missed the excitement of urban life, and they began moving back to their former neighborhoods [where they can get a newspaper or a sandwich without driving five miles].

WORKING WITH PEERS

In the following exercise, combine the simple sentences into one compound-complex sentence. Remember to put a comma before the coordinating conjunction (*and, but, or, nor, for, so, yet*) that joins the two sentences. The first one serves as an example.

1. The film became tangled. The audience began stamping its feet. One man asked for his money back.

   COMPOUND-COMPLEX SENTENCE

   When the film became tangled, the audience began stamping its feet, and one man asked for his money back.

2. Growing your own vegetables can save money. Growing vegetables is a relaxing hobby. The cost of vegetables in the supermarket is rising every day.

3.   We admire our neighbor Mrs. Martinez. She is the school board presi-
     dent. She oversees the finances and curriculum of the schools. She listens
     patiently to parents, teachers, and students.

4.   Close the door. Lock the door securely. Do this each time. You leave the
     house.

5.   The movie had many special effects. One was a disappearing car. The
     car traveled through time. The car needed an enormous amount of
     electricity to recharge it for its return.

☞ Exercise 6

Rewrite the following paragraph to improve the variety of sentences. You may
wish to leave some of them as simple sentences.

   Each afternoon, Tony worked in a neighborhood grocery store. Tony and
his boss, Mr. Tessina, stocked shelves. They waited on customers. They
ordered food and supplies. Sometimes business was slow. Then Tony studied
in the storeroom. Cans and boxes of food were stacked up to the ceiling.
Tony's desk was a packing crate. One afternoon, Tony became very hungry.
He made himself a sandwich to quiet his growling stomach. Into a large roll,
Tony put salami, ham, cheese, tomatoes, pickles, olives, and onions. The
smell of the sandwich floated out of the storeroom. Customers were shopping
for groceries. They smelled the sandwich. The shoppers asked Mr. Tessina
about the delicious smell. He asked Tony to show his snack to the customers.
Tony's sandwich looked tasty to the customers. They placed orders for sandwiches of their own. Within two months, people were standing in long lines at
the new sandwich counter. The grocery store was doing more business than
ever.

WRITING VARIED SENTENCES

Types of Sentences	Number and Kinds of Clauses	Examples
Simple	One independent clause	David can hit homeruns.
		David and Jeffrey can hit homeruns.
		David can hit homeruns and field fly balls.
		David and Jeffrey can hit homeruns and field fly balls.

WRITING VARIED SENTENCES (continued)

Types of Sentences	Number and Kinds of Clauses	Examples
Compound	Two independent clauses—joined either by a coordinating conjunction *(and, but, or, nor, for, so, yet)* or by a semicolon	David can hit homeruns, and Jeffrey can field fly balls. David can hit homeruns; Jeffrey can field fly balls.
Complex	One independent and at least one dependent clause	While David can hit homeruns, Jeffrey can field fly balls. David, who can hit homeruns, can also hit fly balls. David and Jeffrey can hit homeruns exactly as the coach wants them to do.
Compound-complex	Two independent clauses and at least one dependent clause	While David can hit homeruns, Jeffrey can field fly balls, but neither one can slide home head first.

CHAPTER 12

Punctuating Sentences: Commas and Semicolons

In Chapter 11 you practiced writing different kinds of sentences and reviewed how to punctuate them as well. This chapter reviews most of the conventional uses of the comma and semicolon, including those mentioned in Chapter 11. Knowing some basic principles for comma and semicolon use may help clear up any confusion you may have now.

These punctuation principles developed as an attempt to signal pauses, ends of sentences, and other marks of intonation for people reading what someone else wrote. When people speak, their voices supply the needed pauses and variations in tone. For example, if you meet a neighbor on the street, you may say, "Hello, Mrs. Jones." However, if you call the Jones' house on the telephone and a female answers, you may say, "Hello, Mrs. Jones?" with a rising tone in your voice to indicate a question as to the identity of the person you have reached. As you can see, the only way to render the difference between the two sentences in writing is with a change in the end punctuation mark.

Similar reasons exist for using commas and semicolons as ways to signal pauses that separate groups of words. What is acceptable as "correct" comma and semicolon use varies over time, but some agreed-upon, regular system of punctuation seems to be necessary so that readers will be able to understand writers' thoughts. Take, for example, a sentence like "The police officer met Tom O'Malley the block captain for Crime Watch Joseph Brown a witness and Maureen Linder the owner of the house at the site of the burglary." Without any internal punctuation, the sentence could be understood in one of several ways. For instance, the police officer could have met five different people—(a) Tom O'Malley, (b) the block captain for Crime Watch, (c) Joseph Brown, (d) a witness, and (e) Maureen Linder—as in the following sentence:

> The police officer met Tom O'Malley, the block captain for Crime Watch, Joseph Brown, a witness, and Maureen Linder, the owner of the house, at the site of the burglary.

Or the police officer could have met three people—(a) Tom O'Malley, the block captain, (b) Joseph Brown, a witness, and (c) Maureen Linder, the owner—as in this sentence:

> The police officer met Tom O'Malley, the block captain for Crime Watch; Joseph Brown, a witness; and Maureen Linder, the owner of the house, at the site of the burglary.

Can you think of other possible readings of the original sentence? For example, could Joseph Brown be the Crime Watch captain?

Using commas and semicolons correctly helps your reader understand what you are saying and avoids confusion. The nearby box summarizes currently acceptable principles for comma and semicolon use.

COMMAS AND SEMICOLONS

Joining Sentences

1. Use a comma between two complete sentences connected by *and, but, or, nor, for, so,* or *yet.*

   ### EXAMPLE

   Teresa waited in a long line to register, but her patience was rewarded with the course schedule she wanted.

   Exception: If the sentences are *very* short, you can leave out the comma:

   Teresa talked and Brian listened.

2. Use a semicolon between two sentences *not* connected by *and, but, or, nor, for, so,* or *yet.*

EXAMPLE

Teresa waited in a long line to register; her patience was rewarded with the course schedule she wanted.

Note: After a semicolon, you may use a transition such as *however, moreover, therefore, in addition,* or *for example.* If you do, remember to use a comma after the transition:

Teresa waited in a long line to register; however, her patience was rewarded with the course schedule she wanted.

Separating an Introduction from a Main Sentence

1. Use a comma to separate any type of introduction from the rest of the sentence.

EXAMPLES

When I fall in love, it will be forever.

Yes, we have the boots you ordered.

Mario, do you know where we can get a Coke?

In the afternoon after a long day of classes, Marie did not want to go to work.

Before skating on a lake, you should check the thickness of the ice.

For example, there is a type of ski wax for almost every kind of snow.

Separating Words in a Series

1. Use a comma to separate three or more items in a series.

EXAMPLE

Leroy ate a whole pepperoni pizza, a dill pickle, a pint of rocky road ice cream, and a bag of marshmallows.

(Note: Some people leave out the comma before *and* if it doesn't create confusion.)

2. Use a semicolon to separate items in a series if the series also contains commas.

EXAMPLE

Leroy, the quarterback, went to the pizza place with John Garner, the fullback; Ray Browne, the wide receiver; Tony Lancetta, the field goal kicker; and Pete Wozniak, the center.

3.   Use a comma to separate adjectives that describe the same noun *if* the order of the words can be changed or if *and* could be inserted between them.

EXAMPLE

The police were looking for a clever, daring bank robber.

Note: The sentence could also read:

The police were looking for a clever and daring bank robber.

Also the adjectives could be reversed to read "daring and clever."

Use *no* comma if the adjectives can't be changed around or if they can't have *and* inserted between them.

EXAMPLE

The surprising suspect turned out to be a little old lady who drove a red Porsche convertible.

Setting Off Interrupters from the Main Part of the Sentence
1.   Use a comma to set off words or phrases that come in the middle of a sentence and interrupt the flow of the sentence. These interrupters are often signaled by a pause if the sentence is read aloud, and they often can be left out without confusing the reader as to the meaning of the sentence.

EXAMPLES

Toby, my best friend, likes to explore new trails in the woods.

He is, on the other hand, somewhat accident-prone.

Mrs. Gray, the loan officer at the bank, approved my request for a loan.

Family vacations by car are, generally speaking, tests of everyone's patience.

Mr. Gillespie, who teaches physical education, also coaches the sixth grade basketball team.

Major exception: If the word or phrase cannot be left out without creating confusion, then it is not an interrupter and does not need commas. Also, such words or phrases are generally read without pausing.

EXAMPLES

The gloves that were on the table have disappeared.

My friend Toby is always getting hurt.

The woman who asked for a bus transfer was angry when the driver said that he didn't have any.

A stormy sky that suddenly looks green means "watch for tornadoes" in some parts of the United States

Note: As a general rule, don't put a comma before the word *that*.

Setting Off Places, Dates, and Quotations

1. Use a comma between a city and a state or between a date and a year. Also, in a sentence use a comma *after* the state and *after* the year.

    EXAMPLES

    Hopkins, Minnesota, is a suburb of Minneapolis.

    July 4, 1776, is celebrated today as Independence Day.

2. Use a comma to set off a quotation from other words in the sentence.

    EXAMPLES

    Fernando said, "The cause of the drought was the position of the jet stream."

    "Oh, that's interesting," replied Juanita. "I thought it was caused by the greenhouse effect."

    "Couldn't both causes," asked David, "be responsible?"

Joining Sentences

When one complete sentence (that is, an independent clause having at least one subject and one verb) is joined to another complete sentence, the resulting compound sentence needs to be punctuated. (See Chapter 11 for a review of compound sentences.)

There are two options for joining two sentences:

1. _____ , and _____ .

    _____ , but _____ .

    _____ , or _____ .

    _____ , nor _____ .

_____ , for _____ .

_____ , so _____ .

_____ , yet _____ .

2.   a.   _____ ; _____ .

     b.   _____ ; transition word, _____ .

As mentioned in the box, very short sentences joined by *and, but, or, nor, for, so,* or *yet* do not need the comma. Common transition words include *however, moreover, therefore, in addition, consequently, nevertheless,* and *in fact.*

☞   ## Exercise 1

Join each pair of sentences in two ways: by inserting a comma and a conjunction (*and, but, or, nor, for, so, yet*) and by inserting a semicolon and a transition word followed by a comma. The first pair are done for you as an example.

1.   Video games continue to rise in popularity. New games sell out as soon as they arrive.

     a.   *Video games continue to rise in popularity, and new games sell out as soon as they arrive.*

     b.   *Video games continue to rise in popularity; in fact, new games sell out as soon as they arrive.*

2.   Some consumers suspect that the companies create shortages of games deliberately. The companies say that they can't get enough chips to meet the demand.

     a.   _____

          _____

     b.   _____

          _____

3.   Some people question the value of video games. They think that the games are a waste of time, especially for students.

     a.   _____

_____

b.   _____

_____

4.   Doctors even warn game players about overuse of fingers and wrists
during prolonged play. They recommend taking periodic breaks to rest
the hands.

a.   _____

_____

b.   _____

_____

5.   Video game fans say that the games develop eye-hand coordination. The
games provide an escape from stress.

a.   _____

_____

b.   _____

_____

WORKING WITH PEERS

Write at least six sentences on the subject of video games. Try to relate the
sentences to each other so that you are writing a short paragraph. Join at least
two sentences with a comma and a conjunction and two with a semicolon and
a transition word.

Separating an Introduction from the Main Sentence

Many times you will begin a sentence with an introductory idea before
writing the main independent clause of the sentence. Any such introduction
needs a comma after it, before the start of the main clause. There are several
kinds of introductions:

Introductory clause or phrase beginning with a subordinating word such as
after, because, before, since, when, or *while:*

When it rained, we cancelled the soccer game.

Since he was new in town, he took the wrong freeway exit.

Because she wanted to change her major, she made an appointment with her advisor.

While waiting for her advisor, she overheard another student complaining about conflicts between her work and her class schedule.

After working until 9:30, I don't have the energy to study until midnight.

Introductory prepositional phrase at least five words long:

Under the street light on the corner, he could see the suspicious figure dressed in a trench coat.

Using yes or no or addressing a person by name at the beginning of a sentence:

Yes, you may have your loan paid in three installments.

No, I am sorry I can't help you.

David, would you please close the door to the hall?

Using a transition at the beginning of a sentence:

In fact, domed stadiums have become increasingly popular.

However, cities find the cost of building a covered stadium much higher than the cost of one that is open.

Furthermore, architects find domes harder to design.

☞ **Exercise 2**

Add commas after any introductions to each main sentence in the following exercise. Some sentences do not have introductions and are already correctly punctuated.

1. When Jennifer was in high school she had many friends who went everywhere together.

2. In fact Jennifer and her friends even took jobs in different stores at the same mall so they could be together.

3. During the last half of their senior year Jennifer and her friends began planning what to do after graduation.

4. Some of them planned to go away to college; others were going to go to local schools or get full-time jobs.

5. However all of them vowed that their friendship would not change.

6. Nothing much changed during the summer after graduation.

7. Yes the girls had jobs and vacation plans, but they still managed to get together.

8. Around the end of August or the beginning of September Jennifer began to realize that the group's vow to remain friends might be broken.

9. After starting classes at a local college Jennifer found that she did not have the time to socialize with her friends or even work with them at the mall.

10. Furthermore she found that her friends were also too busy with their jobs or school to get together.

☞ Exercise 3

Write at least five related sentences about a change in friendships that you have experienced. Try to use an introduction to the main sentence in at least two of the sentences. Punctuate properly.

Separating Words in a Series

Commas and semicolons separate words, phrases, or clauses in a series so that a reader will be able to see the different elements and won't run them together. The most common example is a listing of three or more objects:

Mike picked up sandpaper, drop cloths, brushes, and paint at the hardware store.

Some writers omit the comma before *and* ("brushes and paint"). That's all right as long as there is no confusion. If you were writing about sandwiches being made in a deli and omitted a comma before the *and,* a reader could misunderstand your list:

The deli worker filled the order for bologna, salami, tuna fish, ham and cheese sandwiches.

(Were there ham sandwiches and cheese sandwiches or combination ham and cheese sandwiches?)

Another example of this use of the comma is a listing of three or more subjects or three or more actions: Inez, Nita, and Maria decided to meet after health class.

They needed time to choose a project for their term report, split up the task of researching the subject, and begin gathering information.

Note: When you write a series, each item in the series has to be the same form, that is, each must be parallel to the others. For example, in the previous sentence, you shouldn't say, "They needed time to choose a project for their term project, splitting up the task . . ., and gathering information." (For further information on keeping elements parallel, see Chapter 15.)

As explained in the earlier box, semicolons are used in a series to mark the major divisions if the series also contains commas: The athletic department awarded most valuable player trophies to Joe Gunder, football; Tony Huong, soccer; Jerry Martinez, tennis; Ray Marshall, basketball; Mary Malone, swimming; and Kaya Dubcek, field hockey.

☞ **Exercise 4**

Use commas and semicolons where needed to separate items in a series in the following sentences.

1. Animals in danger of extinction include elephants Bengal tigers spotted leopards black leopards and gray whales.

2. Tigers leopards and other fur-bearing animals are hunted for their valuable skins.

3. Measures to protect them include prohibiting the hunting of endangered species banning the sale of pelts and outlawing the sale of finished fur coats.

4. However, poor third-world economies a thriving black market and high demand for fashion furs render these protective measures useless.

5. Sometimes, changes in the environment, rather than hunting, threaten a species. Animals about to become extinct for this reason include the giant panda China the gorilla Africa the sea otter United States and the wild yak India.

Another need to separate items with a comma may occur when two adjectives modify a noun. You can join these adjectives with an *and* without a comma:

The quick and lanky basketball player got the rebound and stuffed the basket.

But many times the two modifiers appear without the *and:*

The quick, lanky basketball player got the rebound and stuffed the basket.

The comma here substitutes for the *and.* If you can't use an *and* between two adjectives or can't reverse them, then no comma is needed. For example, in the previous sentence, no comma is needed between *basketball* and *player.* Note the following:

> The efficient executive secretary answered the telephone while preparing the vice president's daily schedule.

Since you wouldn't write "The efficient and executive secretary" or "The executive efficient secretary," no comma is needed.

☞ Exercise 5

Determine whether you need to put a comma between adjectives in the following sentences. Use the test of inserting an *and* between them and reversing their order. If you can do either one, use a comma; if not, no punctuation is needed.

1. Besides animals, birds like the American peregrine falcon are endangered.

2. Exotic colorful birds like the macaw may be trapped for sale as pets, which prevents them from breeding in the wild.

3. Other birds have suffered from the effects of dangerous long-acting pesticides.

4. The beautiful bald eagle and the large whooping crane are two victims of pesticides in the environment.

5. Concerned informed citizens can ask for laws protecting these disappearing creatures.

WORKING WITH PEERS

Write five related sentences about the environment, trying to use items in a series. Use commas and semicolons as needed.

Setting Off Interrupters from the Main Part of the Sentence

As you write, you may include words in a sentence that interrupt the sentence's main idea. For example, you might write:

> Bitterly cold "Bears" weather did not, as it turned out, help the home team.

The clause "as it turned out" interrupts the main idea that the weather did not help the home team. When you speak, such interruptions are indicated by pauses. In writing, commas are used before and after the interruption to show where the main idea stops and then starts again. Interruptions can be one word or several words and usually take one of the following forms.

Transitions

The same words that serve as introductions to sentences can be placed in the middle of or at the end of a sentence to serve as a transition or linking of ideas. Words and expressions such as *however, moreover, of course, in contrast, indeed, in fact,* and *on the other hand* should have commas placed before and after them in a sentence. (Obviously, if a transition comes at the end of a sentence, only a comma before the expression is necessary, since a period will come after it.)

EXAMPLES

Many people on diets will, in fact, give in to their urge for chocolate.

Diet food manufacturers make many products, therefore, in chocolate flavor.

Addressing a Person By Name

Just as you put a comma after addressing a person by name at the beginning of a sentence, so do you set off the person's name with two commas when it appears in the middle of the sentence.

EXAMPLE

Please, David, close the door to the hall.

Contrasts

Words expressing a contrasting idea are set off by commas.

EXAMPLES

Power, not money, was the reason for Smith's run for Senator.

The student planned to take five years, instead of the usual four, to finish college,

Appositives and Nonrestrictive Modifiers

A group of words that restates or adds information to a word that it follows is set off by two commas.

EXAMPLES

Mrs. Schmidt, my first grade teacher, thought I talked too much.

John's father, an immigrant from Scotland, tried to keep alive many Scottish traditions.

The bus driver, who appeared to be in a hurry, barked at the passenger requesting a transfer.

The baker, a small woman with flour-covered hands, braided the bread dough with expert speed.

Note: If the words are needed to identify who is being discussed or to make the meaning clear, then no commas are used. Compare:

a.   Steve, my son's best friend, loves to play basketball.

   But:

My son's friend Steve loves to play basketball. (He could have more than one friend, and the name is necessary to identify the friend.)

b.   My white leather sneakers, which were new last week, are caked with mud.

   But:

The sneakers that were worn by the victim were caked with mud. (Here the words "that were worn by the victim" identify which sneakers are being discussed. In the first sentence, the sneakers were identified as "my sneakers" at the beginning and the words "which were new" just add extra information.)

Usually word groups beginning with *that* are necessary to the sentence and are not set off by commas. Word groups beginning with *which* and *who* can be set off or not, depending on the meaning of the sentence.

☞ Exercise 6

Use commas in the following sentences to set off interruptions from the rest of the sentence. Some sentences have restrictive word groups that are not interruptions and so are correct as written.

1.   People who diet have to be careful that they are not doing themselves harm.

2.   Fad diets which frequently are the subjects of the latest best-selling paperbacks may cause a serious misbalance of body chemistry.

3.   The water diet for example may cause too much potassium to wash out of the system.

4.   The grapefruit diet which required the eating of grapefruit at nearly every meal upset many people's stomachs.

5. Most doctors and nutritionists agree that exercise not just diet alone is the key to effective weight control.

6. Jane Brody a writer for the *New York Times* has made an extensive study of dieting.

7. She reports that people who exercise regularly and restrict their fat intake are generally the most successful dieters.

8. Fat not carbohydrates like spaghetti and bread are the real no-nos for dieters.

9. Whole grain carbohydrates are in fact a good source of fiber.

10. A modern-day Milton Hershey the creator of the Hershey bar would have to invent a low-fat, high-fiber chocolate bar.

WORKING WITH PEERS

Write at least five related sentences about diets or dieting. Follow all the punctuation guidelines discussed so far.

Setting Off Places, Dates, and Quotations

Some special situations call for the use of commas. Most people put commas between the city and the state or between the date and the year, but they may neglect to put a comma *after* the state or the year when either of these is used in a sentence.

EXAMPLES

Orlando, Florida, is a vacation destination for many families.

George wondered why Katmandu, Nepal, was called the ceiling of the world.

Arbor Day was first observed on April 10, 1872, in Nebraska.

Use a comma to set off words directly quoted from other words in a sentence. Study the following diagrams and examples. "C" stands for capital letter.

1. Jane said, "C_____."

2. "C_____," Tony replied.

3a. "C_____," Anna said, "_____."

b. "C_____," Anna said, "C_____."

EXAMPLES

1.   Jane said, "I don't know how to study for biology."

2.   "Neither do I," Tony replied.

3a. "Perhaps what we should do," Anna said, "is form a study group."

b.   "I have an idea," Anna said. "We could form a study group."

☞ Exercise 7

Use commas to set off dates, places, and quotations in the following sentences.

1.   Many Americans have a vivid memory of some dates in recent history, such as the attack on Pearl Harbor, December 7 1941 or the assassination of President Kennedy on November 22 1963.

2.   In fact, anyone old enough to remember those two events can probably answer the question "Where were you when you heard the news?"

3.   Younger people may recall January 28 1986 when the space shuttle Challenger exploded after being launched from Cape Canaveral Florida.

4.   A history teacher once remarked "We seem to remember disasters or tragedies more clearly than victories or triumphs."

5.   While that may be true for national events, I have a good memory for October 4 January 14 and May 27—my family's birthdays.

WORKING WITH PEERS

Write five sentences about places and dates that mean something to you, and include a quotation or two about your feelings or the feelings of others about these dates.

☞ Exercise 8

Punctuate the following paragraph according to the guidelines for commas and semicolons presented in this chapter.

Winter

Some people hate the idea of winter and they avoid contact with the cold as much as possible. They stay inside even on sunny days if the thermometer is below freezing. If a snowstorm threatens they load up on groceries buy bags of salt for their sidewalks and hover near the radio for updates on the bad news. If they can afford it they plan vacations where it never snows. Not everyone however hates winter and snowy weather. School children in places like Minneapolis Minnesota and Buffalo New York pray for blizzards so school will be called off. Ski resort owners say "There is nothing sweeter to us than snow in the forecast." While not everyone would go as far as to say that some people like the crisp clean atmosphere after a snowstorm and find the fluffy soft snow beautiful to see. Of course many Americans don't have an opinion about winter weather they live in places where snow is never seen!

PUNCTUATING SENTENCES: COMMAS AND SEMICOLONS

Guideline	Examples
Use a comma . . .	
1. and a conjunction *(and, but, or, nor, for, so, yet)* to join two or more sentences.	The basketball player grabbed the rebound, but the buzzer sounded before he could shoot.
2. to separate an introduction from the main sentence.	If the player had made the basket, his team would have won.
3. to separate words in a series.	The coach, the fans, and the players on the bench groaned in disappointment. The tall, lean player slumped in defeat.
4. to set off interrupters from the rest of the sentence.	The coach, though disappointed, congratulated the player on a nice try.
5. to set off dates, places, and quotations.	"The next game will be Wednesday, March 1st, in Denver, Colorado," said the coach.
Use a semicolon . . .	
1. to join two or more sentences without *and, but, or, nor, for, so, yet.*	The basketball player grabbed the rebound; the buzzer sounded before he could shoot.
	or
	The basketball player grabbed the rebound; however, the buzzer sounded before he could shoot.
2. to separate items in a series if the series also has commas.	The key players on the team were LeRoy Grooms, guard; Kevin White, center; and Joseph Dorsey, forward.

CHAPTER 13

Punctuating Sentences:
Other Marks

Other marks of punctuation range from the most common, the period, to ones used more infrequently, such as the exclamation mark. Along with commas and semicolons, these marks help the reader understand the writer's ideas, substituting for the pauses and changes in tone used in speech. It is easier to think about these marks in groups.

OTHER PUNCTUATION MARKS

1. Marks signaling the end of a sentence or idea: periods, question marks, exclamation marks.

2. Marks emphasizing or deemphasizing an idea: colons, dashes, parentheses, italics.

3. Marks indicating a special function: apostrophes, hyphens, quotation marks, brackets, ellipses.

End Marks

Period

A period, ., is like a stop sign on a street. It tells the reader that the sentence or idea has come to an end. A period also signals that the sentence is a statement and, if read aloud, should end with a falling tone of voice.

EXAMPLES

I need to get my car washed.

Mario got a new job.

Anna works in the afternoons, and Joe works the midnight shift.

Sometimes a sentence contains a word like *asks* or *wonders* that may make you think it is a question:

I wonder whether it will rain today.

Such sentences are not direct questions, and therefore they use a period, not a question mark. Compare the following pairs:

STATEMENT

George asked if Jill could meet him for lunch.

QUESTION

Jill, can you meet me for lunch?

STATEMENT

I wonder how I did on my biology exam.

QUESTION

How did I do on my biology exam?

Periods are also used in abbreviations like *etc., a.m.,* and *p.m.,* but not in the relatively new postal abbreviations for states, such as *PA, TX,* and *CA.* There are other abbreviations that don't use periods, such as *NASA* and *CIA.* Consult your dictionary when in doubt.

Question Mark

A question mark, ?, signals the reader or the listener that the sentence or idea is a question. If read aloud or spoken, a question ends with a rising tone of voice.

EXAMPLES

Are you going?

Where should we meet?

When?

Do you know how to get there, or should I get a map?

I know the area fairly well, but do you think I should call for directions?

Note that the last sentence starts as a statement but ends in a question and therefore takes a question mark.

Exclamation Mark

An exclamation mark, !, signals commands or strong feelings. If read aloud or spoken, such sentences or ideas usually keep the same tone throughout, neither falling nor rising. They are usually short.

EXAMPLES

Help!

Open a window, quick!

Stand back!

Use only one exclamation mark, and don't use them simply to add emphasis to statements. For example, a direction such as "Please put all used towels in the bin" gets a period not an exclamation mark. Underline, use capital letters, or print your message in a different color for emphasis, but save exclamation marks for strong feelings.

Emphasis or Deemphasis Marks

Colon

The colon, :, is used at the end of a complete sentence to direct the reader's attention to a list, an example, or an explanation. It may also be used in the salutation of a business letter *(Dear Sir or Madam:)*, to separate numbers *(9:30 a.m.)*, to set off a title from a subtitle *(Friday the 13th: Part IV)*, to separate the place of publication from the publisher of a book in a bibliography *(New York: Random House)*, or to set off a heading, as in the following example.

EXAMPLE—LIST

Janine had several things on her shopping list: books, notebook paper, pens, highlight markers, and instant coffee.

Note: A list following a verb such as *is* or *are* does not use a colon because the sentence has not been completed.

EXAMPLE—NO COLON

Bruce admits that he is lazy, disorganized, and easily distracted.

Note: A list following the expression *such as* also does not use a colon.

EXAMPLE—NO COLON

Bruce liked all the foods that were bad for him, such as red meat, butter, ice cream, and french fries.

EXAMPLE—EXAMPLE

Bruce found an activity that suited his diet and personality: eating buttered popcorn while watching his 100-channel remote control TV.

EXAMPLE—EXPLANATION

Janine knew of only one way to pass her biology exam: studying all night.

Dash

A dash, —, shows a bold change of idea, a contradiction, or an interruption in the flow of a sentence. If dashes are overused, they lose their emphasis.

EXAMPLES

Teresa walked out the door—and out of his life.

Sean pleaded—even begged—for her to return. His absences, his broken promises, his short temper—all were enough to make her resist his pleadings now.

Parentheses

Parentheses, (   ), deemphasize ideas. When a sentence with parentheses is read aloud, the reader's voice usually drops in tone to indicate that what is in parentheses is less important or is simply additional information.

EXAMPLES

To get there, follow Route 46 to County Road W (a scenic country road).

John Updike (born 1932) is a contemporary writer of novels and short stories whose book *The Witches of Eastwick* became a popular film.

Italics

Italics are the slanted letters you sometimes see in type that emphasize a word or phrase or indicate the title of a book, movie, play, or other long, full-length work. They are also used to set off foreign language expressions. In typing, italics are represented by underlining of the words involved.

EXAMPLES

Les Miserables, a musical based on Victor Hugo's novel of the French Revolution, was popular worldwide.

I said *not* to call me after 10 p.m.

In Middle English the *k* in knife was pronounced.

Special Function Marks

Apostrophe

Apostrophes, ', are used in contractions to show that a letter is missing *(can't)* and to show possession *(the shoes of my father = my father's shoes).* Using the apostrophe to show possession follows these guidelines:

1.   Use an apostrophe after all singular words:

Mary's car

Thomas's football

one week's vacation

an hour's pay

2.   Use an apostrophe after all plural words that don't form the plural with an *s:*

children's playground

women's work

men's shirts

3.   Use an apostrophe after the *s* in plural words that form the plural with an *s:*

two weeks' vacation

families' yards

thieves' loot

Note: The words that often cause problems are those that sound alike.

who's = "who is"

whose = pronoun, already possessive, that means "belonging to whom"

it's = "it is"

its = pronoun, already possessive, that means "belonging to it"

Other pronouns that are already possessive include *my, mine, your, yours, his, her, hers, our, ours, their,* and *theirs.* Since they are already possessive, they don't need an apostrophe.

Hyphen

The hyphen, -, is used at the ends of typed lines to divide a word at a syllable. Hyphens are also used to join two words that may at one time have been separate words *(water-skier),* but you will probably have to check a dictionary because many similar words do not take a hyphen *(hitchhiker,* for example). Hyphens are used in numbers from *twenty-one* to *ninety-nine* and in certain modifiers and phrases, such as *well-known actor, eighteenth-century portrait, holier-than-thou, devil-may-care.*

Quotation Marks

Quotation marks (" ") enclose words written or spoken by another person. Typically, the quotation is introduced by a short statement *(he said, she explained)* followed by a comma or a colon, but the quote can come anywhere in a sentence.

EXAMPLES

The customer complained, "I should not be charged for something I did not get!"

"I'll see that it gets straightened out," said the credit manager. "I'm sorry that this happened."

"Well, I'm relieved to know that you agree with me, and I appreciate your help," replied the customer, calming down.

Note that most of the time other punctuation goes inside the quotation marks. An exception: Punctuating a question that is not part of the quotation:

Did the professor say, "Class ends in five minutes"?

Remember that indirect quotations do not use quotation marks:

The reporter said that she would not reveal the identity of her sources.

The direct version would read:

The reporter said, "I will not reveal the identity of my sources."

Quotation marks are also used to enclose titles of short works, such as poems, short stories, essays, and songs:

"Kubla Khan"
"The Pit and the Pendulum"
"Letter from the Birmingham Jail"
"Satisfaction"

Finally, quotation marks sometimes are used to enclose words being defined or being discussed as words:

Many people confuse the words "further" and "farther."

Brackets

Brackets, [   ], are used within a quotation to explain something not in the original quotation:

A comic book collector complained, "The character of The Joker [played in the movie version by Jack Nicholson] was originally a humorous practical joker, not a sadistic villain."

Ellipses

Ellipses (. . .) are used to show something left out of a quoted statement. They are helpful when a writer wants to shorten a lengthy quote but wants readers to know that something has been left out.

EXAMPLE—ORIGINAL QUOTATION (BY JOHN F. KENNEDY)

"We stand today on the edge of a new frontier—the frontier of the 1960s—a frontier of unknown opportunities and perils—a frontier of unfulfilled hopes and threats."

EXAMPLE—QUOTATION WITH ELLIPSES

"We stand today on the edge of a new frontier . . . a frontier of unknown opportunities and perils. . . ."

The following exercises will help you apply what you have learned about other marks of punctuation.

End Marks: To help you punctuate the ends of sentences, read the sentences aloud. Your voice tone may help you determine whether to use a period, a question mark, or an exclamation point.

☞ Exercise 1

Use the appropriate punctuation at the ends of the following sentences and quotations.

1. Some people can't wait to see the next movie blockbuster, while others don't care if they ever see another film

2. Are you a member of either group

3. Most of the time it wouldn't matter that one person likes movies while another doesn't

4. However, if the two people are married to each other or are good friends, their difference in movie-going may create conflict

5. "I can't wait to see *Batman*" exclaims one partner

6. "How can you want to see such trash" questions the other

7. I wonder how people resolve this conflict

8. Do you think such a small matter could lead to separation

9. What a shame that would be

10. Fortunately, most people are not extreme in their preferences and are willing to compromise

WORKING WITH PEERS

Write five sentences with your classmates about your attitudes toward movies. Try to include all three end marks, and remember to use commas or other internal punctuation where needed.

Emphasis or Deemphasis Marks: Remember that the colon, the dash, and italics add emphasis to the word, phrase, or sentence, while parentheses are designed to enclose additional, nonessential information. Colons are used after complete sentences to emphasize what follows: a list, an explanation, a quotation. Dashes are used to show an interruption in thought. Italics or underlines emphasize titles of long works, or foreign words or phrases.

☞   Exercise 2

Punctuate the following sentences using colons, dashes, italics, and parentheses where necessary. Place the proper end punctuation as well.

1. Many communities have adopted an increasingly popular solution to their garbage problem recycling waste

2. Plastic bottles, glass jars and bottles, aluminum cans, newspapers all are becoming more economical to recycle.

3. Articles in publications like Scientific American explain new techniques for recycling materials

4. Instead of being a "throwaway society" as one sociologist put it we are becoming a "recycled society"

5. Some people object to sorting cans, bottles, and newspapers it does take more effort than throwing everything together in a Hefty bag

6. To overcome these objections, communities impose fines sometimes up to $500 to enforce their recycling programs

7. Usually though not always such fines convince even reluctant citizens of the need for their cooperation.

WORKING WITH PEERS

Write five related sentences about your feelings about pollution, littering, recycling, or a similar subject. Punctuate correctly.

Special Function Marks: Apostrophes are used in contractions such as *can't* and *won't* to show letters left out and with an *s* to show ownership or possession *(my brother's car, the neighbors' trash cans)*. Hyphens separate words into syllables at the end of a typed line or may join two or more words into one expression *(up-to-date)*. Quotation marks indicate someone's exact words, set off titles of short works, or indicate words used as words. Brackets and ellipses indicate either something added to a quotation that was not originally there or something left out.

☞   Exercise 3

Put apostrophes in their proper places in contractions or in possessives. Add hyphens to words used together to make one expression.

1. Many peoples study habits may be counter productive.

2. They may think theyre studying, but very little learning is going on because they are being constantly distracted.

3. For example, Jerrys TV is always tuned to a baseball, football, or basketball game, and when he thinks hes studying, hes really sneaking a look at almost every instant replay, especially in down to the wire games.

4. Teresas just as bad, but her distraction is MTV: she just cant keep her eyes off many rock groups videos.

5. Some people dont have a television set on but still get distracted by other family members conversations, the constant ringing of the telephone, or other interruptions.

6. What everyone needs is an all purpose study place, either where they live or at school.

7. Such a place shouldnt have distractions from TV or other people.

8. For ninety five out of one hundred people studying without distractions results in better grades.

9. Of course, there are always some students who could study on a merry go round or in a wind tunnel, but such self motivated people are rare.

10. A students study place deserves some real thought and planning.

☞ Exercise 4

Use quotation marks to set off directly quoted statements and titles of short works such as speeches, essays, short stories, and songs. Indirect quotations do not need such marks. As indicated, insert brackets to add an explanation to the quote or ellipses to leave something out.

1. In Martin Luther King's speech I Have a Dream, he says, I have a dream that my four little children will one day live in a nation where they will not be judged by the color of their skin but by the content of their character.

2. He also quotes from the lyrics to the song America, ending with the line Let freedom ring.

3. The end of his speech builds on the last line of the song as Dr. King asks America to Let freedom ring from the mighty mountains of New York. Let freedom ring from the heightening Alleghenies of Pennsylvania!

4. Shorten the two sentences in the quote in number 3 by leaving out the first three words of the second sentence and inserting ellipses. Write the shortened version here:

5.   Enclose in brackets the information *August 28, 1963,* after the word *today* in the following sentence.

Dr. King says, I have a dream today.

WORKING WITH PEERS

Write five related sentences on study habits or on Dr. Martin Luther King, Jr., trying to use the marks of punctuation from this section. Be careful also to put commas and other marks where they belong.

☞   Exercise 5

Punctuate the following paragraph according to what you have learned in this and previous chapters.

Voyager 2

Before the space probe Voyager 2 left Neptune for the edge of the solar system scientists proclaimed its twelve year journey a success The probe took advantage of a once in a lifetime opportunity actually the alignment of planets which occurs only every 176 years to investigate the outer planets in our solar system Using the gravity of each planet as a slingshot Voyager moved more quickly between planets than it could have otherwise For example it would normally take thirty two years to Neptune Voyager did it in twelve What did the probe discover about the outer solar system Voyager found evidence of many unusual things storms ice volcanoes unusual magnetic fields and more planetary rings and moons than were known Chief project scientist Edward Stone says these data form nothing less than the encyclopedia of the planets

OTHER PUNCTUATION MARKS

Guideline	Examples
Use a period . . .	
1. to end a statement.	The hike up the mountain trail is difficult.
2. in an abbreviation.	Mt. McKinley has many popular trails.
Use a question mark to end a direct question.	Have you ever climbed above 7,000 feet?
Use an exclamation mark to show strong feeling in a sentence or in a phrase.	Help! My rope broke!

OTHER PUNCTUATION MARKS (continued)

Guideline	Examples
Use a colon . . .	
1. after a complete sentence to introduce a list or an explanation.	Every mountain hiker needs at least four things: sturdy boots, food, water, and a weatherproof jacket.
	The jacket is needed to protect the hiker from hypothermia: the dangerous drop in body temperature caused by sudden chilling.
2. after the salutation in a business letter.	Dear Ms. Kosloski:
3. in writing the time.	9:00 a.m.
4. in subtitles.	The Other Side of the Mountain: Part 2
Use a dash to show a break in thought.	I once hiked three miles in a snow— what's that sound?
Use parentheses to enclose extra information.	This lightweight poncho (cost $25.99) is ideal.
Use italics to indicate titles of long works like novels, plays, albums, films, and names of magazines.	LIFE Magazine did a picture story on conquering Mt. Everest.
Use apostrophes . . .	
1. in contractions.	He couldn't move another step.
2. to show possession.	He needed the guide's help to crawl into the tent.
	He soon revived in the warmth created by the other hikers' bodies.
Use hyphens . . .	
1. to separate words at syllables at the end of a typed line.	His ascent of the mountain was post-poned.
2. to join two or more words into one.	He made a trade-off: the ascent for his health.
Use quotations . . .	
1. to enclose the direct statements of a speaker or writer.	"I'll live to hike again," Bob said.
2. to set off titles of short works such as short stories, songs, essays, poems	"The Road Not Taken" by Robert Frost was one of Bob's favorite poems.

OTHER PUNCTUATION MARKS (continued)

Guideline	Examples
Use brackets to insert material into a quoted statement.	"Two roads diverged [split apart] in a yellow wood."
Use ellipses to leave out material from a quoted statement.	"I took the one less travelled . . ., and that has made all the difference."

CHAPTER 14

Being Consistent: Subject-Verb Agreement and Pronoun-Antecedent Agreement

Readers prefer to take it easy when they read. They like to glide their eyes over a page and understand what they are reading without having to reread a passage in order to understand the writer's ideas. One way writers help readers is by being consistent in the agreement of subjects and verbs and pronouns and antecedents. If a writer writes

The coaches plan to meet with all their players soon after the term starts.

the reader can follow the sentence smoothly. On the other hand, if inconsistencies exist, as in:

The coaches plans to meet with all his players soon after the term start.

some readers may become confused: Is it one coach? Should it read *The coach's plan is to meet?* What is a *term start?* Not all of us follow standard usage in speech. But in writing, even more confusion may result from failure to be consistent because of the reader's inability to ask questions to clear up any misunderstanding.

The following boxes illustrate the principles of agreement.

SUBJECT-VERB AGREEMENT

General Principle
Singular subjects have singular verbs, and plural subjects have plural verbs.

EXAMPLES

The students meet next week to plan the next campus rock concert.

The last concert was a great success.

What Are Singular Verbs and Plural Verbs?
1. Singular verbs end in *s* in the present tense:

She plans.

The monkey chatters.

The train has already gone.

2. Plural verbs do not end in *s* in the present tense:

They plan.

The monkeys chatter.

The trains have already gone.

What Are Singular Subjects?
1. Nouns not ending in *s*, in *es*, or in one of the other plural endings, such as *-ren (children)*, *-en (men, women, oxen)*, or that change to a plural form, such as *goose/geese.* Dictionaries list plural forms of each word.

2. Pronouns *I, he, she,* and *it;* forms of *-body* and *-one,* such as *everybody, anyone, nobody,* and *none;* and *each, either,* and *neither.*

3. Collective nouns such as *team* and *group* that act like one unit:

The football team practices each Tuesday afternoon.

4. Singular subjects connected by *either-or* still remain singular:

Either the rock band or the football team has scheduled the playing field for this Saturday.

5.   Singular subjects followed by a prepositional phrase are still singular:

George, along with his classmates, walks from the bus stop to the campus.

Note: This usage sounds awkward to many people. You may want to change the sentence to:

George and his classmates walk from the bus stop to the campus.

What Are Plural Subjects?

1.   Nouns ending in *s,* in *es,* or in a plural ending such as *-ren, -en,* or that have changed form *(mouse/mice).*

2.   Pronouns *we* and *they,* and the words *few, many,* and *several.*

3.   Two subjects joined by *and* are plural:

Maria and Kim are part of the field hockey team.

4.   Collective nouns such as team and group that act as individuals—not as a unit:

The band play eight instruments among them.

Note: This usage sounds awkward to many people and, while correct, may be avoided by saying:

The members of the band play eight instruments among them.

5.   Plural subjects connected by *either-or* remain plural:

Either the students or the teachers are wrong about the date for the game.

Special Situations:

1.   If a plural subject and a singular subject are connected by *either-or* or *neither-nor,* the verb agrees with the closer subject:

Neither the players nor the coach is aware of the penalty.

Either the crowd noise or the referees' unclear hand signals have caused the confusion.

2.   Some pronouns *(all, any, more, most, none, some)* are either singular or plural, depending on the context:

All of the money was lost.

All of the members were late for the meeting.

3. If the subject comes after the verb, it still must agree with the verb. Be sure to find the true subject:

Here are the registration forms.

In the line stretching around the corner are students who still are trying to register.

PRONOUN-ANTECEDENT AGREEMENT

General Principle
Pronouns have to agree with the words they replace:

George eats his breakfast in a hurry.

Suzanna likes to linger over her coffee in the morning.

Both of them leave their houses at the same time each morning.

The word *antecedent* means something that comes before something else. For example, your parents and grandparents are your antecedents. In the case of pronouns, the nouns or pronouns they refer back to are their antecedents. In the preceding sentences, *George, Suzanna,* and *Both* are the antecedents for *his, her,* and *their,* respectively.

The same situations that cause problems for subject-verb agreement cause problems here.

1. Words such as *everybody, anyone,* and *none* are singular, and any other pronoun that replaces one of these words also has to be singular:

Everybody learns lessons in his or her own way.

Each student tries to find his or her own study method.

Note: If you find the use of *his or her* awkward, you can make the sentence plural:

All students learn lessons in their own ways.

Don't use only masculine pronouns to refer to words like *everybody* and *anybody.* Such use is sexist and offends many people.

2.   Collective nouns used as a unit are singular and take singular pronouns:

The team played its heart out.

Collective nouns used to indicate individuals take plural pronouns:

The committee raised their hands to vote.

Note: Revising the sentence to read as follows may sound better to many people:

The committee members raised their hands to vote.

3.   Just as the verb agrees with the closer subject in a sentence with *either-or* or *neither-nor,* so the pronoun agrees with the closer antecedent:

Either the coach or the players need an answer to their question before play can continue.

Special Situation: Keep Pronoun References Clear
Make sure the pronoun has a clear antecedent. For example, don't write the following:

I like accounting, so I want to be one.

(One can't be *accounting,* but one can be *an accountant.*) Rather it should read:

I like the work of accountants, so I want to be one.

Or, don't write:

Students forgot to send in their housing forms, but it didn't matter.

(No word in the sentence is an antecedent of it.) Rather, write:

Students forgot to send in their housing forms, but they received room assignments anyway.

Don't write:

Maria told Kim that she would be late for practice.

(Which one will be late?) Instead, write:

Maria told Kim to hurry, or she would be late for practice.

Or write:

Maria said to Kim, "I will be late for practice."

Don't write:

Students' lives are busy, so they must organize their time wisely.

(*They* refers back to *students*, but the possessive form is not a proper antecedent.) Rather, it should be:

Because the lives of students are busy, they must organize their time wisely.

Subject-Verb Agreement

The key to being consistent in subject-verb agreement is knowing which words are singular and which words are plural. Several examples have already been mentioned above. The following examples may be even more helpful in completing the subsequent practice exercises.

Singular Verbs

Put *I*, *he*, or *she* before each of the following verbs.

_____ am

_____ is

_____ has been

_____ was

_____ plans (I plan)

_____ studies (I study)

Note that with the exception of words used with I (*I am, I plan, I study*), all the singular verbs end in *s*.

Plural Verbs

Put *you, we,* or *they* before each of the following words.

_____ are

_____ were

_____ have been

_____ plan

_____ study

Singular Subjects

child	goose	no one
someone	dish	everybody
ox	everyone	somebody
belief	the number	anybody
knife	anyone	woman
boy	each	amount of
mouse	none	

Collective nouns such as *team, squad,* and *committee* act as a unit and hence are treated as singular subjects.

Plural Subjects

children	mice	several
women	geese	a number
oxen	dishes	number of
beliefs	few	scissors
knives	many	
boys	both	

Subjects That Can Be Singular or Plural

all	more	sheep
any	most	deer
some	athletics	

Again, collective nouns are treated as separate individuals.

Note: These are only examples of singular and plural words used as subjects. Check a dictionary if you are in doubt about any other words.

☞ Exercise 1

Change the following sentences to the plural form if they are singular and to the singular form if they are plural. Be sure to change both the subjects and the verbs.

1.	The boy has a paper route.	1.	_____
2.	_____	2.	The geese eat the corn in the field.
3.	A dull knife makes a mess of a turkey.	3.	_____
4.	_____	4.	Women have many career opportunities in the 1990s.
5.	A child mimics adults' behavior.	5.	_____.

WORKING WITH PEERS

In groups, write at least five sentences in the present tense about extracurricular activities for students (plural) on your campus. Then change the sentences to singular form, keeping the verbs in the present tense. Try to use verbs besides *is* and *are, has* and *have.*

☞ Exercise 2

Write the correct form of the verb in parenthesis in the blank provided. Note that all pronouns used in the sentences are correct.

1. Many people simply _____ not realize the power of hurricanes. (do)

2. They _____ to take into account the very low pressure at the eye of the storm and the surges of water driven by hurricane-force winds. (fail)

3. As a result, when a hurricane _____, everyone _____ not left the coastal area, even though an emergency team _____ issued orders to leave. (hit, has)

4. Many of these people _____ to ride out the storm in the comfort of their own homes instead of going to a crowded shelter. (prefer) Some _____ also afraid of looters taking things after the storm _____. (is, pass) An emergency unit in a given area _____ the owners' concerns among themselves before deciding whether to force owners to leave or not. (debate)

5. Many emergency workers _____ that no reason _____ convincing if one's life _____ at stake. (decide, is)

Special Situations

As already noted, some special situations may cause difficulty in being consistent. The subsequent exercises will give you practice in the following troublesome areas:

1. If subjects are connected by *either-or* or *neither-nor,* the verb agrees with the closer subject.

2. If two subjects are joined by *and,* they are plural (unless the two words are really one unit, like *peanut butter and jelly sandwich*).

3. In an inverted sentence (one in which the subject comes after the verb, as in "Here is your order"), be sure to locate the subject and make it agree with the verb. The words *there* and *here* are never subjects. Remember that if you find the verb first and then ask who or what is doing the action or existing, your answer will be the subject of the sentence. Don't just look at the first noun that you see.

4. While subjects are not found in prepositional phrases, sometimes the words that can be either singular or plural (*all, any, some, more, most*) will take their number from a phrase used after the words:

All of the money is gone.

All of the students are bankrupt.

☞ Exercise 3

Fill in the correct verb in each of the following sentences,

1. Herman and Georgio _____ been friends since childhood. (has)

2. Although each of them _____ different things, they _____ each other's preferences. (like, respect)

3. For example, on a fall Saturday that there _____ a baseball game and a college football game, the two friends _____ turns watching each other's favorite sport. (is, take)

4. If Herman _____ to see his favorite horror movie, Georgio will go along even though he _____ science-fiction films. (want, favor)

5. There _____ other ways the two friends cooperate. (is)

6. If either Herman's mother or George's sisters _____ help with heavy shopping bags, both friends _____ in to carry the bags. (need, pitch)

7. All of their other friends _____ how well they get along. (admire)

8. No one ever _____ them argue for more than a few minutes. (hear)

9. However, there _____ a new situation that may test their friendship more than any other _____ to this day. (is, has)

10. Both friends _____ fallen in love with the same girl. (has)

WORKING WITH PEERS

Write a story about a friendship between two people, with each member of your group contributing the next sentence as you go around the group. Sentences should be in the present tense, and group members should try to think of varied sentence structures. However, let your imaginations run freely to think of situations these two friends might encounter.

Pronoun-Antecedent Agreement

As mentioned earlier, pronouns must agree with the words to which they refer, their antecedents. The same basic principle applies: singular pronouns agree with singular antecedents, and plural pronouns agree with plural antecedents. Look at the earlier list of singular and plural pronouns (pages 271–272) to refresh your memory. And remember:

1. If two words are joined by *and,* they will take a plural verb and hence a plural pronoun.

2. If two words are connected by *either-or,* the verb and the pronoun will agree with the closer subject.

3. Collective nouns may be used to indicate either a unit acting as one thing (singular), which will take a singular pronoun *(its),* or as many individuals (plural), which will take a plural pronoun *(their).*

☞ Exercise 4

Fill in the blank with the appropriate form of the pronoun. Circle the ante-cedent with which the pronoun agrees. Note that the verbs used in the sen-tences are correct, which may help you choose the correct pronoun.

1. Everybody who has ever shared an office or a room with someone knows that people can be divided into two groups: _____ are either messy or neat.

2. A neat person always puts _____ clothes away in drawers or closets, while the messy person drops _____ clothes where _____ land.

3. The neat one cleans off _____ desk at the end of a day, while the messy one doesn't bother.

4. When a messy person and a neat person share the same space, _____ may get angry at each other.

5. "The Odd Couple," a movie and a television series, was based on this situation. Felix and Oscar are two divorced men who share an apartment. _____ habits are completely different.

6. Either Felix is running the vacuum cleaner while _____ room-mate is trying to watch a football game, or Oscar is tracking mud on the floor that Felix has just washed.

7. Both men are frustrated with _____ living arrangements.

8. Neither Oscar nor _____ poker-playing friends care about the beer cans or half-empty pizza boxes that _____ leave around the apartment, so everybody is astonished when _____ sees the sign on the door the next night, "Condemned by the Board of Health."

9. Felix has arranged an inspection, and the Board has imposed _____ penalty.

10. Neither the poker players nor Oscar has another place to play, so every-one does _____ best to clean up the apartment. The Board revokes _____ condemnation.

☞ Exercise 5

Write at least five sentences about someone you know who is either messy or neat. Keep sentences in the present tense. Make all subject and verbs agree, and check to see that all pronouns agree with their antecedents.

Special Situation: Clear Pronoun References

As already mentioned, pronouns must have clear antecedents in order for the reader to understand what he or she is reading.

☞ Exercise 6

In the following sentences, make sure pronouns clearly refer to a specific antecedent. You may need to rewrite sentences.

1. George told Barry that he had to declare a major by next week.

2. George said that he had chosen real estate but wasn't sure he wanted to be one.

3. Barry's choice was uncertain, but he was leaning toward marketing.

4. Many students are unprepared to choose majors because it comes so early in their college careers.

5. They shouldn't require students to choose majors until at least the end of their freshman year.

☞ Exercise 7

The following paragraph contains mistakes in subject-verb agreement and pronoun-antecedent agreement. Correct the errors by changing forms or rewriting sentences. Remember that you may have to change subjects, verbs, and pronouns in a sentence to keep it consistent with sentences that come before or after.

Bosses

Everyone who has ever worked can probably define their ideal boss. They are fair, understanding, and able to compromise. The ideal boss is fair in the way they make up schedules. He or she doesn't always give the same people weekend shifts, while others never has to work weekends. The good boss doesn't criticize some people and let others get away with murder. Everyone is held to the same rules and get equal praise or blame. However, being fair don't mean that they can't be understanding if an employee has an unusual problem. Everyone has problems sometimes that prevents them from coming to work on time. Some of these problems include car trouble or public transportation delays, family problems, and sudden illness. The ideal boss understands these problems and doesn't complain as long as it doesn't happen very often. Finally, the ideal boss is not too set in their ways. They are willing to compromise if an employee has a suggestion for a new way to do something. In fact, the ideal boss rewards employees who make good suggestions. It might encourage more employees to think about ways to improve production or sales. These qualities should be practiced by every boss, but most people finds that ideal bosses is the exception, not the rule.

WORKING WITH PEERS

In groups, add ideas to the preceding paragraph's definition of the ideal boss. These could be additional qualities or other ways such a person could show fairness, understanding, or the ability to compromise. Write your group's expanded definition.

BEING CONSISTENT: SUBJECT-VERB AGREEMENT AND PRONOUN-ANTECEDENT AGREEMENT

Guideline	Examples
Singular subjects have singular verbs.	One of the players has been named MVP.
Words ending in *-body* or *-one* are singular.	Everybody is happy that the MVP is the goalie.
Collective nouns are singular if the group acts as a unit.	The team lines up to congratulate the goalie.
Plural subjects take plural verbs.	The players cheer the goalie.
Subjects joined by *and* are plural.	The reporter and the coach smile at each other.
Collective nouns are plural if the group acts as many individuals.	The team take showers, dress, and walk to their cars.
If subjects are joined by *either-or* or *neither-nor,* the verb agrees with the closer subject.	Either the coach or the players leave the locker room first.
	Either the players or the coach leaves the locker room first.
Some words can be singular or plural, depending on the context.	All of the money for the goalie was worth it.
	All of the owners were happy.
Pronouns agree with the words they replace (their antecedents).	Everybody on the team did his best.
	All of the players did their best.
Pronouns must have clear antecedents.	The coach told the goalie that he had won MVP.

CHAPTER 15

Developing Clear Sentences: Placement of Modifiers and Parallel Structure

You may have seen or heard of the film "Throw Momma from the Train," in which two characters actually try to throw one man's domineering mother from a moving train. Did you know, however, that the title may have been based on a Pennsylvania Dutch expression "Throw Momma from the train a kiss?" That expression sounds funny to speakers of standard English because the word order puts kiss at the end of the sentence instead of closer to the word *throw*, as in "Throw a kiss to Momma from the train." In English, word order is very important; if words are changed around, meaning will change. Consider the following pair of sentences:

The cat bit the dog.

The dog bit the cat.

Obviously, the only change in these sentences is the word order, but that change makes quite a difference in meaning.

Consider another pair of sentences:

Only I like Brad. [I am the one person who likes him.]

I like only Brad. [Brad is the one person I like.]

Again, changing the word order produces a change in the meaning of the sentence.

What this means for writers and readers is that if readers are going to understand a writer's ideas, the writer will have to make sure the word order clearly conveys the intended message.

Another aspect of keeping sentences clear can also be thought about in terms of an analogy with trains: A train runs on parallel tracks, and if one of the tracks is missing or twisted out of shape, the train may derail. A sentence may have parallel elements (for example, a list) that must be maintained in parallel form to be understood clearly. Consider the following example:

Maggie enjoys swimming in the summer, skiing in the winter, and to go to rock concerts all year around.

The last part of this sentence "derails," that is, it does not follow the reader's expectations that the list will be completed with another -*ing* phrase. If Maggie enjoys three things, then all three should appear as parallel items in a list:

Maggie enjoys swimming in the summer,

   skiing in the winter,

   and going to rock concerts all year around.

The following boxes illustrate these principles in several situations.

PLACEMENT OF MODIFIERS

General Principle
Put modifiers next to the words they modify.

Modifiers are words that give extra information about nouns and verbs. They may be adjectives (like *red, dull, shiny, large*) that modify nouns; or adverbs (like *slowly, often, never, only*) that modify verbs; or prepositional phrases (like *in the treetops, on the hill, over the river and through the woods*) that modify either nouns or verbs; or verb phrases (like *singing in the shower* or *singed from head to foot*) that also modify nouns.

Compare the following pairs of sentences. Don't write:

The moth-eaten woman's coat was all that she had left.

Instead, write:

The woman's moth-eaten coat was all that she had left.

It's not:

He almost earned $100 parking cars last weekend.

Rather, it's:

He earned almost $100 parking cars last weekend.

(Note that the first version sounds like he missed out on the money entirely!) Don't write:

The police officer in the parking lot searched for the car keys.

(unless you mean to indicate where the police officer was stationed). Rather, write:

The police officer searched in the parking lot for the car keys.

It shouldn't be:

He shot a moose wearing his pajamas.

Instead, it's:

Wearing his pajamas, he shot a moose.

Don't write:

Although singed from head to foot, we saw our cat escape from the pile of burning leaves.

(Who is singed?) Write instead:

Although singed from head to foot, our cat escaped from the pile of burning leaves.

PARALLEL STRUCTURE

General Principle
Use the same grammatical forms in lists, pairs, and other sentence patterns.

EXAMPLE (three verbs all in past tense)

The burglar broke the window, reached in, and opened the door.

EXAMPLE (two nouns as items)

The thief took not only the stereo but also the compact disks.

EXAMPLE (three prepositional phrases)

A government of the people, by the people, and for the people must not perish from the Earth.

EXAMPLE (three verb phrases)

Paula wanted three things out of life: to have a worthwhile job, to have a warm family life, and to contribute to her community.

Placement of Modifiers

As you have seen, words or phrases generally modify the parts of the sentence they are next to. We have to use the word *generally* because adverbs can sometimes be moved around in a sentence without confusion. For example, the sentence "The injured player moved slowly off the field" can also be written "Slowly, the injured player moved off the field" or even "The injured player moved off the field slowly." Where a writer puts the word *slowly* will depend on the emphasis he or she wants to give the word. However, many modifiers can't be moved so easily without creating confusion, or even humor.

☞ Exercise 1

Read each of the following sentences and answer the questions and follow the instructions after each.

1.   Opening the door, the rain-soaked carpet was ruined.

   Who opened the door?
   Put a person's name after the phrase "Opening the door" and revise the sentence:

   Opening the door,

2.   He died almost ten times during the operation.

   Does this mean he died nine times?

Place *almost* so the sentence means that he came close to dying ten times:

3.   Frank bought a car from a used car salesman with a defective carburetor.

Does the salesman have a defective carburetor?
Revise the sentence:

4.   Swinging through the trees, the scientists admired the agile monkeys.

Who was swinging through the trees?
Reposition that phrase so as to modify those that probably were swinging:

5.   Having woven a rope made of bedsheets, the escape was going according to plan.

Who made the rope out of bedsheets?
After the word *bedsheets,* begin the main sentence with *the prisoners* and revise the sentence:

Having woven a rope out of bedsheets, the prisoners

As you can see in Exercise 1, sometimes a modifier is misplaced and easily can be shifted to another position in the sentence to correct the sentence. At other times, however, a modifier may not have anything in the sentence to modify (as in #1 and #5) and the whole sentence must be revised. Such modifiers are called *dangling modifiers* because they are kind of left dangling without any word to modify. They frequently occur when a writer begins the sentence with a phrase that shows some human action (*opening a door, weaving a rope, strolling on a beach, climbing a hill*) and then doesn't supply the person doing the action as the subject of the sentence. Because people have more trouble with these constructions than with some others, the following exercise provides additional practice.

☞   Exercise 2

Complete the following sentences, being careful to supply a subject that fits the action of the opening verb phrase.

1. Strolling on the beach,

2. Having studied carefully for my exams,

3. Arriving at the train station a bit late,

4. Confused and anxious,

5. After falling asleep while watching a movie,

WORKING WITH PEERS

In a small group, write about an incident that uses the following modifiers. In making up sentences, you may use other modifiers as well.

in the dark alley

Hearing footsteps behind him (or her)

in the flash of a car's headlights

almost

only

Darting quickly from the sidewalk

a reddish-haired

Parallel Structure

Most of the time, the key to using clear parallel structure is simply becoming aware of sentence patterns, such as lists, that readers expect to be parallel in form. When writing a draft, sometimes they will begin a list in one pattern and end with a different pattern, as in the following example:

Pete couldn't decide whether to play soccer, to go out for cross country, or if he should join the swimming team.

When writers revise, they may notice the pattern change and correct it. There are some patterns, however, that are easily overlooked when revising. See the following examples and the subsequent exercises.

Parallel Pairs

If you use any of the following pairs, whatever form follows the first word in the pair also must follow the second word:

not only	but also
both	and
either	or
neither	nor

EXAMPLES

Steve needed not only the time to assemble the new bookcase but also the skill to put it together.

He looked at both the package diagram and the instruction manual, to no avail.

He either would have to admit defeat or pretend to know what he was doing.

Neither his ego nor his checkbook would let him pay the store for putting the bookcase together.

☞ Exercise 3

Fill in the blanks of the following sentences, keeping forms parallel.

1. Mark asked his friend not only to _____

   but also _____.

2. Kevin decided to accept either _____ or

   _____ but not both.

3. Leslie found neither _____ nor

   _____ that she had been looking for.

4.   The college offers not only _____ but also

_____ to needy students.

5.   Bret discovered that he could neither _____

nor _____ without feeling great pain.

☞ Exercise 4

In each of the following word groups, one of the items is not parallel with the others. Correct the form of the item so that all are parallel.

1.   short hours,
     high pay, and
     benefits that are generous.

2.   damming up streams, and
     siphoned water off to irrigate crops

3.   both creative and having a sense of independence

4.   singing,
     songwriter, and
     playing guitar

5.   pay any price,
     bear any burden, and
     fighting off foes that may exist

WORKING WITH PEERS

In pairs or small groups, write about some choices you have had to make. Use such constructions as *either . . . or, neither . . . nor, both . . . and,* and *not only . . . but also.* Check your sentences for clear parallel structure.

☞ Exercise 5

The following passage has problems with clear placement of modifiers and clear parallel structure. Correct any errors by rearranging or rewriting sentences as needed.

Balancing Act

Sometimes being a college student is as difficult as being a circus juggler or a tightrope artist. Not only does the student have to do well academically, but also there are finances to consider. Being a student, money is a problem. Of course, many students have jobs, but many jobs pay only minimum wage, so students are forced to work long hours to make enough money. Some students work all day at full-time jobs and going to school at night. Such long hours may cause students to lose sleep and not enough time for studying. In addition to the pressures of school and work, many students have pressures at home as well. Living at home and commuting to school, the family atmosphere may not be right for studying. Other family members may distract students from their work. If the student is older with his or her own family, then meeting the needs of other family members can add another ball to juggle in the air for the student. Students can give up neither their jobs nor should they be asked to give up their families. So what is the solution? Most counselors agree that recognizing the many demands, organizing time wisely, and perhaps registration for a lighter class load may help students become good academic jugglers.

DEVELOPING CLEAR SENTENCES: PLACEMENT OF MODIFIERS AND PARALLEL STRUCTURE

Guideline	Examples
Put modifiers close to the words they modify.	He took only what he needed from the cash box.
Be especially careful with phrases at the beginning of the sentence.	Standing at the front of the room, Marvin broke out in a sweat.
Keep lists, pairs, and other patterns in the same grammatical structure.	Raking leaves, shoveling snow, and mowing grass were all new to the former city-dweller.
Be especially careful with constructions like *not only . . . but also, either . . . or,* and *neither . . . nor.* Remember that whatever structure follows the first term of the pair should also follow the second term of the pair.	Martha was not only an accomplished actress but also a skilled teacher. Either we have to raise taxes to pay for the new city buildings or the city will have to do without them.

CHAPTER 16

Revising for Economy, Emphasis, and Tone

Another way that writers can meet the needs of readers is to revise early drafts so as to improve the economy, emphasis, and tone of their sentences. You are probably used to thinking of economy in terms of using money wisely, but you can think of it also as using words wisely.

Put yourself in your reader's place, reading a ten-page term paper or business report. If the sentences are overly long and use too many words to get across the ideas, the reader will get tired of reading and may not pay as much attention to the content as you would like. For example, how much patience would you have with a paper in which all the sentences read like the following?

> It is the belief and firm conviction of all mental health professionals that treatment of chronically ill male and female patients has declined due to lack of sufficient physical facilities and competent personnel.

Wouldn't you rather read this?

> Mental health professionals believe that treatment of chronically ill patients has declined due to lack of hospital beds and well-trained staff.

In Chapter 11 you learned that varying the kind of sentences you write helps a reader to read and understand your ideas more easily. In this chapter you will learn ways to streamline sentences to eliminate wordiness.

Writing your ideas with the right amount of emphasis also contributes to increased reader understanding. Many writers don't realize that putting important information at the beginning or end of a sentence draws more reader attention than if the idea is buried in the middle. Compare, for example, the following sentences:

> In my opinion, and I'm sure others agree, there are employees working more than twenty hours per week who should get a raise and increased benefits to be effective at the next pay period.

> Employees working more than twenty hours per week should immediately, in my opinion, get a raise and increased benefits.

As you can see, reorganizing ideas and reducing wordiness contribute to improving emphasis. In this chapter you will practice eliminating weak beginnings and endings and reorganizing ideas that need greater emphasis.

Finally, if anyone has ever said to you, "I don't like your tone of voice," you know that sometimes it's not what you say but the way you say it that is important. The words you choose may be formal (for example, "motor vehicles") or informal ("cars"), depending on your audience and purpose in writing. Actually, there are several levels of usage from formal to nonstandard that must be adjusted to fit the audience for a particular piece of writing.

The following boxes illustrate these principles.

REVISING FOR ECONOMY

1. Avoid redundancy (repeating what was just said in different words).

Not:	But:
each and everyone of you	each
final outcome	outcome
round in shape	round

2. Use active, not passive, voice—it saves words. Active sentences have the doer of the action as the subject of the sentence. Not:

    The man was hit by the red Ford Mustang. (nine words)

    But:

    The red Ford Mustang hit the man. (seven words—same idea)

3. Convert nouns ending in *-ing* or *-ion* or *-ment* or another suffix into the verb forms they came from. Not:

The dean made a decision.

But:

The dean decided.

Not:

The student officers were in a meeting.

But:

The student officers met.

Note that the second version of these pairs is shorter and that the verbs *decided* and *met* do the work of both the noun and verb they replace—that's economy!

4. Begin with your main idea, not with a weak beginning such as *it is* or *there are*. Not:

It is the faculty's decision to add a study day before exams.

But:

The faculty decided to add a study day before exams.

Not:

There are many reasons for why people vote.

But:

People vote for many reasons.

REVISING FOR EMPHASIS

1. Put an important idea at the end of the sentence (most important) or at the beginning of the sentence (next most important). The middle gets the least attention from a reader. Compare these versions. In which sentence does the drunk driving receive greater emphasis?

The prominent businessman convicted of drunk driving lost his driver's license.

Convicted of drunk driving, the prominent businessman lost his license.

Note too that besides reducing wordiness, beginning a sentence with the main idea instead of with *it is* or *there are* increases an idea's emphasis.

2. Give an important idea a high grammatical rank and a less important idea a lower grammatical rank.

GRAMMATICAL RANK, FROM HIGH TO LOW

Sentence:	We were happy to meet Pam Courtney at the airport. She is my cousin.
Independent clause:	We were happy to meet Pam Courtney at the airport, for she is my cousin.
Dependent clause:	We were happy to meet Pam Courtney, who is my cousin, at the airport.
Phrase:	We were happy to meet Pam Courtney, my cousin, at the airport.
Word:	We were happy to meet cousin Pam Courtney at the airport.

Notice that the information about Pam's being my cousin decreases in emphasis as the grammatical rank decreases. Notice also that the number of words needed to get across the information declines, thereby reducing wordiness.

REVISING FOR TONE

1. Use the level of usage appropriate for your audience. A formal report, a letter to the editor of a newspaper, and a letter to a friend may each require different word choices.

Level	Description	Example
Formal	Considered Standard English Usage and required in some academic and business writing, formal usage means using no contractions (*won't* for *will not*) or informal or colloquial words or phrases. Jargon, or	The police officers would not allow the alleged perpetrator to call his spouse, only his attorney.

Level	Description	Example
	specialized words used by people in certain occupations or other special situations, may also appear in formal writing. Note that jargon may cause confusion for a reader who doesn't know the terms. Be certain your audience is familiar with any such words, or define them as you use them.	
Informal or colloquial	Also considered Standard English Usage and employed in the media, in public conversation, and in much writing, this level of usage is marked by contractions and a mix of formal and informal words. Colloquial words include such expressions as "I don't get it" for "I do not understand." Dictionaries usually list "inf." or "colloq." next to a word if it is not formal.	The police wouldn't let the suspect call his wife, only his lawyer.
Slang	Words that are considered outside standard usage because they are used by a small group not empowered by a society—such as criminals, teenagers, minority groups, and working class people. Many times, words begin as slang but eventually become considered merely informal if enough people in positions of influence use them. For example, *cop*, meaning "police officer," is still considered slang by most dictionaries, but some consider it informal and more may accept it as standard usage as time goes on. When in doubt, check a word's usage in a dictionary. Slang is generally unacceptable in academic or business writing.	The cop wouldn't let the wise guy call his old lady, only his ambulance-chaser.
Regional or dialectal	Regions in the United States have their own words and phrases that other regions may not understand. For example, in the Pittsburgh area someone might say that her house "needs cleaned." In Indiana, a woman might say she needs to "red up" her house (*to ready it* means "to clean it"). Using words or grammatical structures that are common only to a region is appropriate if the reader is from the region and the purpose of the writing is informal. However, regional expressions are generally not appropriate in academic and business writing.	

Level	Description
	Dialects are also common in the United States. Many times, we notice a dialect only in the way someone pronounces words, as in "pahk" for "park" in Boston. Pronunciation differences won't be evident in writing (unless they somehow produce misspellings). Sometimes, however, dialects use different grammatical forms that are evident in writing. If someone writes, "I became too soon hungry," readers outside a group of Pennsylvania Dutch speakers will notice the nonstandard use. Similarly, if someone writes, "I be hungry" instead of the standard "I am hungry," readers will notice the dialectal usage. Just as with regionalisms, dialectal expressions are appropriate in speech among members of the dialect group but are not appropriate in most academic or business writing.
Nonstandard	This label is usually applied to an ungrammatical use of language, such as "ain't" or "He don't know nothin'." Writers should avoid using nonstandard words and structures.

2. Be sensitive to the connotations of words, that is, the shades of meaning or emotional response words create. Compare, for example, "Please be quiet" with "Shut your trap!"

3. Be aware that some usages may create a sexist tone. Avoid using the masculine forms when you mean all people, as in "Everyone should exercise his vote in this election" or "All men yearn for freedom from tyranny." Recast sentences to include women, or choose words that apply to both sexes: "Everyone should exercise his or her vote in this election," or "All people should be sure to exercise their right to vote in this election."

Revising for Economy

One way to be more economical in writing is to avoid unnecessary repetition (redundancy) and unnecessary words. Redundant or wordy expressions creep into speech and writing without our realizing that we are using them. How many of the phrases in the following exercise do you use without realizing it?

☞ Exercise 1

In the following exercise, substitute shorter expressions for the redundant or wordy ones.

1. in this day and age _____

2. at this point in time _____

3. each and every person _____

4. in the city of Chicago _____

5. pink in color _____

6. ready and able _____

7. very unique _____

8. important essentials _____

9. end result _____

10. totally hopeless _____

WORKING WITH PEERS

Make a list of other phrases that could be considered redundant. Why do you think we use so many unnecessary words?

☞ Exercise 2

Edit the following paragraph to eliminate redundant or wordy expressions.

First Job

If I think back in time to when I was in high school, I remember applying for my one and only job up to that time. I was nervous and anxious as I prepared for the interview, but since I had the basic and required credentials for the lifeguard job, my lifesaving certificate, I hoped and prayed that the pool director would hire me. I felt ready and able to handle any and all emergency situations at the pool. Trying to act more confident and assured than I really felt, I met the pool director, who asked me about my swimming and lifesaving experience. Once I began to answer questions, my nervousness and anxiety went away. I tried to give totally accurate and entirely complete answers. Soon the interview was over, and to my great relief and joy, I heard the pool director ask me when I could start to work.

Another way to streamline your sentences is to use active, rather than passive, verb forms. As was shown earlier, active sentences take fewer words, and the subject is doing the action of the verb, so the sentences seem more vigorous.

EXAMPLE (ACTIVE SENTENCE)

Students raised over $2000 in their volleyball marathon.

The subject, *students,* did the action of the verb, *raised.*

EXAMPLE (PASSIVE SENTENCE)

Over $2000 was raised by students in their volleyball marathon.

The subject, *dollars,* received the action, *was raised;* then the agent of the action, *by the students,* had to be added.

To make sentences active, make the subject of the sentence the doer of the action. Note that there are times when you don't know who did the action ("The store owner was held up at knife point") or when the doer of the action is not the point of the sentence ("The car was repainted after the accident"). At such times, passive verb forms are necessary. The following exercise will give you practice in noticing and changing passive verbs into active ones.

☞ Exercise 3

Change each of the following sentences from passive to active forms. Look for the doer of the action in the phrase after the verb and move it to become the subject of the sentence.

1.   The leaves were raked by the neighbors.

2.   However, the leaves were soon blown by the wind back onto the neighbors' lawns.

3.   Scenes of pine trees, or even cactus and palm trees, were pictured by the neighbors in their frustration.

4.   These leaf-rakers were envied, however, by some city-dwellers who had few trees to enjoy.

5.   On the other hand, freedom from lawn chores was appreciated by others who live in treeless areas.

A second way to let verbs help you streamline your sentences is to convert some nouns into verbs. Notice that certain nouns, like *development, argument, interference,* and *reliance,* are really verb forms with a suffix added to make them nouns. Notice, too, that when you use such words, you may be adding words to your sentences. Compare the following two sentences:

The lawyer and his client got into a heated argument.

The lawyer and his client argued heatedly.

If your writing seems wordy, check sentences for nouns ending in *-ment, -ance, -ence, -ion,* or *-tion.* Try to convert them to their verb forms, and rewrite the sentence. The following exercise will give you practice.

☞ Exercise 4

Streamline the following sentences by converting nouns ending in *-ment, -tion, -ance,* and the like into verbs and revising the sentence.

1.   The city engineer made an argument for a new water treatment plant.

2.   The city could no longer maintain its reliance on the present plant.

3.   The old plant makes treatment of water inefficient, resulting in shortages.

4.   Furthermore, the present plant makes the distribution of water uneven throughout the city, which could be the causation of low-pressure areas and fire safety problems.

5.   The development of a new plant will be the solution for these problems.

Finally, you can reduce wordiness by eliminating weak beginnings from sentences. Starting a sentence with "It is" or "There are" adds two extra words and delays the main idea to the middle of the sentence (a weak position). Writers often start sentences in this way in a draft because they don't yet know what to say, so they begin weakly just to begin. During the revision process, you can spot such sentences and make them less wordy and more emphatic.

☞   Exercise 5

Revise the following sentences by omitting the "It is" and "There are" beginnings. You will need to supply another main verb for the sentence.

1.   There are many reasons why people commute to colleges near their homes.

2.   It is reasonable to say that they save money by living at home.

3.   There are also those that work full-time and go to school at night.

4.   It is possible that some may like the privacy of their own homes, and don't wish to share a dorm room with a stranger.

5.   For whatever reasons, there are increasing numbers of student commuters.

Revising for Emphasis

As the box explained, an idea receives the greatest emphasis at the end or beginning of a sentence, so writers don't want to clutter up those positions with extra words. As you have seen, eliminating weak beginnings helps. Be aware, too, of too many prepositional phrases or transitional expressions that can clutter up the end or beginning of a sentence. Revise sentences so the main content receives the emphasis.

☞ Exercise 6

Revise the following sentences by changing the position of the italicized words to either the beginning or the end of the sentence. Eliminate weak beginnings and extra phrases.

1.   There is no doubt in anyone's mind that *a major earthquake will occur in California* in the next thirty years.

2.   Although new buildings have been successfully "quake-proofed," *many older buildings and highways may collapse in a quake that registers above 7 on the Richter scale* according to geologists who have studied matters of this kind.

3.   There is another problem with building construction, which is the fact that *some houses and office buildings have been built on landfill* near the ocean or on the sides of mountains instead of solid rock, which can better withstand a quake.

4.   For example, during the 1989 San Francisco earthquake, *the Marina district suffered more damage than other residential areas* because houses there were built on unstable landfill.

5.   In contrast to the Marina district situation, *other buildings in the city built on solid rock foundations had much less damage* as a rule, which, of course, is subject to occasional exceptions.

As you read in the earlier box, the grammatical rank of an idea also contributes to the emphasis placed on it—the higher the rank, the greater the emphasis.

A sentence is the highest rank, and therefore an important idea should be written as a sentence. However, sometimes writers use the highest rank to convey a relatively unimportant idea, thereby adding unnecessary words to a sentence. After all, why should you use a sentence when a clause or phrase or word will do?

☞

Exercise 7

In each of the following, the italicized idea is written as a complete sentence that could be reduced to an independent clause and attached to another sentence by *and, but, or, nor, for, so,* or *yet;* a dependent clause, beginning with a word like *who, which,* or *that;* a phrase; or even a word. Deemphasize the idea in italics to its most concise form while still preserving the idea.

1. The San Francisco earthquake struck at 5:04 p.m. *The third game of the World Series was just about to start.*

2. *TV commentators were doing their pregame show.* They didn't know what was happening at first.

3. Confusion was widespread. *It was only natural.*

4. Some fans at Candlestick Park asked vendors to keep pouring beer. *They didn't realize the severity of the quake.*

5. The stadium shook and rolled. *It did not collapse.*

Another way to illustrate the idea of changing the grammatical rank of ideas is to put everything in a paragraph into separate sentences. Such a paragraph will sound a bit like a Dick and Jane first-grade reader, but it will show you how much you depend on combining ideas to make smooth-sounding sentences while emphasizing just what ideas need to be emphasized.

WORKING WITH PEERS

In pairs or small groups, combine the following sentences into a paragraph that emphasizes the main points and deemphasizes or eliminates lesser ideas.

Earthquake Preparation

1. There was an earthquake in San Francisco.
2. It was in 1989.
3. It taught many lessons.
4. One lesson was to have bottled water, canned food, and batteries.
5. Every citizen learned this lesson.
6. City officials learned another lesson.
7. This lesson was to have more fire and rescue equipment.
8. Some of the equipment should be cranes and high ladders.
9. This equipment could rescue people from highways and tall buildings.
10. Engineers learned other lessons.
11. One was building shock absorbers into buildings and highways.
12. Some buildings with rollers or flexible hinges swayed.
13. But they did not break.
14. Another lesson was to seek solid foundations for buildings.
15. Nothing can prevent an earthquake.
16. Preparation can lessen its effects.
17. Preparation may be expensive.
18. Loss of lives and property is expensive too.

Revising for Tone

As you have learned, there are five levels of usage: formal, informal or colloquial, slang, regional or dialectal, and nonstandard. Effective writers use the level of usage suited to their audience and their purpose. The football coach doesn't write a recruiting letter to a prospect in the same language that he or she would use in a request for funds from the president of the college. Being able to adapt your language to different situations will enable you to communicate with a wide variety of people in many different circumstances. In contrast, if you can use only nonstandard, dialectal or regional expressions, or slang, you will be at a disadvantage in more formal writing situations.

☞ Exercise 8

Change the following expressions into formal usage. Check your dictionary if needed.

1. The cops busted the crack dealer.

2. The movie was awesome.

3. The feds were on to the money-laundering scheme.

4. George tried to get money off his brother.

5. Margie should of went home, instead of hangin' on the corner.

6. Mel was feelin' poorly and took to his bed.

7. The people be clappin' their hands while the band be playin'.

8. I been thinking that Marie shouldn't of took the scarf from Judy's drawer.

9. Jeff spent his summer down the shore after graduating high school.

10. Hot damn! I won the lottery!

WORKING WITH PEERS

In pairs or groups, list words or expressions in the following categories and then compare your lists with those of other classmates.

Current Slang	Regional or Dialect	Jargon (in business, law, medicine, etc.)

☞ Exercise 9

Revise the following passage by reducing wordiness, giving ideas proper emphasis, and making the level of usage appropriate for academic writing.

City Dilemma: The Homeless

No matter whether someone is a resident or a visitor who comes to shop or look for things to buy in a big city, one is dismayed at finding homeless people without shelter sleeping on the streets and avenues. At first, there is the response of asking the question "Why don't the cops bust these bums?" But that answer is too easy and oversimplified. Laws protect the rights and privileges of people to do what they please as long as they are not engaging in criminal conduct or unlawful behavior. While some people and residents would point out that sleeping on steam grates or using public spaces as toilets should be outlawed, the law ain't clear about such goings on. In addition, there is the problem of overcrowded courts and jails. There is simply no room for all the homeless in the pokey. Also there is the problem that many of the homeless are mentally ill and really need treatment, not jailing. But mental hospitals need more funding and better facilities too, and they have not been adequately funded or given money to provide these services. Then, too, if the homeless person does not agree that he or she needs treatment, strict laws governing involuntary commitment hogtie the shrinks. Do-gooders and other charities have opened flophouses to shelter the homeless, and other groups tend to their food and medical care, but these efforts are not enough. There are many experts who think that a joint city, state, federal effort is needed and required to help the homeless.

REVISING FOR ECONOMY, EMPHASIS AND TONE

Guideline	Examples
Reduce wordiness by . . .	
1. Eliminating redundancies.	*Not:* It is each and every student's right to have received expert instruction.
2. Using active not passive verbs.	
3. Converting some nouns into verbs.	*But:* Students deserve expert teaching.
4. Eliminating weak beginnings.	
Give ideas proper emphasis by . . .	
1. Placing important thoughts at the beginning or end of a sentence.	*Not:* If you want to know what I think, we should hire professors who value teaching at least as high as something else.
	But: We should hire professors, in my opinion, who put teaching first.
2. Increasing grammatical rank of important ideas and decreasing grammatical rank of less important ideas.	
Use a level of usage appropriate to the writer's audience and purpose:	
Formal (academic and business writing)	I would like to borrow money for my college tuition.
Informal or colloquial (everyday use among strangers)	Could you lend me money for college?

REVISING FOR ECONOMY, EMPHASIS AND TONE (continued)

Guideline	Examples
Slang (among friends)	Can you spare some dough for the U?
Regional or dialectal (among groups that share the language)	I be needin' some 5's and 10's for bookin' it.
Nonstandard (use only when standard use is out of place)	Ain't you got money I can get off you for college?

CHAPTER 17

Using Standard English Forms: Verbs, Adjectives, Adverbs, Pronoun Cases

In Chapter 16 you learned about levels of usage and the need to adjust your level of usage to your audience. As explained in that chapter, formal usage is required most frequently in academic and business writing situations. Knowledge of Standard English forms will enable you to write at the appropriate level of usage. Many of these forms may be familiar to you, but there may be some forms not common in speech that you have to learn to use in writing. For example, the distinction between *who* and *whom* is one almost everybody needs to practice because it is still required in formal writing situations but is almost universally ignored in speech. Since language use is dynamic and ever-changing, at some point the *who-whom* distinction may disappear. But until it does, people needing to communicate in formal situations still must know it.

While learning Standard English forms depends more on memory of those forms than on learning rules, there are some basic principles, which are discussed in the following box. Lists of the most troublesome forms of Standard English verbs, adjectives, adverbs, and pronoun cases follow in the chapter.

STANDARD VERB FORMS

All verb forms are derived from the three principal parts of the verb: the present tense, the past tense, and the past participle. The *present* tense is the base form of the verb, often written as an infinitive (*to* + verb, as in *to go, to walk, to swim*). The *past* tense shows action or state of being that has already happened; it frequently ends in *-ed* (e.g., *walked*). However, there are many verbs, called *irregular* verbs, that do not end in *-ed*, and their forms must be memorized or checked in a dictionary. The past participle is the form used to make other, more complicated tenses (e.g., *has walked, will have walked, had walked*) and always uses a helping verb (auxiliary) with it.

EXAMPLE (present)

I take my car for regular oil changes.

EXAMPLE (past)

I took my car to the service station yesterday.

EXAMPLE (present perfect—action that happened more than once in the past)

I have taken my car to have the oil changed every six months.

EXAMPLE (past perfect—action that happened before some other past action)

I had taken my car to be serviced just before it broke down.

There are many other verb tenses, but all are formed from the three principal parts just illustrated.

STANDARD ADJECTIVE AND ADVERB FORMS

Adjectives are used to describe nouns and pronouns, as in:

the red pony   the quiet room   the clean window   silly me

Adverbs describe verbs; they also describe adjectives and other adverbs:

Describing Verbs	Describing Adjectives	Describing Other Adverbs
ran *quickly*	*really* quiet room	ran *quite* quickly
went *soon*	*spotlessly* clean window	went *very* soon

Problems with standard adjective and adverb forms usually occur in two situations:

1.   People may use the adjective form when they should use the adverb form:

Not:	But:
He ran quick.	He ran quickly.
The construction job paid good.	The construction job paid well.
The child asked a question in a real quiet voice.	The child asked a question in a really quiet voice.

2.   After a linking verb, an adjective form is usually needed to describe the subject:

The car's paint job was bad.

Some verbs referring to the senses (*feel, look, hear, taste*) and certain others (*grow, become, seem*) may act as linking verbs and need adjective forms after them:

The patient looked bad to me.

(*Bad* describes *patient.*)

The marathon runner grew faint.

(*Faint* describes *runner.*)

The banquet food tasted good to me.

(*Good* describes *food.*)

The athlete felt good about the performance.

(*Good* describes *athlete.*)
Exception: When *well* refers to *health*, it may be used after a linking verb:

How is your father feeling? He is well, thank you.

After a few days' rest, the student felt well again.

STANDARD PRONOUN CASES

In English, a noun keeps the same form whether it is a subject or an object:

> The train was on time.
>
> Don't miss the train.

Nouns do change form if used to show possession:

> The train's sleeping car was filled.

> Pronouns, however, have three distinct forms, called *cases:*

Subject case	I	you	he	she	it	we	they	who
Possessive case	my	your	his	her	its	our	their	whose
	mine	yours		hers		ours	theirs	
Object case	me	you	him	her	it	us	them	whom

So, for example, in standard English you would use the following forms:

> *They* were late. (subject)
> Did you miss *them*? (object)
> *Who* saw the accident? (subject)
> To *whom* did you report accident? (object)
> This is *she*. (predicate noun—same case as subject)

Note that *whom* has the same ending as *him* and *them*. This similarity may help you choose the correct case—try substituting *him* or *them* in normal sentence order to see whether *who* or *whom* is the correct form.

> Did you report the accident to them?

Standard Verb Forms

If you have been around young children, you may have heard them say, "She throwed the ball." They were applying to regular verbs what they had learned about *-ed* endings from listening to others speak. Of course, you know that *throw* doesn't behave like the regular verbs and that the Standard form is *threw*. Children learn the difference if the people around them speak Standard English. However, if they are not exposed to Standard English, they may continue to use other verb forms.

The following table gives you the three principal parts of many troublesome verbs. It may help you to think of the three as used in a sentence with a subject such as *I*. In some cases, there may be more than one accepted form. Check your dictionary for verbs not in this table.

PRINCIPAL PARTS OF SOME TROUBLESOME VERBS

Present ("I . . .")	Past ("I . . .")	Past Participle ("I have . . .")
agree	agreed	agreed
am (he is, we are)	was (we were)	been (he has been)
arise	arose	arisen
become	became	become
begin	began	begun
bite	bit	bitten, bit
blow	blew	blown
break	broke	broken
bring	brought	brought
burst	burst	burst
buy	bought	bought
catch	caught	caught
choose	chose	chosen
come	came	come
dive	dived, dove	dived, dove
do	did	done
draw	drew	drawn
dream	dreamed, dreamt	dreamed, dreamt
drink	drank	drunk
drive	drove	driven
eat	ate	eaten
fall	fell	fallen
find	found	found
fly	flew	flown
forget	forgot	forgotten
freeze	froze	frozen
get	got	got, gotten

PRINCIPAL PARTS OF SOME TROUBLESOME VERBS (continued)

Present ("I . . .")	Past ("I . . .")	Past Participle ("I have . . .")
give	gave	given
go	went	gone
grow	grew	grown
hang (people)	hanged	hanged
hang (objects)	hung	hung
know	knew	known
lay (to place)	laid	laid
lie (to recline)	lay	lain
pay	paid	paid
prove	proved	proved, proven
ring	rang, rung	rung
rise (to go up)*	rose	risen
run	ran	rung
say	said	said
see	saw	seen
set (to place)	set	set
shake	shook	shaken
shrink	shrank, shrunk	shrunk, shrunken
sing	sang, sung	sung
sit (in a chair)	sat	sat
speak	spoke	spoken
steal	stole	stolen
sting	stung	stung
swear	swore	sworn
swim	swam	swum
take	took	taken
tear	tore	tore
throw	threw	thrown
wear	wore	worn
write	wrote	written

*Note that *raise* (to lift up) is a regular verb.

☞ Exercise 1

Fill in the blank with the Standard form of one of the verbs in the table of troublesome verbs. Be careful to choose the tense indicated by the sentence.

1. Herbert _____ in his easy chair last Sunday and watched football.

2. It would have _____ a power failure to move him from the spot.

3. When his family _____ to him, he answered only with a grunt.

4. Finally, his wife _____ that she had _____ tired of his obsession.

5. She felt that Herbert should _____ attention to his family for at least part of Sunday.

6. She _____ a one-game limit.

7. Her remarks _____ Herbert's attention at last.

8. At first he _____ that she was ruining his life, but then he

   _____ to notice his kids' sad looks.

9. Reluctantly, he _____ that they _____ right.

10. As he _____ back to his easy chair, he _____ that the

    new limit could _____ next Sunday!

☞ Exercise 2

The following groups of sentences will give you practice with *lie/lay, sit/set, rise/raise,* and forms of the verb *to be.*

1. *lie/lay*

   a. The hens at Farmer Brown's _____ more eggs after Mr. Brown piped in music to the hen house.

   b. Jeremy couldn't remember where he _____ down his car keys.

   c. The new mother wearily _____ down for a nap after feed-
      ing her newborn daughter.

   d. Before being arrested, the protestors had _____ on the
      sidewalk of the government building.

2. *sit/set*

   a. Please _____ the tables for a party of fifty guests.

   b. _____ at the head table will be the mayor and the governor.

   c. If you can _____ still long enough, you will be rewarded
      with dessert.

   d. Last evening, the badly injured man _____ patiently wait-
      ing for treatment in the emergency room.

3. *rise/raise*

   a. The caretaker _____ the flag at school each morning.

   b. The people had to be evacuated when the flood waters

      _____.

   c. The professor has _____ to a position of national
      importance.

   d. Some people are said to _____ themselves by their own
      bootstraps.

4. *am, is, are, was, were, has been, have been*

   a. Monsters _____ commonly feared by children.

   b. One such monster _____ the one hiding in the closet or
      under the bed.

   c. If we would admit it, most of us _____ have been
      _____ frightened by thoughts of such creatures.

   d. However, after being reassured that there _____ no mons-

      ters in the room, we _____ able to go to sleep.

WORKING WITH PEERS

In small groups, write a children's story using as many irregular verbs as you can. Share your story with the other groups in the class.

Standard Adjective and Adverb Forms

As explained in the earlier box, adjectives describe only nouns and pronouns, whereas adverbs describe verbs, adjectives, and other adverbs. It may help to think of these words as occupying a particular place in a sentence. Look at the following sentences to see the usual places that adjectives and adverbs appear.

1.   The _____ car crashed _____ into the wall.
            (adj.)   (adv.)

2.   The driver was taken _____ to the hospital with
                                    (adv.)

     _____ _____ injuries.
            (adv.)   (adj.)

3.   The car was a _____ wreck.
                              (adj.)

4.   _____, the driver survived.
            (adv.)

When a word has both an adjective and an adverb form, such as *real* and *really, frequent* and *frequently,* and *serious* and *seriously,* then the *-ly* ending indicates the adverb form. Sometimes, the forms change completely, as in the case of *good* (adjective) and *well* (adverb).

Remember that after a linking verb *(is, am, are, was, were, has been, have been)* and after sense verbs, such as *see, look, smell, taste, feel,* the adjective form is probably needed to describe the subject. You may want to think of a linking verb as an equals sign with one side equal to the other:

Joan is small.	Joan = small
The perfume smells strong.	perfume = strong
This sandwich tastes good.	sandwich = good

The major exception to this rule is (as previously mentioned) when the word *well* means "in good health," when it may be used after a linking verb.

EXAMPLE

I was sick, but I feel well now.

Sometimes you will have to use your judgment to decide which form is correct:

Dressed in a suit for his interview, George looked good.

(*Good* is an adjective describing *George*.)

Before he left, George looked carefully for his notebook.

(*Carefully* is an adverb describing *looked*.)

After other kinds of verbs, use the adverb form to describe how something was done (*well, completely*), when it was done (*soon, immediately*), or how much (*very, really*).

☞ Exercise 3

Fill in the blank with the correct word of the pair of words in parentheses.

1. Tina _____ (real, really) did _____ (good, well) on her first day in the job.

2. She dressed _____ (conservative, conservatively) in a navy blue suit, which she thought would show that she wanted to be taken

   _____ (serious, seriously).

3. Her boss greeted her _____ (warm, warmly) and told her that

   he _____ (sure, surely) needed her help.

4. Even before lunch, Tina had analyzed a problem _____ (cor-

   rect, correctly) that had stumped others for a _____ (real, really) long time.

5. She felt _____ (good, well) about her ability to do the job.

☞ Exercise 4

Write five sentences in which you use the words *good* and *well*. Include some sentences with linking or sense verbs and some with action verbs.

Standard Pronoun Cases

The forms of the personal pronouns in the box at the beginning of the chapter are divided into subject, object, and possessive forms. There are really just a few situations that confuse many people.

1. Sometimes when two pronouns or a noun and pronoun are together, people have trouble with the correct form:

    Joe and *(I, me)* left for school early.

    We met Marty and *(she, her)* on the way.

    Joe gave Marty and *(she, her)* a smile and said, "*(We, Us)* earlybirds may not get the worm, but we will get seats on the bus!"

    Although you could analyze the sentence to determine whether the word needed is a subject or an object, an easier way is to try the word alone. The correct form is often then apparent:

Correct	Incorrect
I left for school early.	Me left for school early.
We met her on the way.	We met she on the way.
Joe gave her a smile.	Joe gave she a smile.
We may not get the worm.	Us may not get the worm.

2. If a sentence expresses a comparison, it may end with a pronoun, as in:

    She is shorter than *(I, me)*.

    To help decide what the correct form of the pronoun should be, finish the comparison:

    She is shorter than I am.

3. Linking verbs act as equals signs, as was explained earlier. That means that a pronoun after a linking verb should be in the subject form, since it equals the subject:

    This is she.

    It is I.

The robber was he.

The winner was who?

Since many people do not use this construction when they talk, they need to pay attention to the need for this form in formal writing situations.

4.   The use of *who* and *whom* is another example of a distinction being made in formal writing that is not frequently made in speech. To repeat: *Who* is a subject form, and *whom* (like *him* and *them*) is an object form. Because sentences using these words frequently either are questions or contain dependent clauses, there are some special techniques to help choose the correct form:

a.   Put reverse-order sentences in normal order:

(Who, Whom) do you trust?   becomes   You do trust *(who, whom)*?

You should choose *whom* because it is an object, like *them*.

b.   If the *who/whom* choice is in a dependent clause, look at the usage in that clause only:

Give the ball to *(whoever, whomever* can make the first down)*.

Here, the choice is *whoever,* because it is the subject of *can make*.

☞ Exercise 5

Circle the correct form of the pronoun.

1.   Felicia and (she, her) have the same math instructor.

2.   My father gave my sisters and (I, me) our allowance on Saturday. They were older and got more money than (I, me).

3.   Do you know anyone (who, whom) collects baseball cards?

4.   You should write to (whoever, whomever) is in charge of billing for the insurance company to straighten out your bill.

5.   To (who, whom) should I speak?

6.   My friends bought lunch for (she, her) and (I, me) when we were broke. They were nice to save (we, us) students from starving to death before our paychecks came.

7.   May I speak to Jerry, please? This is (he, him).

8.   The prosecutor turned to the jury and asked, "Do you wonder about (who, whom) I am speaking? I am talking about the defendant."

9. My brother, (who, whom) is two years younger, is eight inches taller than (I, me).

10. (We, Us) kids used to empty the refrigerator as soon as it was filled up.

☞ Exercise 6

Write five sentences using pronouns in the following situations: in pairs *(he and she, him and me);* in comparisons *(she is smarter than I);* or in constructions requiring *who* or *whom.*

☞ Exercise 7

Edit the following paragraph for errors in the use of Standard forms of verbs, adjectives, adverbs, and pronoun cases.

Choosing a Career

One of the real important decisions I must make soon is what kind of job I want to prepare myself for. My advisor, Mrs. Brownlee, talked recent to my classmates and I, lying out our options. One guy that I seen around asked, "How am I supposed to decide my future when I can't even figure out today?" All of us other students laughed because we knowed how he feels. Then Mrs. Brownlee asked he and the rest of us if we had ever took an interest inventory to see what our interests was. Janice and Bruce had went to a better high school than us, so him and her had been gave the test. The rest of we students wanted to know what the advisor meaned by an interest inventory. She explained that you choosed different likes and dislikes from a list of questions like "Would you rather hike alone in the woods or join with a group of hikers?" The answers to these questions would show those who like to work with people or those for who working with people would be a bad idea. Mrs. Brownlee said that the counseling service gave these tests free to whomever signed up for an appointment. I thinked that this was a real good idea for me to do since I didn't know whether I would do good in business or some other field.

USING STANDARD ENGLISH FORMS

1. Learn the principal parts of irregular verbs, paying particular attention to commonly confused verbs like *lie/lay, sit/set,* and *rise/raise,* and the forms of the verb *to be.*

2. Use adjective forms to describe nouns:

   The quiet man ate his small meal.

   Use adverb forms to describe verbs, adjectives, and other adverbs. Many adverbs end in *-ly:*

   He is really tired.

3. Since linking verbs and sense verbs act as equals signs, connecting the subject of the sentence to the adjective that follows the verb, use the adjective form:

   Marvin was cold.
   She felt guilty.

4. Use a subject pronoun as the subject of a sentence or following a linking verb:

   She is the doctor.
   It is he who called.

5. Use an object pronoun to receive the action of the verb:

   The car hit him.
   Whom did the car hit?

6. When two pronouns or a noun and pronoun are used together, test the pronoun use by using each word separately:

   Mary and she are going to the play on Friday.
   It occurred to us students that the term was nearing the end.

7. When a pronoun is used at the end of a comparison, finish the comparison to determine the form:

   Linda swims faster than she (does).

CHAPTER 18

Using Correct Spelling

Some people think that being a good or bad speller is the essence of being a good or bad writer. I have heard people say, "I am a terrible writer; I can't spell." By now, you should be aware that writing involves putting ideas into words in ways meaningful to a reader and that spelling is only a small part of editing a written manuscript. In fact, with today's spelling checkers on word processing programs, bad spellers are getting more help than ever before.

It may interest you to know that one's ability to spell may be innate—experts believe that a person's ability to spell ranges from perfect recall of the printed word (the people with so-called photographic memories) to almost no recall of what a word looks like in print (people who are severely dyslexic). Most of us fall somewhere along this continuum, with good, mediocre, and bad spellers sprinkled among us.

Even if spelling is related to visual recall ability, you can do some things to help you spell better. One suggestion is to keep a list of the *correct* spelling of words you have misspelled and to look at it frequently to help your visual-recall memory. Add to the list everytime you get a paper returned. Sometimes say and spell the words on your list out loud so that your brain pathways receive the sound of the spelling of the words. This process also helps your memory. Another suggestion is to learn some of the rules that govern English spelling that will help with some of the most frequent errors. Finally, learn the words that sound the same or nearly the same but are spelled differently, so that they are not a frequent source of error.

Selected Rules of English Spelling

1. *i* before *e* except after *c* or when sounded like *a* as in *neighbor* and *weigh:*

believe	ceiling	neighbor
piece	perceive	weigh
relief	deceive	sleigh

    Exceptions: their, either, neither, leisure, seize, weird, financier, species

2. If a word ends in silent *e* and you add a suffix beginning with a vowel (*a, e, i, o, u, y*), then drop the *e:*

care + ing = caring	name + ing = naming
place + ed = placed	imagine + ed = imagined
fame + ous = famous	noise + y = noisy

    If a word ends in silent *e* and you add a suffix beginning with a consonant (anything but *a, e, i, o, u, y*), then keep the *e:*

hope + less = hopeless	lone + ly = lonely
force + ful = forceful	state + ment = statement

    Exceptions: Words ending in *-ce* or *-ge* keep the *e* if you add *-able* or *-ous:* noticeable, courageous, advantageous. *Also,* truly, awful, dyeing, ninth.

3. Double the last letter of a word ending in a vowel-consonant combination *(vc)* when you add a suffix that starts with a vowel:

    drag + ed = dragged   equip + ing = equipping
      vc   *v*   *vc*   *v*

    But:

    equip + ment = equipment
      vc   *c*

    (suffix begins with consonant)

Exceptions: If the word is accented on the first syllable, don't double the final letter:

differ + ent = different   open + ed = opened
   vc   *v*   *vc*   *v*

4. If a word ends in *y* with a consonant before it, change the *y* to *i* when adding a suffix not beginning with *i*:

busy + ly = busily   icy + er = icier
  cv   *cv*

try + ed = tried   study + es = studies
 cv   *cv*

But:

buy + er = buyer   monkey + s = monkeys.
 vv   *vv*

And when the suffix starts with *i*:

enjoy + ing = enjoying

carry + ing = carrying

study + ing = studying

5. Adding a prefix to a word does not change the spelling of the root word:

mis + spell = misspell   un + necessary = unnecessary

6. Most nouns add *s* to form the plural, but some nouns add *es* or change form or stay the same.
     Add *es* to nouns ending in *s, sh, ch, x,* or *z*:

boxes   kisses   catches   bushes   buzzes

     Add *es* to nouns ending in a consonant and *o*:

heroes   tomatoes   potatoes

Exceptions:

pianos   banjos   photos   autos

Change the form of certain words:

knife-knives   wolf-wolves   thief-thieves

child-children   man-men   mouse-mice   fungus-fungi

Keep the same form:

sheep   deer   moose

SIMILAR-SOUNDING WORDS

Word: Meaning	Examples
accept: to agree	I accept the invitation.
except: excluding	He lost everything in the fire except his dog.
advice: counseling, recommendation (noun)	Marv took the professor's advice.
advise: to suggest, to make a recommendation (verb)	The teacher advised him to study.
affect: to influence (verb)	Being called names doesn't affect me.
effect: result (noun)	The terrible effects of the wind were apparent.
all ready: prepared	They were all ready for the party.
already: indicating before some other time	He had already left the house before I could remind him of the appointment.
all together: in a group	The club worked all together on the marathon.
altogether: entirely	He was altogether exhausted after running.
altar: place of worship (noun)	The altar was covered with flowers.
alter: to change (verb)	The driver needed to alter his direction when he saw the tree in the road.
aloud: to speak or make a noise that can be heard	She read aloud from the script.
allowed: to be given permission	Students were allowed to leave the room after they finished the exam.

SIMILAR-SOUNDING WORDS (continued)

Word: Meaning	Examples
angel: a spirit	Angel food cake is so light that even an angel could eat it.
angle: two lines or directions coming together; a point of view	The airplane had a sharp angle of descent.
	The senator took a new angle in the debate.
berth: a place to rest	She took a berth on the train.
birth: a new life, or beginning	The birth of a child is often a joyous occasion.
brake: to stop, or something that stops	He put on the brakes.
break: to cause destruction, or something that is disrupted	The gas company reported a break in service.
capital: the city where a government meets; money for a business; or a descriptive word meaning "execution for a serious crime"	Legislators met today in the capital to discuss raising more capital for state businesses and to vote on whether to allow capital punishment.
capitol: the building where a legislature meets	The architect met with legislators to discuss renovating the capitol.
cite: to quote	The speaker cited the new law.
sight: ability to see	He sighted the ship's mast.
site: a location	What will be built on this site?
close: to shut or end (verb)	Please close the door.
clothes: things to wear (noun)	Do clothes make the man or woman?
coarse: rough	The coarse beach sand hurt our feet.
course: path; or school subject	The course of life never is smooth.
	Mike was having trouble with his chemistry course.
conscience: one's moral sense	The thief's conscience began to bother him.
conscious: aware	She became conscious of people staring at her.
	The patient soon became conscious after surgery.
desert: sandy, dry place (noun)	Some people love the desert landscape.

SIMILAR-SOUNDING WORDS (continued)

Word: Meaning	Examples
desert: to leave (verb)	The soldier tried to desert but was caught.
dessert: a treat at the end of meal	The chef made a wonderful chocolate dessert.
dining: eating	The dining room was empty.
dinning: making noise	The engine whine was a dinning in her ears.
dying: to stop living	The old man was dying.
dyeing: adding or changing the color of something	People try to look younger by dyeing their hair.
emigrate: to leave a country	His relatives emigrated from Puerto Rico.
immigrate: to enter a country	He immigrated to America to start a new life.
fair: a festival (noun)	We loved the county fair.
fair: reasonable (adjective)	The teacher was a fair grader.
fare: fee for transportation	City council raised the bus fare.
forth: forward	The hero went forth to seek his fortune.
fourth: after *third*	The child was fourth in line to the throne.
hear: to receive sound	Do you hear me clearly?
here: in this place	I will stand over here.
hole: an opening	The squirrel dug a hole in the ground.
whole: entire, complete	Mark ate a whole pizza.
its: pronoun showing ownership	The cat licked its fur.
it's: contraction meaning "it is"	It's a lovely day.
know: to understand or recognize	Do you know the author?
no: negative	I have no money.
loose: not tight	She likes loose jackets.
lose: to abandon an object; or to not win a contest	Losing your ticket will mean losing the lottery, even if you choose the right numbers.

SIMILAR-SOUNDING WORDS (continued)

Word: Meaning	Examples
passed: completing a course; overtaking someone; or approving a law (verb)	Joan passed the course by answering a question about a law that had just been passed. When she passed her friend in the hall, she gave her a thumbs-up sign.
past: a time gone by (noun or adjective)	That is in the past.
	She is the past president of the association.
past: a direction (preposition)	He drove past her house.
peace: quiet; not war	The country longed for peace.
piece: a portion	I would like a piece of pie.
personal: individual	I have personal business.
personnel: people who work for a company (noun or adjective)	All personnel should fill out benefit forms. A personnel officer will answer your questions.
principal: head of a school (noun)	The principal is your pal.
principal: amount of money (noun)	The loan includes prinicpal and interest.
principal: main or chief (adjective)	My principal reason for quitting the team was my grades.
principle: a belief or value	She is a woman of strong principles.
precede: to go before	The queen preceded her husband.
proceed: to continue	The meeting will not proceed without more members being present.
quiet: not noisy	Susan was a quiet person.
quite: completely or very	Aaron was quite tired.
stationary: not moving	The statue looked alive but remained stationary.
stationery: paper used to write on	He ordered new stationery for the office.
than: a word used to show comparisons	My sister is taller than I.
then: indicates time	Then the pitcher made a motion to first base.
there: a place	Put the box there, please.

SIMILAR-SOUNDING WORDS (continued)

Word: Meaning	Examples
their: ownership	Those are their books.
they're: contraction meaning "they are"	They're going to the concert.
to: toward	The mayor walked to his office from the rally.
too: also	The city council president went too.
two: the number after *one*	The two of them talked as they walked.
weather: the climate	The weather is cold and windy.
whether: indicates a choice	He could not decide whether to wear his coat or not.
were: past tense of *are*	Were you at the meeting?
where: a question of place	Where is my key?
who's: contraction meaning "who is"	Who's going to claim this coat?
whose: shows ownership	Whose car is blocking my driveway?
your: shows ownership	Your letter arrived yesterday.
you're: contraction meaning "you are"	You're scheduled to work on Saturday night.

☞ Exercise 1

Correct any errors you find in the following sentences.

1. Anyone who recieves stolen merchandise is just as guilty as the one who stole it.

2. Although he had studyed for the test, he thought a passing grade was still hopless.

3. Some people are unable to study in a noisey place.

4. African monkies have frequently been used in medical research.

5. The releif on his face was noticable when he recieved his check.

6. Nieghbors were quite willing to help out the homeless victims of the earthquake.

7. It never occured to Susan that Mary was geting tired of waiting for her.

8. Marian has created several new dishs featuring cheap vegetables like potatos and tomatos.

9. With their radioes blaring, the hunters tryed to scare the mooses into the trap.

10. The hospital cheif of staff was planing to request a new emergency room.

☞ Exercise 2

Fill in the correct missing letters in the following words.

th __ __ f   kni __ es

ch __ __ f   n __ __ ther

w __ __ gh   c __ __ ling

n __ __ ghbor   n __ __ ce

w __ __ rd   notic __ __ ble

donk __ __ __   wom __ n (plural)

marr __ __ s   monk __ __ s

☞ Exercise 3

Choose the correct form in parentheses.

1. I will (accept, except) the invitation to speak unless (adviced, advised) not to.

2. The spy made sure his pursuers were out of (cite, sight, site) when he turned off the main road to take the dirt path to the nuclear power (cite, sight, site).

3. The politician did not realize what the (affect, effect) of his decision to run would be on his family.

4. If the neighbors are going to have any (peace, piece) and (quiet, quite), Tom is going to have to (clothes, close) his windows when he plays the guitar.

5. Mario took four (coarses, courses) in his first semester and (than, then) took five subjects the next term.

6. Carson City is the (capital, capitol) of the (desert, dessert) state of Nevada.

7. Some people manage to (loose, lose) an umbrella almost every time they use one.

8. (Your, You're) going to be late to (their, there, they're) wedding if you don't hurry.

9. The (weather, whether) front remained (stationary, stationery) for (to, too, two) days, causing (to, too, two) much rain for the streams (to, too, two) handle.

10. In the (passed, past), investment brokers may have violated ethical (principals, principles), but the disastrous (affects, effects) of insider trading caused SEC (personal, personnel) to investigate stock trades closely.

11. (Know, No) new legislation has to be (passed, past); present laws just need to be enforced.

12. In the (forth, fourth) semester at many colleges, students must choose (their, they're, there) major.

13. If (your, you're) buying a house, you need to figure the monthly payments by adding up (principal, principle), interest, taxes, and insurance.

14. Many people (died, dyed) trying to (emigrate, immigrate) from countries behind the iron curtain.

15. The travel agent was more (than, then) pleased to make our reservations for a (berth, birth) on the cruise ship, especially since the commission (affected, effected) the size of her pay check.

WORKING WITH PEERS

In pairs or small groups, make up ten sentences like those in Exercise 3 that use pairs of commonly confused words. Exchange your sentences with another group, and circle the correct forms.

☞ Exercise 4

Correct spelling errors in the following passage, and change the form of any words used incorrectly.

Capturing the Tourist Dollar

Increasingly, citys are triing to broaden there appeal beyond the usual convention crowd. They beleive that tourism should be a source of revenue and jobs year around and want to make a city vacation as popular with familys as the Grand Canyon, Yellowstone Park, or even Disney World. Some citys, like Boston and Baltimore, have been successful developeing they're waterfront areas. Whereas in the passed these areas where run-down docks and rotting warehouses, today they feature attractive shops and restaurants and activitys like the National Aquarium in Baltimore. Some places were whether is a problem, like Minneapolis, Minnesota, have built skyways and domed stadiums and even put an entire zoo under cover to attract visitors.

Las Vegas, long an attraction to gamblers, has begun to lure familys to with inexpensive all-you-can-eat buffets, family room packages, and family-oriented entertainment like Circus Circus. While many tourists will always think of a vacation in terms of a national park, the seashore, the mountains, or some other natural spot, some will explore the new city wonders.

Identifying Parts of Speech

Noun

A noun is the name of a person, a place, an object, or an idea. A noun can be one word, a verbal ending in *-ing* or *to* + verb, or a clause. Examples are italicized in the following sentences.

Mary and *George* live in *Chicago.*

A *democracy* requires educated *citizens.*

The *windows* needed to be cleaned.

Pitching is a special *skill.*

To be a quarterback takes practice.

He waited for *whoever was in charge.*

Pronoun

A pronoun is a word used in place of a noun. Pronouns include: *I, you, he, she, it, we, they, me, him, her, us, them, mine, yours, ours, its, theirs, who, whom, one, everyone, someone, anyone, no one, everybody, somebody, anybody, nobody, this, these, that, those, which, each, either, neither, what.* Examples are italicized in the following sentences:

They live in Chicago.

It requires educated citizens.

Those needed to be cleaned.

Verb

A verb expresses an action or a state of being and can be tested by putting a noun or pronoun before it to make a small sentence ("She swims." "Mary has gone." "He runs."). Examples are italicized in the following examples.

The students *work* at several jobs.

The club *raised* money through a volleyball marathon.

Hard work *is* necessary for success.

The store manager *had been* a football player in college.

Adjective

An adjective describes a noun or pronoun by answering the questions "Which?", "What kind of?", or "How many?". Sometimes a verb form ending in *-ed* or *-ing* is used as as adjective, and sometimes a clause is an adjective. Examples follow:

That dress will be put in a museum. (Which dress?)

The *helium* balloon burst. (What kind of balloon?)

The *frightened* children fled the *swimming* snake. (What kind of children? What kind of snake?)

The children *who were frightened* fled the lake. (Which?)

Four students head the *student* government. (How many students? What kind of government?)

Note: As in the preceding sentence, *students* is a noun when it names something but can become an adjective when it describes a word like *government*. Words may change their part of speech as they take on different functions.

Adverb

An adverb describes a verb, an adjective, or another adverb by answering the questions "When?", "Where?", "Why?", "How?", "How much?", or "How often?". Adverbs may be one or more words, including clauses. Here are some examples.

George draws *well*. (draws how?)

George *frequently* draws *well*. (draws how and how often?)

Put the paper *there*. (put where?)

Put the paper *where it can dry out*. (put where?)

Recently, Juan received a raise. (received when?)

The monster raised its arm *quite threateningly*. (How raised, how much threateningly?)

The children were *very* happy. (how much happy?)

Note: Adverbs are more movable than many other parts of speech. You may find them next to the word they describe or at the beginning or the end of a sentence. Ask yourself what word they are describing. If it's a verb, an adjective, or an adverb, then you know the word itself is an adverb.

Preposition

A preposition is a word that expresses a relationship and is always followed by a noun or pronoun in what is called a *prepositional phrase*. The following examples of prepositional phrases have their prepositions italicized.

under the house	*during* the storm
over the house	*after* the storm
through the house	*before* the storm
into the house	*of* the court
around the house	*to* the station
next to the house	*by* the law

Note: Prepositional phrases are used in sentences to describe nouns or pronouns (therefore acting as adjectives) and to describe verbs (therefore acting as adverbs).

Conjunction

A conjunction joins together two words, two clauses, or two sentences. Most common are the coordinating conjunctions *and, but, or, nor, for, so,* and *yet.*

Certain words that sometimes serve as other parts of speech may also serve as subordinating conjunctions that introduce dependent clauses. In the following sentences, each italicized word is a conjunction introducing a dependent clause.

Because there had been so much rain, crops rotted in the field.

He walked to the corner, *where* he caught a bus.

Susan agreed to join her friends *unless* she found out that she had to work.

Identifying Parts of the Sentence

Verb

The verb in a sentence expresses an action or a state of being. It may be one word, two or more verbs connected by *and,* or a main word together with auxiliaries such as *may, can, has, have, is,* and *are.* An *-ing* word must have an auxiliary with it to be a verb. Here are some examples.

The dog *buried* the bone.

The dog *chased* and *caught* a rabbit.

The dog *is being chased* by the neighbor's cat.

The cat *may have* some wildcat ancestors.

The cat *is winning* the race.

Subject

The subject of a sentence is the noun or pronoun that performs the action of the sentence or is spoken about in the sentence. It may be one word, two or more words linked by *and,* a verbal like *swimming,* or a clause:

The *telephone* revolutionized communication.

Hurricanes and *tornadoes* are still highly unpredictable.

337

Hurrying along an icy sidewalk is dangerous.

Whoever is next may use the computer.

Direct Object

The direct object in a sentence is the noun or pronoun that receives the action of the verb. It can be one word, two or more words connected by *and,* a verbal ending in *-ing,* or a clause. The best way to find it is to repeat the subject and verb and ask the question "what?". Examples:

The dog buried the bone. (The dog buried what? *bone*)

The dog chased and caught a rabbit. (The dog chased and caught what? *rabbit*)

The dog bit him. (The dog bit what? *him*)

The dog dodged whatever was in her way. (The dog dodged what? *whatever was in her way*)

The dog hates bathing. (The dog hates what? *bathing*)

Indirect Object

Sometimes a sentence with a direct object has an indirect object that receives the direct object, such as:

I gave my friend some money. (I gave what? *some money* [direct object] to whom? *my friend* [indirect object].)

The indirect object is almost always a person or group of people. More examples:

The quarterback threw the *receiver* (indirect object) the ball.

The boss paid *me* (indirect object) my wages.

I made my *mother* (indirect object) a sweater.

We gave the *Boy Scouts* (indirect object) a donation.

Predicate Noun and Predicate Adjective

In sentences with state-of-being verbs *(is, am, are, was, were),* words following the verb rename or describe the subject of the sentence. The verb can be thought to act as an equals sign:

The doctor is Lynn Smith.   The doctor = Lynn Smith

The doctor is young.   The doctor = young

In these two sentences, *Lynn Smith* is a predicate noun and *young* is a predicate adjective. Examples follow.

Herbert Morris is the star *scholar* (predicate noun).

The cat was *black* (pred. adj.) and *white* (pred. adj.).

The winner is *whoever claims the prize first* (pred. noun).

This season's sport is *swimming* (pred. noun).

Acknowledgments

Page 46: "Timeless Beauty," from *Dateline America* by Charles Kuralt. Copyright © 1979 by CBS, Inc. Reprinted by permission of Harcourt Brace Jovanovich, Inc.

Page 47: "The Ngong Farm," excerpt from *Out of Africa* by Isak Dinesen. Copyright © 1937 by Random House, Inc., and renewed 1965 by Rungstedlundfonden. Reprinted by permission of Random House, Inc., and Florence Feiler Literary Agent.

Page 49: "Muroc," excerpt from *The Right Stuff* by Tom Wolfe. Copyright © 1979 by Tom Wolfe. Reprinted by permission of Farrar, Straus & Giroux, Inc.

Page 89: "Main Street America—1900," from Frederick Lewis Allen, *The Big Change: America Transforms Itself, 1900–1950*. New York: Harper & Row, Publishers, Inc.

Page 90: "Who's in Town in August," *New York Times* editorial, August 27, 1987. Copyright © 1987 by The New York Times Company. Reprinted by permission.

Page 91: "No Name Woman," excerpt from *The Woman Warrior: Memoirs of a Girlhood Among Ghosts* by Maxine Hong Kingston. Copyright © 1975, 1976 by Maxine Hong Kingston. Reprinted by permission of Alfred K. Knopf, Inc.

Page 139: "Oranges: Florida and California," excerpt from *Oranges* by John McPhee. Copyright © 1966, 1967 by John McPhee. Reprinted by permission of Farrar, Straus & Giroux, Inc.

Page 140: "They Sing, They Dance, They're Utterly Different" by John Pareles from *The New York Times,* October 11, 1988. Copyright © 1988 by The New York Times Company. Reprinted by permission.

Page 145: "How I Learned to Read and Write" (editor's title), Malcolm X, *Autobiography of Malcolm X.* New York: Ballantine Books, 1977.

Page 195: "Bulimia: Binge-Eating Cycles Followed by Purges and Guilt" by Jane E. Brody from *Personal Health Column, The New York Times,* March 30, 1983. Copyright © 1983 by The New York Times Company. Reprinted by permission.

Page 199: Excerpt from "The Imagination of Disaster" by Susan Sontag from *Against Interpretation,* 1966. Reprinted by permission of Wylie, Aitken & Stone, Inc.

Page 203: "Snarling Cars" by Paul Blumberg. Reprinted by permission of the author.

Index